BIOGRAPHY
OF
BROKEN
FORTUNES

D1496817

BIOGRAPHY
OF
BROKEN
FORTUNES

Wilkie and Bob,
Brothers of William, Henry,
and Alice James

JANE MAHER

ARCHON BOOKS

1986

For Pat

© 1986 by Jane Maher. All rights reserved
First published 1986 as an Archon Book,
an imprint of The Shoe String Press, Inc.,
Hamden, Connecticut 06514

Printed in the United States of America

The paper in this book meets the guidelines for permanence and
durability of the Committee on Production Guidelines for Book Longevity
of the Council on Library Resources.

Library of Congress Cataloging-in-Publication Data

Maher, Jane, 1947-
Biography of broken fortunes.

Bibliography: p.
Includes index.
1. James, Garth Wilkinson, 1845-1883. 2. James,
Robertson, 1846-1910. 3. James family. 4. United
States—Biography. I. Title.
CT275.J292M34 1986   929'.2'0973   86-1041
ISBN 0-208-02109-4

The author is grateful to the following for permission to quote from copyrighted
works:

☐ Cambridge University Press, *Freedom, The Black Military Experience*, Series II,
edited by Ira Berlin.

☐ Dodd, Mead & Co. *Alice James: Her Brothers—Her Journal* by Anna Robeson
Burr; and *The Diary of Alice James*, edited by Leon Edel, copyright © 1964 Leon Edel.

☐ Houghton Mifflin Co. and Jonathan Cape Ltd., *Alice James*, by Jean Strouse,
copyright © 1980 Jean Strouse.

☐ Little, Brown & Co. *The Letters of William James*, edited by Henry James III; and
The Thought and Character of William James, by Ralph Barton Perry.

☐ Pantheon Books, a division of Random House, *The Negro's Civil War*, by James M.
McPherson.

☐ St. Martin's Press, *One Gallant Rush*, by Peter Burchard.

☐ Viking Penguin, *William James*, by Gay Wilson Allen, copyright © 1967 Gay
Wilson Allen.

☐ Yale University Press, *New Masters: Northern Planters during the Civil War and
Reconstruction*, by Lawrence N. Powell.

2283611

In your letter . . . you speak of an autobiography. . . . It would have to be the biography of broken fortunes.

Robertson James to his sister-in-law
Alice H. James, February 24, 1898

CONTENTS

ACKNOWLEDGMENTS

I am grateful to Rodney G. Dennis, Curator of Manuscripts, the Houghton Library, Harvard University, and to Alexander R. James for permission to quote from the extensive collection of James family letters, and to the staff of the library for their help and cooperation. I am also grateful to the Harvard University Archives for permission to quote from the letters of Henry James III and R. B. Perry, and to the Bancroft Library, University of California, Berkeley, for permission to quote from the letters of Margaret James Porter.

Special thanks to Mr. Peter Drummie of the Massachusetts Historical Society and to Mrs. Marcia Moss of the Concord Free Public Library for their help and cooperation during the course of my research. Thanks also to Mr. Byron Anderson of Milwaukee, Wisconsin, for his dedication and hard work in researching the lives of Garth Wilkinson and Robertson during the period they resided in Milwaukee.

It is impossible to thank the relatives of Garth Wilkinson and Robertson sufficiently for their hospitality and support during the course of my research, and for their permission to quote from the material in their private collections: Mr. and Mrs. Henry James Vaux, Mr. George Vaux, and Mr. and Mrs. Slater Brown, Robertson's descendants; and Mr. David E. James, his wife, Andrea, and his sisters, Leslie and Liza, Garth Wilkinson's descendants.

Very special and sincere thanks are due to my friends who assisted me in every way possible: Alice Chiappetta, Jennifer McClure, Anne Peronti, Veronica Ryan, and Leanne Smith.

INTRODUCTION

Garth Wilkinson James and Robertson James, nicknamed Wilkie and Bob by family and friends, appear as failed, shadowy figures in the biographies of their illustrious brothers, Henry and William. Their valiant Civil War service is treated as an exception to their otherwise obscure and often difficult lives. Wilkie is described as the most affable and carefree of all the Jameses, but ruefully inept in financial and business matters. Bob is described as an alcoholic, a philanderer, as one who was weak natured with a tendency toward morbid self-absorption.

A biography—of sorts—was written about Wilkie and Bob in 1934. Mary James Vaux, Bob's daughter, feared that Wilkie, Bob, and Alice were being neglected in the books which were being written about the Jameses. Thus she commissioned a biographer, Anna Robeson Burr, to write about the three youngest James children. In addition to an essay describing all five James children, Burr printed Alice's diary. The book, *Alice James: Her Brothers—Her Journal,* published at Mrs. Vaux's expense, was a commercial success. The essay is such a simplistic sketch, however, that it is of little use. In defense of Burr, one must remember that she was writing in memoriam, and she was being paid by the daughter and niece of her subjects.

Burr's book, along with the other James biographies, answers none of the difficult questions which exist about the two youngest James brothers. Is it significant that William and Henry prospered despite early poor health, while Wilkie and Bob, who were healthy and robust, suffered for most of their adult lives from a variety of symptoms and problems? Was the abolitionist Sanborn School simply another of Henry James, Sr.'s, educational experiments, or were Wilkie and Bob exposed to an ideological viewpoint which determined their future actions? Why were Wilkie and Bob permitted, even encouraged, to enlist, while Henry and William had been sternly discouraged? What effect did the Civil War service and their failed attempt to run a plantation in Florida have on Wilkie and Bob and their relationship with the other members of the family? Why did both men settle in Milwaukee, in surroundings alien to the background and education which the James children had shared? Was Bob's sometimes repugnant behavior and alcoholism another form of the disease which plagued Alice all of her adult life?

The answers to such questions and the story of the lives of Wilkie and Bob contribute to a better understanding of one of America's most extraordinary families. To understand any one member of the James family, one must be aware of the forces, both supportive and competitive, which were being generated by every other member. As Henry James wrote of his family in his *Autobiography,* they were "such a company of characters and such a picture of differences, and withal so fused and united and interlocked, that each . . . pleads for preservation."[1]

1
A PRIVATE VENTURE
IN IDEALISM:
The Children's Education, 1842–1862

Henry James, Sr., was descended from Irish ancestors; his father, William, had immigrated to America in 1789 and had become one of the wealthiest, most influential men in Albany.[1] Mary James, born Mary Walsh, was of Scotch-Irish descent; her family was prosperous enough for her to be residing in Washington Square when she met her future husband. At the time, Henry James, Sr., was studying theology at Princeton, but he soon grew disgusted and abandoned not only his studies but conventional religion. His ability to convince his wife to join him in this rupture with organized religion, and her willingness to be convinced, is indicative of their entire life together: he was a brilliant, spirited, somewhat eccentric idealist who would dedicate his life to understanding and explicating the teachings of the Swedish philosopher Emanuel Swedenborg; she was the pragmatic wife who would cater to his needs and accept his ideas without question.

Henry James, Sr.,'s exuberance and restlessness can be seen even in the arrival of his children: all five were born within seven years, in four different locations. William was born in 1842 in a room at the Astor House, one of New York's finest hotels; Henry was born in 1843, and Garth Wilkinson in 1845, in Washington Place, New York; Robertson was born in 1846 at 50 Pearl Street, Albany; and Alice was born in 1848 at 54 West 14th Street, New York.

Henry James, Sr., displayed an excruciating concern over his children's well-being, and it was always he who showered his children with affection and attention, hopelessly spoiling them despite his wife's protests. Alice recalled in her diary that her father, without Mrs. James's knowledge, would allow the children to see their Christmas presents, which were hidden away in a closet, a week or so before Christmas. "I can't remember whether he used to confess to Mother after, or not, the dear, dear creature!" Alice wrote.[2] At another time, Alice described her father as "the same dear old good-for-nothing home-sick papa."[3]

Mrs. James was stern and efficient in her management of the household, and she was far more aloof with her children, appreciating the value of benign neglect. She wrote the following account to her English friend and Wilkie's godmother, Mrs. J. J. Garth Wilkinson, after whose husband Wilkie had been named. (In turn, the Wilkinsons named their daughter Mary after Mrs. James.)

> Your little Wilkie has come out for himself since the birth of little Rob. He seemed thereupon to take the hint, and seeing that he was about to be shoved off, concluded to let us see how well he could take care of himself. He began to walk when the baby was two weeks old, took at once into his own hand the redress of his grievances which he seems to think are manifold, and has become emphatically the *ruling* spirit in the nursery. Poor little soul! My pity I believe would be more strongly excited for him were he less able or ready to take his own part, but as his strength of arm or of will seldom fails him, he is too often left to fight his own battles.[4]

From every other account of his childhood, Wilkie seldom had need of strength of arm or of will. All recollections of him depict a sociable, affable spirit, and some of the most beautifully rendered passages in Henry's *Autobiography* are about Wilkie's wonderful, lively nature. Henry remembered that Wilkie possessed "an instinct for intercourse,"[5] and Wilkie's tendency to "go in for everything and everyone" kept Henry "abundantly occupied."[6] He seemed to Henry to live in "a happy hum of relations."[7]

Admiration for Wilkie's geniality was not limited to his family. Thomas Sergeant Perry recalled his characteristic sociability: "I remember walking with Wilky hanging on my arm, talking to me as if he had found an old friend after a long absence."[8] (Although Wilkie used the *ie* spelling, many family members and friends used a *y* at the end of his nickname.)

No such lighthearted accounts exist to describe Bob. Even when Bob was very young, his brothers teased him for constantly saying "One oughtn't joke on such a serious subject."[9] Late in his life, Bob attempted to write an autobiography, but like many of the other things he tried, he did not complete it. The following fragment, all that exists of his attempt, is indicative of Bob's conviction that he had been sorely neglected as a child.

> I was born in the year 1846, in Albany, N.Y. I never remember being told anything extraordinary about my babyhood but I often like to contemplate myself as a baby and wonder if I was really as little appreciated as I fully remember feeling at the time. I never see infants now without discerning in their usually solemn countenance a conviction that they are on their guard and in more or less hostile surroundings. However that may be, in my own case, at a very early age the problems of life began to press upon me in such an unnatural way and I developed such an ability for feeling hurt and wounded that I became quite convinced by the time I was twelve years old that I was a foundling.[10]

Despite his belief to the contrary, anecdotes do exist to prove that Bob was appreciated. Henry recalled that he and his brothers repeatedly appealed to their father to name a profession which would prove acceptable, even impressive, to their friends. The boys were particularly anxious to respond to one boy whose father was a stevedore, since the word seemed so "fine and mysterious" to them. Henry recalled that it was Bob who not only retorted that his father wrote, but he even supplied "the further fact that he had written *Lectures and Miscellanies James.*"[11]

Anna Robeson Burr recorded another favorite family story about the "ingenious little Robertson": "On one occasion, Bob accompanied his aunt to an hotel, where his brother Henry was to join them. When the latter arrived, he was puzzled to find no mention of 'Miss Catherine Walsh' on the register. Investigation revealed the following entry: 'R. James and Lady.' "[12]

Bob was not above using his ingenuity, however, to escape schoolwork. When the family decided to return to America from Europe, the news was kept from Bob until the last possible moment, "for fear he would do no studying whatsoever."[13]

Even when Bob was very young, he was different from the other children; he was not satisfied simply with *being*, a quality which Henry James, Sr., encouraged above all in his children. When Bob was only nine years old, his father described him as clever and promising, with ten times the go-ahead of all the rest of his children. Go-ahead, or ambition, was not a convenient thing to possess in the James family, where one was encouraged to pursue interesting possibilities—but not too closely, not too thoroughly, for one might then run the risk of eliminating the exploration of other interesting possibilities. In 1860, when Bob was fourteen, he wrote to William of a plan he had devised for his future, a plan which William recounted to the family for their amusement: "I got a singular note from Bobby the other day. He says he wants to go into a dry good store when we get home. Mr. O'Conover's son knows plenty of boys in New York knowing French, 15 years old, getting $1,000 and some $5,000. He wishes me to 'tell Father to consider the proposition.'

Poor little Bobby."[14]

Bob was teased by and compared with his older brothers for most of his childhood. Henry James, Sr., took his children to Europe, where he believed they would receive a better education, thus depriving all his children of the opportunity to associate and form friendships with other children. As early as 1849, unhappy with the education which his children were receiving in New York, Henry James, Sr., began to wonder "whether it would not be better to go abroad for a few years with his children allowing them to absorb French and German and get a better sensuous education."[15] The Jameses did not actually move to Europe until 1855; however, even before the "sensuous education" began, Henry James, Sr., moved his family from place to place, seeking larger quarters, better locations, more stimulating company. F. W. Dupee, one of the biographers of Henry James, explained the moves in this way:

> The elder James's dislike of convention exploded in sheer physical restlessness. He was forever hunting improved quarters for the family and better teachers for the children; perhaps he believed that a state of permanent domestic revolution, in addition to fostering their independence of local prejudice, would help to keep his family from hardening into an aggressive social group—in short into the usual family.[16]

There is no doubt that the Jameses never hardened into a "usual family." Henry James, Sr., saw to that. In response to his sons' repeated pleas to name a profession, he replied, greatly amused: "Say I'm a philosopher, say I'm a seeker of truth, say I'm a lover of mankind, say I'm an author of books if you like; or best of all, just say I'm a student."[17] Henry James, Sr.'s, Whitmanesque response was altogether accurate. Unencumbered by the need to earn a living, he dedicated his life to studying theology, to writing lectures and books, and, in Henry's words, to caring for his children's "spiritual decency unspeakably more than for anything else."[18] Henry James, Sr., believed that a family was of value "only as it contributed to a more comprehending and sympathetic participation in the concerns of society."[19] But he did not believe that such participation could be mechanically enforced through any rules; his educational watchword was "spontaneity."

In practice, however, spontaneity seemed to the children more like indecision on their father's part. Henry James described his father's experiment as "no plotted thing at all, but only an accident of accidents,"[20] and he defined their early education as "small vague spasms of school."[21]

In 1855, when the Jameses left for Europe, William was thirteen and Henry was twelve, appropriate enough ages to absorb the sensuousness of it all. But Wilkie was ten, Bob nine, and Alice only seven, making it impossible for Henry James, Sr., to satisfy the needs of all his children at once. A cathedral or museum might please William or Henry, both of whom were precocious and interested in art, but one wonders what the younger children derived from it all. A hint of the effects on Wilkie and Bob is given in one of Alice's diary entries. She wrote of a family outing: "All I can remember of the drive was a never-ending ribbon of dust, stretching in front, and the anguish, greater even than usual, of Wilkie's and Bob's heels grinding into my shins."[22]

From all accounts, Europe was a somewhat difficult experience for all of the children. Less than a month after arriving in Switzerland in 1855, the parents decided that the schools were overrated and decided to have all of the boys tutored with Alice. Toward the end of the year, the family traveled to England, and until the spring of 1856, they stayed in one place. Their next stop was Paris, where Alice and Bob began to study music and to learn French with amazing speed. That Christmas, as a present to his parents and his

Aunt Kate, Bob gave them his French workbook, which contained meticulously copied exercises in poetry, grammar, and mathematics. However, the parents complained of the prices, the quality of the schools, and the unfriendliness of the people and soon began considering other alternatives. Henry remembered these changes and moves as "an incorrigible vagueness of current in our educational drift."[23]

When Bob was twelve, he traveled over the Alps with a tutor and some other youngsters. Henry followed Bob's excursion with "envious fancy," but Bob seemed less enthusiastic about the trip and again made a reference of sorts to abandonment. He noted in a letter to William that during a rain storm, the *cocher,* who had "indulged in certain potations," had "insinuated that we had all better have been with our mothers."[24]

These early wanderings about Europe were always described by Bob with ambivalence. When he recalled his European education, he seemed to recognize in it an indication of the poor luck he would have for the rest of his life. He remembered

> The College Municipale and its stone vaulted ceiling where Wilkie and I went and failed to take prizes. But the day when the Mayor of the City distributed these I do remember, and somehow I think that tho' it was not a prize we both had souvenirs or a reward of some kind—for I recall a beautiful book with gold figures. But around the mayor who stood on a platform with great civic splendor and officials in uniform, I see yet the fortunate scholars ascend the steps of his throne, kneel at his feet, and receive crown or rosettes, or some symbol of merit which *we* did not get. The luck had begun to break early![25]

For a melancholy, sensitive boy who valued prizes, awards, ceremony, and recognition, it must have been difficult for Bob to move from place to place, hardly settling into one school in Switzerland before being transferred back to England, then back to Geneva and then back again to the United States, only to return once again to Switzerland.

Even Wilkie was beginning to feel the effects of the constant traveling and separations. In an attempt to justify his loneliness, he wrote to his father during one of the many times the family was apart: "How do you find Paris and London? I would give a great deal to be there with you, to be arm in arm with you in Regent's Street or St. John's Wood. But I suppose those sweet days have passed and that we are now not to depend so much upon the pleasures that unity or friendship can afford, because we are growing older and must prepare to harden ourselves to deny ourselves the mere affections, so that in the world to come we may have peace and as much of these pleasures as we like."

Even if Wilkie wrote the above in a somewhat jocular attempt to imitate his father's moralizing, he soon forgot both his attempt at humor and his resolve to harden himself. In the same letter he added: "Father, you cannot imagine how much we miss you, and what a blank space your absence makes in this house. Even away off at school I feel it. I have a sort of unprotected feeling (not physically so, but mentally)—I feel as if there were something missing—but I have no doubt it does an immense deal of good to both sides to have occasionally these little separations."[26]

Wilkie's "unprotected feeling" was justified. Details are scarce, but at some point in the family's travels about Europe, Wilkie was bitten by a snake and almost died. Bob mentioned the incident many years later in a letter to his sister-in-law Alice, in which he recalled some of his memories of the past: "The Lake of Geneva, the distant and sombre blue range of the Jura—the village priest who thrust a heated knife into Wilkie's adder-bitten finger and saved him from death in the mountains."[27]

All of the James children were affectionate in their letters to their parents, but Wilkie was exceedingly loving and playful. He began one of his letters, written in 1858, when he was thirteen years old, with the salutation: "Dearest of the Daddybusses and Mommybusses on Earth."[28]

Homesickness, or perhaps just Henry James, Sr.'s, restlessness, brought the family back to America in 1857, and the boys were enrolled in the Berkeley Institute in Newport. A year later, however, William wrote to a friend: "Father has come to the conclusion that America is not the place to bring up such 'ingenuous youth' as myself and my brothers."[29] Consequently, in 1859, the Jameses returned once again to Geneva, to attend schools which Henry James, Sr., had decided, the year before, were overrated.

The family returned permanently to America in 1860. Henry

Sr. wrote that he was returning the boys to the United States so that they could have "friends of their own sex, and sweethearts in the other,"[30] but Henry Jr. gave another reason. Referring to William's expressed desire to return to his study of painting under William Morris Hunt in Newport, he wrote: "We went home to learn how to paint."[31]

Henry James, Sr., felt there was nothing peculiar in his vacillations between Europe and America. His friends and relatives questioned his motives, perhaps even his sanity, in transporting his wife, his five children, his sister-in-law, and his servants to Europe and back two times via a long and arduous sea journey. (In addition, he had taken his family abroad in 1843, before Wilkie, Robertson, and Alice were born.) In response to an inquiry about his abrupt change in plans, Henry James, Sr., conceded that he *had* changed his mind but then explained:

> The truth is . . . I have but one *fixed mind* about anything: which is that whether we stay here or go abroad, and whatever befalls our dear boys in this world, they and you and I are all alike, and after all, absolute creatures of God, vivified every moment by Him, guided every moment by an infallible wisdom and an irreproachable tenderness, and that we have none of us therefore the slightest right to indulge any anxiety in any conceivable circumstances to the slightest whisper of perturbation.[32]

At another time, Henry James, Sr., defended his unconventional behavior as a means to a particular end: "I desire my child to become an upright man, a man in whom goodness shall be induced not by mercenary motives as brute goodness is induced, but by love for it or sympathetic delight in it."[33]

Given Henry James, Sr.'s, unflagging devotion to his children's moral development, the task of managing the more practical, mundane elements in the house fell to Mrs. James. (Henry James, Sr., once explained to a correspondent that he was writing for Mrs. James, because she was busy removing inkspots from the boys' clothing.)

Henry, Mrs. James's favorite son, praised his mother's virtues. "She was our life," he wrote, "she was the house, she was the keystone of the arch. She held us all together. . . . Her sweetness, her mildness, her great natural beneficence were unspeakable."[34] Despite such glowing evidence of Mrs. James's selflessness, Wilkie, the most uninhibited member of this unconventional family, gave another view of Mrs. James, a view which was described by William in a letter he wrote to his parents.

> I stopped this letter before tea, when Wilkie the rosygilled and Frank Higginson came in. I now resume it by the light of a taper and that of the moon. Wilky read H's letter and amused me "metch" by his naive interpretation of Mother's most rational request that I should "keep a memorandum of all moneys I receive from Father." He thought it was that she might know exactly what sums her prodigal philosopher really gives out, and that mistrust of his generosity caused it. The phrase does a little sound that way, as H. subtly framed it, I confess.[35]

Wilkie's interpretation was not at all naïve. He was simply mimicking his mother's habit of accusing her sons of spending too much money. William and Henry invariably wrote contrite defenses of their expenditures to their mother, hoping that she would forgive them and assuring her that they would be more careful in the future. Henry once declared to his mother that he would "feel like a profligate monster" if he were ever to draw too much money from his father's account.[36] Wilkie was the only one of the five children who was feisty enough to joke about the less lofty traits of Mrs. James.

Such traits were essential, however, in a household in which the father refused to live conventionally. Henry James, Sr., was literally conducting "a private venture in idealism," a very expensive enterprise for a man with five children.[37] Mrs. James never disagreed with anything her husband decided to do; she did, however, maintain tight control over the family finances. In discussing the works of Henry James, Sr., F. O. Matthiessen notes that he "was always talking about potentiality rather than actuality."[38] He conducted his personal life in much the same way, leaving the actual for his wife.

Wilkie again alluded to this arrangement in a letter which he wrote when he was sixteen. It reflects his tongue-in-cheek attempt to convince his mother that he had used her money wisely. (In addition, Wilkie imitated his father's tendency to apply any incident, however inconsequential or mundane, to the universal.) And, the letter is a perfect example of that talent which Henry so admired in Wilkie: his ability to turn the tables on any given subject at any given moment.

Dear Parents,
    I have just come in from Boston where I have been overcoat hunting. I could find nothing to suit me anywhere at ready made places, all common miserable undistinguished looking coats with no absolute merit but cheapness, and cheapness you know is not even always a merit. Willie and I concluded after a "long consul de guerre" to return to his tailors to be fitted for one there. Twenty-three dollars was the cheapest we could find so we were forced to acceed. We went to the other tailors, some $28 other $25 and one $30 so we did our best.
    I got a good strong sack coat for sixteen dollars at Nason's and could not find anything suitable for less than that. We knew we overstepped your estimate, but we thought you would do the same if you had been in our shoes. Such is the practical statement, the mere facts, now let's moralize. Certainly nothing can be more intensely demoralizing to the human mind than this perpetual struggle between money and the pocket. The former is constantly running out or wanting to run out and the other is constantly trying to keep it in. Espionage of all sorts is detestable but this miserable espionage of the pocket over the money is doubly so, because it has not even the charm of dealing with flesh and bones, but merely broadcloth and paper.
    Fancy the life of a poor retail shopkeeper. How he must curse the person who does not like his goods, still how we inwardly cursed the man at Oak-Hall today who would not cease pestering with his ugly clothes and ugly voice. However, it is not demoralizing unless you choose to make it so yourself. If you would loose a little of your sympathy and put yourself on the same par with the merchant then it would be all right. But a decent person cannot do that therefore he hangs his head when he enters a shop and prepares for battle.[39]

Wilkie delighted in teasing William, who worried constantly that his parents would consider him a spendthrift. William found the following note from Wilkie one day on returning to his room in Cambridge: "Father will send money tomorrow. He is going to break your head for spending so much."[40] Too upset to realize that Wilkie was joking, William sent his mother a detailed list of his expenditures and apologized for such "youthful weaknesses" as gingerbread, oysters, and a hair shampooing which "the barber unctuously seduced [him] into."[41]

All of the boys, especially William, the oldest and most confident, teased each other in this way. Edward Emerson described a typical scene in the James home:

> "The adipose and affectionate Wilkie," as his father called him, would say something and be instantly corrected by the little cock-sparrow Bob, the youngest, but good-naturedly defend his statement, and then Henry (Junior) would emerge from his silence in defense of Wilkie. Then Bob would be more impertinently insistent, and Mr. James would advance as moderator, and William, the eldest, join in. The voice of the moderator presently would be drowned by the combatants and he soon came down vigorously in the arena, and when, in the excited argument, the dinner knives might not be absent from eagerly gesticulating hands, dear Mrs. James, more conventional, but bright as well as motherly, would look at me, laughingly reassuring, saying, "Don't be disturbed, Edward; they won't stab each other. This is usual when the boys come home."[42]

The tendency has been for biographers to group Henry and William together, then Wilkie and Robertson, leaving Alice, as the youngest and the only girl, to survive as best she could. This was not always the case, particularly during the childhood years. Rather, Henry and Wilkie were often together; Henry remembered that William's "orbit was other and larger."[43] Wilkie, who was less than two years younger than Henry, was his "extremely easy . . . playfellow, off and on, for a few years."[44] Bob usually remained at home with Alice. Many years later, Bob still remembered his hours with Alice in the nursery, pretending to be married, calling each other Mary and Henry. Together, they contracted measles and scarlet fever. Bob was often tutored at home with Alice while the three older boys went off to day schools in New York, and later to boarding schools when the family lived in Europe. It was in 1860, shortly before the Civil War, when the James family returned permanently to America, that Wilkie and Bob were drawn together to a far greater degree than ever before. They were sent to the Sanborn School in Concord, Massachusetts, in one of Henry James, Sr.'s, final attempts at providing a "sensuous education" for his children. After years of traveling about Europe seeking the perfect educational environment, Henry James, Sr., said of the school, an experiment in coeducation which had been recommended to him by its sponsor, Ralph Waldo Emerson: "I can't but felicitate our native land that such magnificent experiments go on among us."[45]

Since it was not a common practice for girls to board away from home, Alice was eliminated as a prospective student. William, and soon after, Henry, began to study art under the tutelage of William Morris Hunt in Newport. Put another way, William was now old enough to resist yet another of his father's educational schemes. Initially, Henry James, Sr., probably wanted Henry and Wilkie to attend the school, since he had written to a friend that "the other youngsters" were "getting to an age, Harry and Wilky especially, when the heart craves a little wider expansion than is furnished it by the domestic affections."[46] A coeducational school sponsored by Emerson would be just the thing. Henry might have been lured to follow William to Hunt's studio as much to avoid yet another boarding school as by his interest in art. That left only Wilkie and Bob, who at fifteen and fourteen were too young to remain idly at home; in a sense, they attended the Sanborn School by default.

Clearly, Bob did not want to attend the school. While the family was still in Europe, he had told William of his desire to own a drygoods store of his own. Although the family was amused by his juvenile plan, it is evident that attendance at yet another school, where he would not learn a particular trade or profession, could not have pleased him. There are very few family letters from this period when the family was together in Newport, but Henry Jr. supplied crucial information in his *Autobiography* concerning Bob's state of mind. In discussing the various plans which his parents made upon the family's return from Europe, he noted that "Wilky . . . had been placed with the youngest of us, Bob, for companion, at the co-educational school . . . established by Mr. F. B. Sanborn."[47] Bob was sent to the Sanborn School primarily so that Wilkie would not have to board alone, much as he had been kept at home with Alice while the other boys attended day schools or boarding schools in Europe.

In a letter praising the Sanborn School, Henry James, Sr., wrote: "I am sure of one thing, which is that if I had had such educational advantages as that in my youth I should probably have been now far more nearly ripe for this world's business."[48] It is doubtful that any education could have made such an irrepressible optimist "ripe for this world's business," but Henry James, Sr.'s, remark does reflect the fact that he sought freedom and unconventionality for his children primarily because he himself had been deprived of it. Henry James, Sr., never forgot the restrictions placed upon him in his childhood. "Nothing is so hard for a child," he remembered, "as *not-to-do;* that is, to keep his hands and feet and tongue in enforced inactivity. It is a cruel wrong to put such an obligation upon him, while his reflective faculties are still undeveloped, and his senses urge him to unrestrictive action."[49]

As a result, Henry James, Sr., devised his own educational theory, which he described to Emerson in a letter which he wrote after Emerson's son, Edward, had visited the James home.

Only one word about Edward, the good boy who smiles like opening violets, but who is not near so robust as he ought to be, because he is allowed to study too hard, in order that he may enter college one year rather than another. I hated to see the beautiful boy so imprisoned by these baneful books: but of course I did not broach any heresy in his hearing. Our true learning is to unlearn always, and our best doing to undo. . . . But anyhow it is a sin and shame to starve the physical life out of any deference to the intellectual.[50]

Emerson, to some degree, agreed with Henry James, Sr. He wanted a school for his children which would be a departure from the gloomy education which he had received. "We are shut up in school and college recitation rooms for ten or fifteen years," he wrote, "and come out at last with a bellyful of words and do not know a thing."[51]

Emerson and Henry James, Sr., had other reasons to be concerned with the quality of schools. American education as a whole was in a dismal state. The average American did not go beyond the fifth grade. Teachers were often unqualified; they received little pay and even less respect. Although Massachusetts became the first state to pass compulsory school-attendance laws, the public schools were attended primarily by the children of immigrants. Henry James, Jr., recalled that parents, in seeking appropriate schools for their off-spring, "welcomed almost any influence that might help at all to form their children to civility."[52]

In 1854, Emerson, concerned with his children's education, or lack of it, had arranged for Franklin B. Sanborn, a student at Harvard, to revive the Concord Academy, a school which had once been run by Henry David Thoreau and his brother John. However, Sanborn was zealously devoted to the abolitionist cause, and he would ultimately become better known as a friend and supporter of John Brown than as an educator. From the start, the question of slavery took precedence over the school, and Sanborn was often away either visiting John Brown and his family or raising funds and support for Brown's cause. Sanborn was one of only six men to know in advance of the raid on Harper's Ferry.

The raid occurred on October 16, 1859, and Sanborn fled to Canada soon after, having discovered that incriminating letters written by him had been seized. Sanborn's friends, among them Thomas Wentworth Higginson, who later became an officer in the first regiment comprised of former slaves, soon informed Sanborn that it was safe to return to Concord. Within days, Sanborn resumed his duties at the school, but he was still preoccupied with raising funds for Brown's family. Sanborn never questioned the morality or the efficacy of the raid on Harper's Ferry, nor did he ever abandon John Brown's cause. As late as 1885, he was still helping with the management of the funds raised, mostly from blacks, for the support of Brown's widow.

John Brown was hanged on December 2, 1859, and soon after Sanborn arranged for two of Brown's daughters to attend his school. He lost no time in raising a subscription to pay the girls' expenses, and the girls moved into the boardinghouse of a Mrs. Clark, where Wilkie and Bob would board when they arrived in the autumn of 1860.

On April 3, 1860, Senate deputies attempted to arrest Sanborn at his home in Concord to make him testify about his involvement with Brown and the raid on Harper's Ferry. The newspapers were full of the incident, and Sanborn himself proudly described the event in minute detail in his autobiography.

Sanborn's case was quickly decided by the Supreme Court of Massachusetts, with John A. Andrew, the future governor who would raise Wilkie's and Bob's regiments, as his counsel. Among Sanborn's supporters in the courtroom were Wendell Phillips and Walt Whitman. Sanborn was soon released and freed from any further obligation to testify before the Senate. The citizens of Boston presented Sanborn's sister with a revolver in recognition of her tact and courage in defending her brother against the deputies who had attempted to kidnap him.

When Wilkie and Bob arrived at the Sanborn School, there is no doubt that they heard much about the incident. Anna Robeson Burr speculated about the effect which Sanborn's involvement with Brown must have had on the boys.

> What waves of emotion beat upon the impressionable children at the Sanborn School. Had not Mr. Sanborn been John Brown's intimate friend? Did not everybody know that Sanborn had spent the summers in 1856 and 1857 traveling in the South and studying the conditions at first hand? He had returned an open advocate of the Underground Railway. . . . For many months New England had resisted the voice of the Abolitionist, but it was listening now. Under such a wave of feeling, children are not told of Government policy and caution and compromise, they are told of injustice and cruelty and the word of God. In the eyes of Wilky and Bob, there could have been no greater hero than John Brown, and no doubt they listened with hunger to the accounts of his visit to Concord before their own arrival[53]

Other Jamesian biographers have agreed with Burr's theory, albeit less histrionically. Although her theory provides a convenient explanation for Wilkie's and Bob's enlistment and service in all-black regiments, particularly since Henry and William did not enlist, the evidence which exists proves that Wilkie and Bob became bored and restless at the school. They chose enlistment not as a result of the Sanborn School but as an alternative to it. For Wilkie and Bob, the Sanborn School was yet another experiment in their father's attempt to provide his children with a sensous education, one in a long line of such experiments which included eccentric tutors, quaint hotels, drawing, language, and music lessons, excursions across the Alps, and visits to art galleries, theaters, cathedrals, and museums.

It is not clear whether or not Henry James, Sr., was even aware of the potential influence which Sanborn's abolitionist convictions and actions could have on his two youngest sons. He knew that the boys would be boarding with the daughter of John Brown, (one of the daughters had left before Wilkie and Bob arrived), and of course he was opposed in principle to slavery. But on the day that Henry James, Sr., escorted Wilkie and Bob to Concord, he seemed more concerned with the coeducational aspect of the school than with anything else. He recorded his impressions of Mrs. Clark's boarding-house in a letter to his friend, Mrs. Caroline Sturgis Tappan:

> Mrs. Clark is a graceless enough woman outwardly, but so tenderly feathered inwardly, so unaffectedly kind and motherly toward the urchins under her roof, that one was glad to leave them in that provident nest. She had three or four other school-boarders, one of them a daughter of John Brown—tall, erect, long-haired and freckled, as John Brown's daughter has a right to be. I kissed her (inwardly) between the eyes, and inwardly heard the martyred Johannes chuckle over the fat inheritance of love and tenderness he had after all bequested to his children in all good men's minds. An arch little Miss Plumley also lives there, with eyes full of laughter and a mouth like a bed of lillies bordered with roses. How it is going to be possible for my two boys to pursue their studies in the midst of that bewilderment I don't clearly see. . . . We asked to see Miss Waterman, one of the teachers quartered in the house, in order to say to her how much we should thank her if she would occasionally put out any too lively spark she might see fall on the expectant tinder of my poor boys' bosoms; but Miss W. herself proved of so siliceous a quality on inspection—with round tender eyes, young, fair and womanly—that I saw in her only new danger and no promise of safety. My present conviction is that a general conflagration is inevitable, ending in the total combustion of all that I hold dear on that spot.[54]

A general conflagration was inevitable, but not of the type which Henry James, Sr., feared. In 1860, he did not suspect that within three years Wilkie and Bob would be fighting for the Union in the South. A civil war over the issue of slavery seemed far from his mind as he continued his description of the Sanborn School:

We were duly wafted to our educational Zion and carefully made over our good and promising and affectionate boys to the school-master's keeping. Out in the field beside his house Sanborn incontinently took us to show how his girls and boys perform together their worship of Hygeia. It was a glimpse into that new world wherein dwelleth righteousness and which is full surely coming upon our children and our children's children; and I could hardly keep myself, as I saw my children's eyes drink in the mingled work and play of the inspiring scene, from shouting out a joyful *Nunc Dimittis*.[55]

Henry James, Jr., recognized the lack of logic inherent in his father's belief that, somehow, an isolated experiment in education conducted by an abolitionist could cause "that new world wherein dwelleth righteousness." He wrote: "A less vague or vain idealist couldn't, I think, have been encountered; it was given to him to catch in the fact at almost any turn right or left some flagrant assurance or promise of the state of man transfigured. The Concord school could be to him . . . such a promise"[56]

Henry James, Sr.'s, usual dread of separation returned, however, and in the same letter to Mrs. Tappan he wrote: "The short of the story is that we left them and rode home robbed of our plumage, feeling sore and ugly and only hoping that they wouldn't die, any of these cold winter days, before the parental breast could get there to warm them back to life or cheer them on to a better."[57]

Even allowing for Henry James, Sr.'s, customary hyperbole, his comments reflect his excruciating preoccupation with his family's welfare. He once told Emerson that he "wished sometime that the lightning would strike his wife and children out of existence and he should suffer no more from loving them."[58]

Despite his last-minute misgivings, Henry James, Sr., left Wilkie and Bob in excellent company; they were attending school with the children of some of New England's most renowned intellectuals and idealists. Other students at the school included Hawthorne's son, Julian. In addition to Edward Emerson, his sisters Ellen and Edith took turns attending the Sanborn School or commuting to Cambridge to attend a private school for girls. Sam Hoar, the son of the famous Judge Hoar, attended the school, along with Frank Stearns, son of the abolitionist George Stearns. The Alcott girls did not attend the school, but they participated in most of the activities; Julian Hawthorne remembered playing and dancing in the Alcott home. Wilkie and Bob participated in dances and charades, and in theatricals directed by Louisa May Alcott. Under her direction, Wilkie portrayed the Duke of Buckingham. There were unchaperoned horseback-riding parties of "boys and girls judiciously selected."[59]

The faculty was a blend of Concord's famous and eccentric residents: Elizabeth Hoar lectured on Milton, and Elizabeth Ripley taught German. Ellery Channing once helped at the school while Sanborn was away. Louisa May Alcott's sister Nan was the drawing instructor. Thoreau himself escorted the students on walks through the woods and gave lectures on wild apples which Sanborn described as "full of juice and queer wit."[60] When the students weren't in class, they often observed Thoreau about town, "land surveying, in all weathers and all wild places."[61] He could often be seen sitting on the front porch of the Minot House, which afterward became one of Concord's most famous landmarks. (Bob painted a picture of the house many years later; it still hangs in the Concord Free Public Library.) There were French and fencing lessons provided by a retired *sous lieutenant* of Louis Philippe's army, and Sanborn took fencing lessons along with his students.

Henry James, Sr., had wondered how his boys would be able to pursue their studies in the midst of the coeducational "bewilderment," but Hawthorne's wife, Sofia, was not at all amused. She refused to send her daughters, Una and Rose, to the school, and she wrote angrily to Sanborn: "We entirely disapprove of this commingling of youths and maidens at the electric age in school."[62] She complained of the change she perceived in her son. "Julian was a sacredly folded bud when we brought him home to America, with a genuine reverence for women, and now he is forcibly bloomed into a *cavaliere servente* before his wisdom teeth have had time to prick through."[63]

Julian Hawthorne gave a different account of his experiences. Referrring to the girls in the school, he recalled that he "was out of it." He continued: "In my tenth year, in Liverpool, I had been ardently in love with a Minnie Warren, who danced away from me into the Unknown, and the scene of our passion saw us no more. By the time I got to Sanborn's I was as bashful as an oyster, and shut my shell, though not unconscious of what went on around me."[64]

Wilkie, on the other hand, was far from out of it. Hawthorne noted:

There were a few distractingly lovely girls—Grace Mitchell, Maggie Plumley, and others with whom the entire left side of the aisle was in love; but the inflammation was serious with a few only. Edward Emerson's big blue eyes would kindle into ecstasy as he bent them on Maggie, and Wilkie James, who came to us from Europe, with all the *savoir-faire* of that region, could not preserve his poise in Grace's presence.[65]

This account of Wilkie's infatuation is noteworthy for another reason: it is part of the only record which exists to describe the boys during their attendance at the Sanborn School, since so few family letters exist from this period. Julian Hawthorne provided flattering descriptions of both Wilkie and Bob.

Christened Garth Wilkinson and Robertson, they were known in school speech as Wilkie and Bob. They were very good looking, open-hearted fellows, had been at school in Switzerland and Paris, were at home in England, spoke several languages, put on no airs, but were simple and hearty as sailors on leave. They had the best of manners and no unfortunate habits. Bob, the younger, was robust and hilarious, tough, tireless as hickory, great in the playground, not much of a scholar. Wilkie was the glass of fashion and the mould of form, but never the least clothes conscious or la-de-da; good natured to the marrow.
    These were two perfectly delightful characters, though, of course, unknown outside their circle of personal friends. Robust Bob was full of fun and pranks and audacities, but in all a perfect gentleman in purpose and practice. He was hugely popular in the school. But Wilkie was incomparable: besides being the best dressed boy in the school, and in manners and talk the most engaging, his good humor was inexhaustible. He was of middle height, broad-shouldered and symmetrical, with a good head, well set, and a smiling countenance. Peg-top trousers were in fashion then: Wilkie's were the widest and most enviable. He was sixteen years old when he came to us, but

appeared older by two or three years, being self-possessed and having the bearing of a man of the world. In the company of the ladies he was entirely at his ease, and devoted; they all loved him.[66]

The only other account which exists about the boys' experiences at the Sanborn School is also from Julian Hawthorne's memoirs, and it describes a rowing contest in which Wilkie again displayed his "incomparable temperament."

Wilkie James had a light roomy boat, furnished with a beautiful pair of varnished oars. Wilkie, inadvertently, at first took his seat on the thwart nearest the bows, and facing in that direction; but a farmer's lad admonished him from the bank, and Wilkie scrambled into the right position, the craft rolling alarmingly as he did so. I didn't know, till after the race was over, that Wilkie had never before sat in a vessel propelled by oars. He had supposed that oarmanship came by nature.

Mr. Sanborn, up on the bridge, was now preparing to wave the starting flag. Surreptitiously almost, a low, unimportant object was forging up alongside "the Oriole," Wilkie's elegant boat, with an old pair of pants and a sleeveless undershirt containing poor Sam Hoar. He had made the punt and oars himself, and was now foolish enough, with no better equipment, to go up against Wilkie. To be sure, he seemed to know how to row; but what of that?

Sanborn waved the flag, and the race was on! . . . Just as Wilkie's shiny oars touched the water, a . . . breeze deflected the high bow of his boat, to correct which he dug one oar deep in the water. But the handle was thus driven violently into his stomach, and forced him off the thwart into the boat's bottom. . . .

Meanwhile, Sam, pulling long and smooth, was out in front. . . . By the time Wilkie got set again, Sam was approaching the finish. Wilkie, flushed and bruised, arrived at last as good natured as ever and heartily gave his blistered hand to his rival, and laughingly apologized to the girls for making such an ass of himself.[67]

Many years later, both Wilkie and Bob would come to appreciate the value of their Concord experiences, particularly as Hawthorne, Emerson, Thoreau, and Louisa May Alcott achieved fame. But at the end of the school year, despite Julian Hawthorne's descriptions of such picaresque adventures, neither Wilkie nor Bob wanted to return to the school. Wilkie did return for one more year, but Bob simply refused to do so. He threatened to run away to sea, and his restiveness was a severe strain on his parents, who were becoming more and more preoccupied with Alice as they realized that the nervous symptoms she had begun to display were serious.

When Wilkie returned to the school, he complained of loneliness to William, who was at the time a student at Harvard. William wrote to his parents about Wilkie, saying: "He says it is pretty lonely at Concord and he misses Bob's lively and sportive wiles very much in the long and dreary evenings tho' he consoles himself by thinking he will have a great time to study."[68]

Apparently, Wilkie had notified his friends at the school that he, too, would not be returning, for in the same letter, William referred to Edward Emerson's surprise and pleasure in learning that Wilkie was, after all, on his way back to Concord.

Wilkie's restlessness did not subside, however, and he sought a change. With his usual verbal playfulness, he notified his parents that he wanted to leave the Sanborn School to travel to Europe with Edward Emerson, who was recovering from a severe case of scarlet fever.

Mr. Emerson I think will send Edward abroad, he wants very much to have somebody to go with him. Now it has struck me for the last two weeks that I am the person destined by fate to fulfill this fraternal office. Edward Emerson and I are two direct opposites, if we could be rolled up together into one substance, what a substance we would make. Emerson (perhaps you have noticed) is very thin, I am (perhaps you half have observed) rather inclined to corpulence. E. is very studious, I am studious, but perhaps not very so. E. is broken down in health, I am robust, strong, and active (especially the active). Edward is full of whatever I lack, and vice-versa. He could lean on me for support, I could do the same, in fact what could not be said upon the subject. I could finish my already commenced knowledge of the German and French language and come home already [sic] to enter a Boston Tailor Store with the signs *"Ici on parle Francais,"* and the *"Hier spricht mann Deutsch."* However there is time enough hereafter during my coming ideal visit to Newport to settle all preliminaries.[69]

Despite Wilkie's optimism, the trip to Europe never materialized, presumably because of Edward Emerson's health.

Wilkie had told William that he would use his time without Bob to study; however, Wilkie simply wasn't a scholar. His fondness for reading increased as he grew older, but in 1861 Wilkie was still the one James for whom reading was not pleasurable. Henry Jr. noted that when Wilkie was young, "the act of reading was inhuman and repugnant to him."[70] Wilkie's reading habits were the source of a family joke which Henry James, Sr., recalled several years later in a letter written to Henry Jr. He reported that Mrs. James had "gone to enjoy a little 'reading' as Wilky used to call it in Aunt Kate's bed this afternoon."[71] Henry James, Sr., then wondered whether he heard his wife reading aloud, or if perhaps he heard instead the sound of slumber. William, who often drew caricatures of his family, drew a picture of Wilkie sleeping and titled it "Garth Wilkinson James hard at work reading."[72]

Wilkie often walked the almost fifteen miles from Concord to Cambridge to visit William, less for exercise than for companionship. After one of these visits, William wrote the often-quoted letter describing Wilkie's antics, in which he "wrought little but disaster during his stay . . . breaking down my good resolutions about food, keeping me from all intellectual exercises, working havoc on my best hat by wearing it while dressing, while in his nightgown, while washing his face, and all but going to bed with it."[73]

Wilkie was simply too sociable to be a scholar. He preferred the company of others to solitary reading, and his increasing restlessness and boredom at the Sanborn School is evident in a letter he wrote from Concord to Tom Ward, a friend of William:

> I have just returned from Boston where I have been spending the last two or three days and having nothing to do now . . . I send you these few lines to tell you that I am not entirely dead,

but expect to be before the time that you come back. The dullness is perfectly inconceivable. There is scarcely a soul to be seen today. The weather is very damp and rainy, and what with that and the above mentioned inconceivable dullness, you can imagine what sort of time I am having. If I had anything new to say I would do so, but the culinary odors announce the approach of dinner, and accordingly I must close.[74]

Wilkie was rarely so lethargic or depressed. Given his state of mind and his apathy toward school, enlistment would be as much a solution as a decision.

Bob remained at home during this time. He left the Sanborn School at the end of the spring term of 1861, and he did not enlist until the summer of 1863. During his interval, he acquired a small sailboat, which he christened *Alice* after his sister. Ellen and Edith Emerson visited the Jameses in Newport in the summer of 1862, accompanied by their brother, Edward, and Ellen described in her letters pleasant sailing and swimming expeditions.

William, in his letters home, teased Bob about his tiny boat and his refusal to return to school. "I pine to see the honest Jack Tar of the family," he wrote, "the Rough Bob, with his rude, untutored ways."[75] Bob visited William occasionally in Cambridge; on one occasion, William addressed Bob in a postscript, asking: "Bob, you young thief, where are my gloves?"[76] Bob often sailed to Portsmouth from Newport, and he visited the soldiers encamped there.

Wilkie completed the spring term of 1862 at the Sanborn School; soon after, in September of 1862, he enlisted. Bob remained at home for several more months; then in May of 1863 he too enlisted, although he would not be seventeen, the minimum age for enlistment, for three more months (his birthday was not until August 29).

It was at this time that a pattern began to be established which would remain in effect for the rest of the parents' lives: education and career decisions made about Wilkie and Bob were not necessarily based on their individual interests or needs, as they certainly were with Henry and, especially, William. Rather, the parents, particularly Mrs. James, contrived for Wilkie and Bob to remain together. Both Mr. and Mrs. James possessed great parental devotion, but their financial and emotional resources were not limitless. At this time, they seem to have concluded that William and Henry were the sons with the most intellectual promise. If the younger sons remained in similar locations and later in similar occupations, they would have each other for support and companionship while the parents concentrated on William's and Henry's educational and career choices, and later on Alice's emotional and physical ailments.

It is impossible to determine how aware the Jameses were of this tendency; however, in the nineteenth century it was not uncommon for parents to be preoccupied with the eldest son. Whether or not a conscious decision had been made, Mrs. James at this time began to refer to Wilkie and Bob collectively as "the boys" in her letters, and she continued to do so even after they were married and had children of their own.

Henry James, Sr.'s, behavior over the issue of the enlistment of his sons was blatantly contradictory. An undated fragment of a letter written by him concerning the enlistment of William and Henry states his unequivocal disapproval: "Affectionate old papas like me are scudding all over the country to apprehend their patriotic offspring, and restore them to the harmless embraces of their mamas." He justified his attitude, saying: "No existing government, nor indeed any now possible government, is worth an honest human life and a clean one like theirs, especially if that government is like ours in danger of bringing back slavery again under one banner: than which consummation I would rather see chaos itself come." And he concluded the letter by noting: "I tell them that no young American should put himself in the way of death until he has realized something of the good of life: until he has found some charming conjugal Elizabeth or other to whisper his devotion to, and assume the task if need be, of keeping his memory green."[77]

Despite such convincing arguments, Henry James, Sr., permitted Bob to lie about his age in order to enlist. On the day Bob joined his regiment, Henry James, Sr., wrote to Elizabeth Peabody: "He went off in good spirits, and though it cost me a heartbreak to part with one so young on a service so hard, I cannot but adore the great Providence which is thus lifting our young men out of indolence and vanity, into some free sympathy with His own deathless life."[78] One suspects that Henry James, Sr., had one particular young man in mind when he wrote this, since Bob had been home, idly, for almost two years.

What, one must ask, became of the need for "some charming conjugal Elizabeth or other"? Some biographers have concluded that Henry James, Sr., was less reluctant to part with his two younger sons because the Emancipation Proclamation had been issued. Until that time, the country's abolitionists had been deeply disturbed over Lincoln's position. "If I could save the Union without freeing any slave," Lincoln had written, "I would do it; and if I could save it by freeing all the slaves, I would do it; and if I could save it by freeing some and leaving others alone, I would also do that."[79] However, Lincoln finally issued a preliminary proclamation freeing all slaves in September of 1862, the same month in which Wilkie enlisted.

Wilkie's recollections of his enlistment, delivered many years later before an association of Union officers, certainly describe a parent whose feelings had altered drastically from the time Henry James, Sr., was "scudding" to restore his sons to the harmless embraces of their mother.

> When I went to the war I was a boy of seventeen years of age, the son of parents devoted to the cause of the Union and the abolition of slavery. It seems unnecessary to tell you that my experiences of life were small. I had been brought up in the belief that slavery was a monstrous wrong, its destruction worthy of a man's best effort, even unto the laying down of life. I had been spending the summer in Newport, Rhode Island, when the war got fairly under way. To me, in my boyish fancy, to go to the war seemed glorious indeed, to my parents it seemed a stern duty, a sacrifice worth any cost. Not for glory's sake, nor for the vantage of a fleeting satisfaction then, did they give me to the cause, but altogether for the reverse of these, from the sad necessities of a direful evil, from which the alarmed conscience of the North was smiting her children into line for the defense of the country's life. . . . My father accompanied me to the recruiting station, witnessed the enrollment, and gave me, as his willing mite, to the cause he had so much at heart.[80]

And when Bob left in July of 1863 to begin service with his regiment, Henry James, Sr., wrote to his friend Elizabeth Peabody: "I seem never to have loved the dear boy before, now that he is clad with such an aureole of Divine beauty and innocence; and though the flesh was weak I still had the courage, spiritually, to bid him put all his heart in his living or dying, that so whether he lived or died he might be fully adopted of that Divine spirit of liberty which is at last renewing all things in its own image."[81]

An explanation of Henry James, Sr.'s, contradictory, even arbitrary, behavior might simply be that Wilkie and Bob *wanted* to enlist, while William and Henry did not. Biographers have exhaustively examined the theory of Henry's "obscure hurt," an injury to his back which presumably precluded enlistment. However, Leon Edel discovered a discrepancy between the date which Henry later gave for his injury and the actual date on which it occurred. William's biographers have cited his nervousness, his emotional turmoil, and, most important, his weak eyes as valid reasons for his not enlisting. Many years later, William's son edited his father's letters and wrote defensively in the introduction: "The physical and nervous frailty, which President Eliot had noticed in James during the first winter at the Scientific School, and which later manifested itself so seriously as to interfere with his studies, kept him from enlisting in the Federal armies during the Civil War. The case was too clear to occasion discussion in his letters."[82]

Obviously, a question always remained, an embarrassment of sorts, over the fact that the two younger brothers went to war, while the two older ones remained at home.

Henry James, Sr.'s, own behavior had something to do with the existence of this paradoxical situation. From the time his children were born, he viewed them as nothing less than living proof of his theories, his beliefs, his goodness. He persistently defined their actions in terms of his beneficent influence and example as their father. Thus, when William and Henry demurred on the issue of enlistment, Henry James, Sr., provided a suitable theory to explain and condone their actions—a theory which reflected his influence over their decision. When Bob and then Wilkie refused to continue to attend the school which Henry James, Sr., had chosen for them, and decided to ·enlist as an alternative, Henry James, Sr., immediately converted their decision into the theory that it was he who, for the good of the nation, had bid his sons to put their hearts and souls into the cause. By 1862, Henry James, Sr., could no longer control his sons' decisions to the degree that he had done in the past, but he could continue to interpret their decisions to suit himself.

2
A BRAVE FIGHT:
Wilkie's Civil War Service, 1863-1865

In 1861, signs of the war were everywhere. Henry Lee Higginson, a student at Harvard, recorded the patriotic mood which swept New England:

> Never in my whole life have I seen anything approaching in the slightest degree the excitement and enthusiasm of the past week. Everything excepting the war is forgotten, business is suspended, the streets are filled with people, drilling is seen on all sides and at all times. . . . You should have seen the troops, real, clean-cut, intelligent Yankees, the same men who fought in '76, a thousand times better than any soldiers living. Everyone is longing to go.[1]

Given the mood of the North at the onset of the Civil War, biographers have concluded that Wilkie and Bob, in contrast to their older brothers, simply did the popular thing by enlisting. One Bostonian said that "not to [enlist] would be to incur lasting disgrace, in comparison with which the hardship and boredom and danger of a campaign would be a festive pastime."[2]

Although this statement reflects the mood prevalent in 1861 shortly after the South's attack on Fort Sumter, by the end of 1862, when Wilkie enlisted, the patriotic fervor had subsided considerably, and it became necessary for both sides to stage war meetings and to offer bounties to stir up lagging enthusiasm. When Oliver Wendell Holmes wrote such patriotic verse as the following:

> Listen young heroes! your country is calling!
> Time strikes the hour for the brave and the true!

> Now, while the foremost are fighting and falling.
> Fill up the ranks that have opened for you.

he was romanticizing a chronic problem which both the North and the South faced: replacing soldiers who had completed their nine months' or three years' service, those who had been killed, wounded, or captured, and those who had deserted.

By 1863, Lincoln was forced to resort to conscription, even though he knew it would be an unpopular method of procuring soldiers. There were three national draft calls in 1863 and 1864; however, the conditions were so lenient that draftees could buy their way out for three hundred dollars or find a replacement. As a result, of the 776,829 names called in all three national drafts, only 46,347 men were actually held for military service. One Massachusetts soldier wrote of his resentment over the scarcity of men willing to fight for their country: "The president has called for 300,000 volunteers, which makes the quota from our state 15,000, and where they are to come from, I am sure I don't know, if the percentage of able-bodied men is as small as shown to be in the last draft."[3]

The terms and conditions of the draft laws so angered poor immigrants who could not afford to buy their way out that draft riots erupted in some large Northern cities. "The blood of a poor man is as precious as that of the wealthy" became the cry of the rioters.

By the time Wilkie and Robertson enlisted, Northerners were no longer so exuberant over their cause or so confident of success. Returning soldiers told how infection and disease among the troops had done more damage than the actual fighting, and men were taking a far more somber attitude toward enlistment. Newspapers detailed the widespread corruption which enabled enlistment officers to earn bounties by signing up men in one state who had recently deserted from another. Furthermore, if Wilkie and Bob had been interested in simply doing the popular thing, they certainly would not have consented to serve as officers in all-black regiments.

The arming of blacks was adopted in October of 1862 only as a result of the North's dire need to fill its rapidly thinning ranks. Until then, Lincoln's administration had refused to accept the offers of blacks to serve in the Union army, insisting that slavery was not an issue of the war and realizing the aversion which many white soldiers would have toward serving with blacks. However, volunteering was at such a standstill, and conscription was so unpopular and unsuccessful, that Lincoln's secretary of war, Edwin M. Stanton, finally declared that the Union would arm "persons of African descent, organized into special corps. Such volunteers would be enlisted for three years, or until sooner discharged."[4] Each state loyal to the Union was thus permitted to raise its own black regiments.

The outcry against Stanton's proclamation was widespread. Northern soldiers were willing to fight for blacks but not with them. "We don't want to fight side and side with the nigger," wrote a corporal of the Seventy-fourth New York Regiment. "We feel we are too superior a race for that."[5] And a writer for the *New York Times* predicted that the presence of black soldiers would undermine the determination and zeal of the white soldiers: "I am quite sure there is not one man in ten but would feel himself degraded as a volunteer if negro equality is to be the order in the field of battle."[6]

Stanton's declaration was, however, the opportunity for which ardent Northern abolitionists had been waiting impatiently. Prominent blacks such as Frederick Douglass had been calling for the arming of black men since the beginning of the war. As early as 1861 he had asked in an editorial:

> What upon the earth is the matter with the American Government and people? Do they really covet the world's ridicule as well as their own social and political ruin? What are they thinking about, or don't they condescend to think at all? So, indeed, it would seem from their blindness in dealing with the tremendous issue now upon them. . . .
>
> Our Presidents, Governors, Generals and Secretaries are calling, with almost frantic vehemence, for men. "Men! men! send us men!" they scream, or the cause of the Union is gone; . . . and yet these very officers, representing the people and Government, steadily and persistently refuse to receive the very class of men which have a deeper interest in the defeat and humiliation of the rebels, than all others. . . . What a spectacle of blind, unreasoning prejudice and pusillanimity is this?[7]

Governor John A. Andrew of Massachusetts, the abolitionist who had defended Sanborn in 1860, traveled to Washington to obtain the order under which he could raise all-black regiments in his state. He returned at once to Boston to begin recruiting, "before the government could reconsider the matter."[8] He set to work immediately, thus embarking upon one of the most idealistic endeavors ever accomplished in America. It required extraordinary cooperation and support from abolitionists throughout the North, and it resulted in the formation of the Fifty-fourth and Fifty-fifth Massachusetts regiments, regiments which made history because of their courage and valor despite blatant displays of prejudice and hatred from white soldiers and civilians.[9]

Since the black population of Massachusetts was not adequate to furnish the number of men required, abolitionists zealously recruited and raised funds throughout the North: in Boston, New Bedford, Nantucket, Fall River, Newport, Providence, Pittsfield, New York City, and Elmira. When George L. Stearns, a staunch supporter of John Brown, addressed a recruitment meeting in Rochester, New York, the son of Frederick Douglass was his first recruit. Prominent abolitionists such as William Lloyd Garrison, Wendell Phillips, and Frederick Douglass addressed meetings, and their fiery oratory quickly inspired blacks to volunteer. They met with such success that the Fifty-fourth Massachusetts Regiment quickly filled up, and the Fifty-fifth was begun.

Since few enlisted men were interested in becoming officers of black troops, Andrew had the freedom to choose his officers "from persons nominated by commanders . . . in the field, by tried friends of the movement . . . and those [he] personally desired to appoint."[10] Andrew chose his officers carefully, knowing that he was selecting men to lead blacks who had no military experience and little, if any, education. And he knew that the majority of the American public would be observing their every action, waiting, and in many cases, hoping to see them fail.

Andrew wrote immediately to Francis G. Shaw, a lifelong supporter of the abolitionist cause. Andrew asked Shaw to present to his son, Robert Gould Shaw, an offer to become commander of "the first colored regiment to be raised in the free States." Andrew then wrote of the regiment:

> Its success or its failure will go far to elevate or depress the estimation in which the character of the colored Americans will be held throughout the world. . . . I am desirous to have for its

officers, particularly its field officers, young men of military experience, of firm antislavery principles, ambitious, superior to a vulgar contempt for color, and having faith in the capacity of colored men for military service. Such officers must necessarily be gentlemen of the highest tone and honor; and I shall look for them in those circles of educated antislavery society which, next to the colored race itself, have the greatest interest in this experiment.[11]

Robert Gould Shaw, who at the time was a second lieutenant in the Second Massachusetts Regiment, initially rejected Andrew's offer, considering his impending marriage and questioning his competence to deal with such an enormous task. He soon changed his mind, however, and Governor Andrew then set about finding twenty-nine other officers who would bring "exceptional character, experience, and ardor to their allotted work."[12]

Governor Andrew was not always able to secure young men with extensive military experience, but he certainly found men of exceptional character. The list of officers of the Fifty-fourth and Fifty-fifth regiments contains the names of some of New England's most illustrious families: Shaw, Russell, Higginson, two Appletons, two Hallowells, two Jameses. Two sons of Frederick Douglass served in the Fifty-fourth. Edward Emerson was offered a commission, but he was never able to pass the physical examination, despite repeated attempts. Henry James, Jr., on visiting the training camp of the Fifty-fourth for the first time, recalled that the officers seemed to "bristle . . . with Boston genealogies."[13]

The officers whom Governor Andrew chose were certainly courageous; they had to be. Most white soldiers refused to have anything to do with these regiments, and the locations of recruiting stations had to be kept secret "to avoid molestation." Major Hallowell of the Fifty-fourth remembered the general response: "Public opinion in the North was either avowedly hostile to this scheme or entirely sceptical as to its value. In Philadelphia recruiting was attended with some little danger, and with so much annoyance that the place of rendezvous was kept secret and the squads were marched under cover of darkness to the depot. . . . In Boston, there were contemptuous remarks by individuals from both extremes of society."[14]

Wilkie recalled that he endured "many sharp rebukes and more or less indignity" when it became known that he was to embark upon such a "crazy scheme."[115] And many years later, Bob described the indignity he endured when he consented to be transferred to the Fifty-fifth Regiment: "It is difficult to realize the contempt which was shown those humble blacks . . . , a feeling which also extended to the white man who well nigh forfeited all social recognition in consenting to officer them. The Governor . . . met with more than one rebuff in offering commissions to those in the field whose valor was not proof against the scorn of what is called the respectable class."[16]

The white officers who consented to lead the first black regiments into battle were subject not only to ridicule from white soldiers and civilians, but to far greater danger than that of officers commanding white troops. The Confederate Congress, infuriated with the decision of the North to arm blacks, declared that

> Every white person being a commissioned officer, or acting as such, who, during the present war, shall command negroes or mulattoes in arms against the Confederate States, or who shall arm, train, organize, or prepare negroes or mulattoes for military service against the Confederate States, or who shall voluntarily aid negroes or mulattoes in any military enterprise, attack, or conflict in such service, shall be deemed as inciting servile insurrection, and shall, if captured, be put to death.[17]

Even the avowed supporters of Governor Andrew's project gaped at the novelty of it all. "Every day, but especially on Sunday, large numbers of visitors were present," wrote one of the officers in the Readville camp in Massachusetts where the black recruits trained. "Many ladies graced the camp with their presence. People came from distant places to witness the novel sight of colored soldiers in quarters and on the drill ground."[18]

William H. Simpkins, a young soldier from Massachusetts and a friend of Wilkie, who volunteered to become an officer of the Fifty-fourth, could have been speaking for all of the white officers when he wrote to his family notifying them of his decision:

> I have to tell you of a pretty important step that I have just taken. I have given my name to be forwarded to Massachusetts

for a commission in the Fifty-fourth Negro Regiment. . . . This is no hasty conclusion, no blind leap of an enthusiast, but the result of much hard thinking. It will not be at first, and probably not for a long time, an agreeable position, for many reasons too evident to state. . . . Then this is nothing but an experiment after all; but it is an experiment that I think it high time we should try, an experiment which the sooner we prove fortunate the sooner we can count upon an immense number of hardy troops that can stand the effect of a Southern climate without injury; an experiment which the sooner we prove unsuccessful, the sooner we shall establish an important truth and rid ourselves of a false hope.[19]

Clearly, to become an officer of these black regiments was a brave, honorable undertaking. Even if Wilkie and Bob sought escape from home and school by enlisting, they did not seek escape from the ideals which made their family so exceptional. For years they had heard their father speak for equality and justice; now they would risk their lives for it. Wilkie and Bob soon became totally committed to their black troops and the cause which they represented; their actions and letters attest to this. Both men would endure suffering and failure later in their lives, partly as a result of their Civil War service. In contrast, the Civil War was the one time in which their idealism, intelligence, bravery, and enthusiasm served them well.

Over thirty of Wilkie's letters written to his parents during the Civil War have survived, and they reflect the same epistolary talent evident in the letters of Henry and William.[20] They remind one of William's letters written when he traveled to Brazil, and of Henry's letters written during his first trip alone to Europe. The circumstances, however, were very different. William wrote to his parents describing the natives, and Henry described the cities and galleries of Europe; Wilkie described battles and the effects of malaria. William and Henry continued to complain about their health and homesickness; Wilkie's health was excellent, although he marched for miles with his troops, and when he mentioned homesickness, he said: "The U.S. Army has taught me not to sigh over such frivolities."[21]

Wilkie enlisted on September 12, 1862. Less than a month later he was assigned, with the Forty-fourth Infantry, to Newbern, North Carolina. His first letter home, dated November 7, 1862, reflects his quick adjustment to army life. In the same letter, he sought to warn his parents, particularly his father, that the war would be more prolonged than anyone had imagined. "You don't know what enemy we have to conquer," he wrote. "Every Secessionist I have seen and all the rebel prisoners I have seen here talk in such callous earnestness about the war."[22]

Within two months of his enlistment, Wilkie was involved in his first battle, and his description of it confirms the verdict of General von Moltke, the German military historian who declared that the Civil War, in terms of training and strategy, was little more than "two armed mobs chasing each other around the country, from which nothing could be learned."[23] "The men . . . think war is a mean piece of business," wrote Wilkie to his parents,

> especially the way it is carried on in this state. We march twenty or thirty miles and find the enemy entrenched in rifle pits, or hidden away in some out of the way place, we send our artillery forward, and after a brisk skirmish ahead, the foe is driven back into the woods, and then we march on for twenty more miles, and find the same luck. Men on the last march were praying for a fight, so that they might halt and throw their knapsacks. I assure you I am not inclined to make friends with bullets, but at Whitehall after marching some fifteen or twenty miles, I really felt at the time relieved when I heard cannonading ahead.[24]

Wilkie had enlisted in Boston with his friend Cabot Russell; they were both assigned to the Forty-fourth, and they would transfer together to the Fifty-fourth, where Cabot would lose his life and Cabot's father would save Wilkie's. But for the time being, they were still very much boys, despite such sudden exposure to war. Wilkie described their antics in a letter home: "We both of us lay beside each other on our bellies on the shore of the river, each of us fancying we saw men in the trees, and pelting away whenever we got a chance."[25]

In January of 1863, Wilkie wrote home about "a malignant fever," malaria, which so disastrously affected both armies during the War. "Two weeks ago, we buried two of our company in three days, and a great many have been taken sick with it."[26] Wilkie himself manifested symptoms of malaria several years later when he was in Florida.

The Forty-fourth was a nine-month regiment, and Wilkie, like all other soldiers, began to count the days. "I am very well and in capital spirits, now and then rather blue about home," he wrote, "but only five months more and thank heaven."[27] Wilkie was devoted to the Northern cause, however, and he anticipated the necessity of remaining, since each new batch of recruits was smaller and less qualified than the last.

> If things don't look more promising than they do now by the end of next May, I fear very much we shall not see home, for [the] government will I expect make an appeal to the 300,000 nine-month's men to stay three months longer, that their services are really needed. What could they say to an appeal emanating from such a high place and for such a high cause. For myself, I am content to stay if the country needs it, but it would come hard I assure you.[28]

An appeal came which was even more compelling than Wilkie had anticipated. Governor Andrew requested that Colonel Lee, commander of the Forty-fourth, recommend three men who would be willing to serve as officers in his all-black regiment. Wilkie and Cabot Russell had befriended William Simpkins, a clerk from West Roxbury, Massachusetts, who had also enlisted with them in Boston and who was currently serving with them in the Forty-fourth. When Lee suggested their names, they readily consented, despite "many sharp rebukes . . . from the men with whom they had fought side by side on the various fields of North Carolina."[29]

Wilkie was pleased that he would be serving under Robert Gould Shaw, whom he described in an address he delivered many years later to a group of veterans in Milwaukee: "Reared early in the atmosphere of freedom, under the precepts of the best of parents, nurtured while young in the path of liberal opinion and radical resistance to all forms of human oppression, he received what to me seems the best heritage of youth, namely, a mind clear to perceive the inequalities of his fellow beings, and a heart willing to temper every uttermost anguish of the slave in every form."[30]

Wilkie, Russell, and Simpkins left the Forty-fourth and traveled to Readville, not far from Boston, to begin training the black troops and to participate in an officers' training program. The black recruits were being chosen very carefully, as their behavior would be carefully observed. Luis Emilio, an officer of the regiment who later wrote a history of its deeds, noted that the medical examination of the black recruits was "most rigid and thorough, nearly one third of the number . . . being peremptorily rejected. As a consequence, a more robust, strong, and healthy set of men were never mustered into the service of the United States."[31]

Colonel Shaw was pleased with the new recruits and wrote from Readville: "Everything goes on prosperously. The intelligence of the men is a great surprise to me. They learn all the details of guard duty and camp service infinitely more readily than most of the Irish I have had under my command. There is not the least doubt that we shall leave the State with as good a regiment as any that has marched."[32] By May of 1863, more blacks had been recruited than were needed for the Fifty-fourth, and the Fifty-fifth Massachusetts, the regiment in which Bob would serve, was formed.[33]

Wilkie was again near his family, and Henry visited him at camp. He recalled in his *Autobiography* the "Readville scene," "which most came home to me as a picture, an interplay of bright breezy air and high shanty-covered levels with blue horizons, and laughing, welcoming, sunburnt young men, who seemed mainly to bristle, through their welcome, with Boston genealogies, and who had all alike turned handsome, only less handsome than their tawny-bearded Colonel."[34]

But of his last visit to Readville, Henry wrote: "The whole situation was more wound up and girded then, the formation of negro regiments affected us as a tremendous War measure." The occasion was for him "vaguely sinister and sad—perhaps simply through the fact that, though our sympathies, our own as a family's, were, in the current phrase, all enlisted on behalf of the race that had sat in bondage, it was impossible for the mustered presence of more specimens of it, and of stranger, than I had ever seen together, not to make the young men who were about to lead them appear sacrificed to the general tragic need."[35]

Henry was describing the inherent conflict many felt about the enterprise: admiration of the "romantic chances" coupled with fear for the young men who were about to lead black men who had not yet proven themselves into battle in the South. Henry marveled, however, over Wilkie's transformation and adaptability. He wrote of his wonder that "this soft companion of my childhood should have such romantic chances and should have mastered, by the mere aid of his native gaiety and sociability, such mysteries, such engines, such arts. To become first a happy soldier and then an easy officer was in particular for G.W.J. an exercise in sociability."³⁶

When the regiment was ready to begin active service in May of 1863, it was ordered to Port Royal Island, off the coast of South Carolina. Its departure was accompanied by enormous fanfare. Henry was unable to witness the march of the Fifty-fourth through the streets of Boston; he was "helplessly absent" because of illness. He recorded anyway the "great reverberations of music, of fluttering banners, launched benedictions and every public sound."³⁷ He was probably unaware of the instances of bigotry which accompanied the departure of the regiment, instances which would occur again and again during the course of its brave service.

Wilkie recalled that "prejudice of the rankest sort" was displayed by some during the march, and he never forgot "the alternating cheers and groans, the alternate huzza and reproach which attempted to deafen each other on our march down State Street."³⁸ Peter Burchard, in his biography of Shaw, notes that "unknown to the public, reserves of police were held out of sight to supress expected rioting."³⁹

Despite the racist undercurrent, of which few were even aware, the march of the Fifty-fourth through Boston on the morning of May 28, 1863, was one of the proudest moments in Massachusetts history. Burchard describes the scene in detail:

> Shaw and his regiment threaded their way . . . through the narrow, history laden streets. . . . The streets were bright with national, state and regimental colors. There was no sign of disrespect, no signal of rioting. One of the marchers remembered, "All along the route, the sidewalks, windows, and balconies were thronged with spectators, and the appearance of the regiment caused repeated cheers and waving of flags and handkerchiefs. . . ." As he passed the house of Wendell Phillips, on Essex Street, Shaw saluted William Lloyd Garrison, who was standing on Phillips' balcony, his hand resting on a bust of John Brown, tears streaming down his face. Just past Phillips' house, a woman swept into the street and thrust a bright bouquet into Shaw's hand. . . . Shaw passed into Beacon Street where, in

front of the State House, he paused to greet Governor Andrew and his staff. . . .

Ellen Shaw [Shaw's sister], who watched from the second floor balcony . . . wrote later, "I was not quite eighteen when the regiment sailed. My mother, Rob's wife, my sisters, and I were on the balcony to see the regiment go by, and when Rob, riding at its head, looked up and kissed his sword, his face was as the face of an angel and I felt perfectly sure he would never come back."

Frederick Douglass was in Boston that day to watch his sons march by, and John Greenleaf Whittier, pacifist though he was, came out this day for his first sight of armed men since the beginning of the war. Whittier was deeply stirred by the sight of the marching Negro soldiers.

The Common was entered by the Charles Street Gate, and on the parade ground, the regiment passed in review before the Governor and the tightly packed throng. At noon, the regiment marched across the Common to the West Street gate and made its way to Battery Wharf. Shaw, still riding at the head of his regiment, moved through a corridor of madly cheering onlookers.[40]

Henry James, Sr., was present at Wilkie's departure, despite his lameness and the distance he had to travel to Boston from Newport. Bob recalled, almost forty years later, that as the regiment halted before the house of Oliver Wendell Holmes, "Dr. Holmes . . . came out of his front door supporting my dear old father, who had arrived to say Godspeed to his boy."[41]

Governor Andrew had been wise in choosing officers who "were superior to a vulgar contempt for color."[42] Soon after the regiment landed at Port Royal, Shaw found it necessary to defend his troops concerning the issue of pay. He wrote to Andrew: "You have probably seen the order from Washington which cuts down the pay of colored troops from $13 to $10. Of course if this affects Massachusetts regiments, it will be a great piece of injustice to them, as they were enlisted on the same footing as all other Massachusetts troops. . . . I shall refuse to have the regiment paid until I hear from you on the subject."[43]

The fear felt by some Northerners over arming black soldiers

was equally indefensible, and again Shaw wrote to Governor Andrew to express his disbelief: "Another change that has been spoken
of was the arming of negro troops with pikes instead of firearms.
Whoever proposed it must have been looking for a means of
annihilating negro troops altogether . . . or have never been under a
heavy musketry fire, nor observed its effects. The project is now
abandoned, I believe."[44]

Under such circumstances as these, the Fifty-fourth saw action
for the first time in "vain and inglorious incursions along the coast of
Georgia" under Colonel Montgomery, who received his orders from
General Hunter. Wilkie, along with the other officers, was disgusted
by the "acts of rapine and devastation" ordered by Montgomery. He
noted in his Milwaukee address that "Colonel Shaw speedily rebelled
at this, and after witnessing the burning of the town of Darien, in
Georgia, from a prosperous seaport town to a mere waste of ashes,
demanded of General Hunter to be relieved from this species of war
and soldierly demoralization."[45]

The Fifty-fourth remained on St. Simon's Island for several
weeks, drilling. General Hunter was replaced by General Gillmore,
and on July 10, 1863, the Fifty-fourth Regiment was ordered to
proceed to James Island, where several regiments were converging in
an attempt to capture Charleston Harbor. Wilkie wrote to his father
of the impending battle, and he expressed his admiration for the
black soldiers, admiration which would steadily increase as time
passed:

> Our work seems already marked out. We are to have the honour
> of charging the first rebel batteries on Morris Island, and to
> push on as far as we can get. It will no doubt be a fearful fight;
> all we ask for the 54th is a good fair fight, no matter how many
> we lose and how good the stuff is. The men behaved admirably
> so far, and you can't commence to imagine how pleasing it is to
> us to reap such success. They are cut out for soldiers in every
> way. Every negro ought to be armed, it is a crying shame that
> the govt. doesn't take the thing in hand more earnestly and
> devote itself to it. It is already beginning to break its faith with
> the negro. They promised him the same pay as the white soldier,
> and they only give him $10 a month—$3 of that for clothing
> making only $7 in cash instead of the white man's $13. But the

negro will bear it; they are patient and used to being roughed. By the time you receive this Charleston I hope will be ours. . . . I feel confident of success, but all depends upon our fight—I feel as much on *my* "fight" as I ever did.[46]

Within hours after Wilkie wrote to his father, the Fifty-fourth received what Wilkie called its "baptism of fire," and he proudly described it in his Milwaukee address:

> For the first time . . . we had met the enemy, and had proven there, fully to our satisfaction at least, that the negro soldier was a fighting soldier. Attacked at early dawn on the 16th of July, on the left of our line, while holding the advance of the Federal position, we had, in a sharp encounter, repulsed a squadron of rebel cavalry and driven them back. . . . How can I . . . ever forget this day! It was my first real experience of war, a day absolutely broken of all that had gone before it, the past annihilated, the future containing all that was in store.

Wilkie continued his description of the Fifty-fourth's bravery and expressed his jubilation over the soldiers' behavior in a battle which cost the regiment sixty men in killed, wounded, and missing.

> It had become a living, breathing suspicion with us . . . that all white troops abhorred our presence in the army, that the 24th Massachusetts Infantry would rather hear of us in some remote corner of the Confederacy than tolerate us in the advance of any battle in which they were themselves called upon to act as reserves or lookers on. . . . Can you not readily share with me that indescribable sensation which a youthful soldier feels, who, placed in a like situation, leading heroic negro soldiers on to victorious battle for the first time in the history of the war.[47]

The Fifty-fourth's heroic assault won the regiment public acclaim, particularly since the Tenth Connecticut Infantry had been able to escape because of the tenacious fight waged by the Fifty-fourth. A newspaper correspondent reported: "The boys of the Tenth Connecticut could not help loving the men who saved them from destruction. I have been deeply affected at hearing this feeling expressed by officers and men of the Connecticut regiment; and probably a thousand homes from Windham to Fairfield have in letters been told the story how the dark-skinned heroes fought the good fight and covered with their own brave hearts the retreat of brothers, sons, and fathers of Connecticut."[48]

Emilio recalled the incident in his history of the regiment: "It was a supreme moment for the Fifty-fourth, then under fire as a regiment for the first time. The sight of wounded comrades had been a trial; and the screaming shot and shell flying overhead, cutting the branches of trees to the right, had a deadly sound. But the dark line stood staunch, holding the front at the most vital point. Not a man was out of place."[49]

It was Wilkie, the adjutant of the regiment, who returned to Colonel Shaw with the message from General Terry saying that he was "exceedingly pleased with the conduct of [the] regiment. They have done all they could do."[50] Cabot Russell had almost been killed when "a mounted officer charged up . . . and cut twice at his head with a sword." Simpkins's company bore the force of the attack, and Simpkins had his "trousers and rubber coat pierced with bullets." He was miraculously uninjured. Emilio described the shock when "some of our dead first appeared to be mutilated; but closer inspection revealed . . . that the fiddler crabs, and not the enemy, did the work."[51]

Flushed with victory, Wilkie wrote to his father of the attack. The letter, dated July 18, 1863, was written only hours before Wilkie was critically wounded in the Fifty-fourth's futile attack on Fort Wagner.

Dear Father,

We are sailing down the Edisto River, on our way to the front. I have only time to say that we came out of the fight on the 16th with 47 killed and wounded. The regiment behaved nobly; and I would give my right arm to keep up the good name it has won. Some of the bravest little episodes were performed by the men. Sergeant Wilson, for example, of Capt. Rapell's company, killed three men out of four who assailed him, and was himself cut down by the fourth man, whom he also wounded severely with his bayonet. We are now on our way to Morris Island, the new attack on Fort Wagner commencing tomorrow at dawn. I hope and pray to God that the regiment will do as nobly there as it did at James Island.

Henry James, Sr., with his customary pride in his children, forwarded Wilkie's letter to the *Newport News,* which printed the letter, prefaced by the comment that "there is no better soldier than the negro, when the soldier's discipline is afforded him."[52]

The regiment landed at 1:00 AM on July 17 and was ordered to march, in a driving rain, throughout the night. Emilio described the scene:

> . . . the men wer obliged to move in single file, groping their way and grasping their leader as they progressed, that they might not separate. . . . Along the foot-bridges the planks became slippery with mire from muddy feet, rendering the footing insecure. . . . Great clods of clay gathered on the feet of the men. Two hours were consumed in passing over the dikes and foot-bridges alone. In distance the route was but a few miles, yet it was daybreak when the leading companies reached firmer ground. The men flung themselves on the wet ground, and in a moment were in deep sleep. . . . Footsore, weary, hungry, and thirsty, the regiment was halted near the beach opposite Folly Island about 5 A.M., on the 17th. . . . Rations were not procurable, and they were fortunate who could find a few crumbs or morsels of meat in their haversacks. Even water was hard to obtain. . . . By noon, the heat and glare from the white sand were almost intolerable.[53]

Within hours, the regiment would be ordered to lead the assault on Fort Wagner, a fort which was virtually impregnable. Emilio described it as "the strongest single earthwork known in the history of warfare."[54] Some historians have claimed that the Fifty-fourth was selected to lead the other regiments in the attack because the Union was more willing to sacrifice black soldiers than white ones. And Henry James, Sr., who followed every movement of Wilkie's regiment, wrote of the decision: "I think it was very cruel to put that regiment in the front of the charge, knowing the fury it would provoke."[55] He was, of course, referring to the rage engendered among Southern troops at the sight of black soldiers.

However, Robert Gould Shaw was honored that his regiment would lead the charge. He walked among his troops and spoke quietly to them: "I want you to prove yourselves. The eyes of thousands will look on what you do tonight."[56] Emilo echoed his colonel's words, saying that the Fifty-fourth's position in the front of the charge was "the post of honor."[57]

Gen. Truman Seymour, who was wounded in the attack, defended the decision to place the Fifty-fourth at the head of the charge: "It was believed that the Fifty-fourth was in every respect as efficient as any other body of men; and as it was one of the strongest and best officered, there seemed to be no good reason why it should not be selected for the advance. This point was decided by General Strong and myself."[58]

Immediately before the attack, Seymour addressed the men: "Boys, I am a Massachusetts man, and I know you will fight for the honor of the State. I am sorry you must go into the field tired and hungry, but the men in the fort are tired too. There are but three hundred behind those walls, and they have been fighting all day. Don't fire a musket on the way up, but go in and bayonet them at their guns".[59] Actually, there were seventeen hundred well-equipped Confederate soldiers behind those walls, waiting for the Union troops.

This initial attack of Fort Wagner was one of the worst debacles of the Civil War. It was poorly planned and even more poorly executed. In order to reach the fort, the men in Wilkie's regiment were forced to wade in water waist-high while the men in the fort shot at them. Before the Fifty-fourth had even begun to fire, Colonel Shaw was shot through the heart while shouting "Forward, Fifty-fourth."[60]

Through interviews with survivors, Emilio was able to ascertain the fate of Wilkie's best friends, Russell and Simpkins: "They climbed the parapet, and were at once fired upon. Captain Russell fell wounded, and Simpkins asked him if he would be carried off. When he declined, and asked to lie straightened out, Simpkins [did] this, and while kneeling over his friend's head, facing the enemy, was himself hit. Putting his hand to his breast, he fell across Russell, and never spoke or moved again."[61]

The charge of the Fifty-fourth, wrote Emilio, was "made and repulsed before the arrival of any other troops."[62] The battle raged on, but the Fifty-fourth regiment was decimated and forced to retreat. A Confederate lieutenant later furnished a description of the carnage:

> The dead and wounded were piled up in a ditch together sometimes fifty in a heap, and they were strewn all over the plain for a distance of three-fourths of a mile. They had . . . negro regiments, and they were slaughtered in every direction. One pile of negroes numbered thirty. . . . The negroes fought gallantly, and were headed by as brave a colonel as ever lived. He mounted the breastworks waving his sword, and at the head of his regiment, and he and a negro orderly sergeant fell dead over the inner crest of the works. The negroes were as fine-looking a set as I ever saw,—large, strong, muscular fellows.[63]

Wilkie was as brave as his colonel during the attack, and he recounted his experiences in his Milwaukee address:

> As I turned to cheer the men, under the example of Col. Shaw, whose footsteps I almost followed, Fort Wagner made herself known to us in tones which left no doubt as to our proximity. . . . To Shaw, in his boyish ardor, it undoubtedly seemed as if the worst had come and gone, and with the spectacle of a line fiercely broken there seemed no time for any other consideration save to urge on his men to swifter assault. After this mighty shock there followed perhaps five seconds of calm. . . . To every soul in that surging column it must have seemed an eternity. A broken line, a mighty cheer! The flash of hand grenades and musketry from the parapets of Wagner, the renewed storm of grape and canister from her remorseless guns, and all individuality vanished from the line behind me! It was the moment for the final summons! the work had been swiftly done, the thunder was the final oration.
>
> Gathering together a knot of men after the suspense of a few seconds, I waved my sword for a further charge toward the living line of fire above us. We had gone then some thirty yards, groping, but determinedly onwards, the ranks obliquely following the swords of those they trusted, and the onward thread of that little group who waved their lurid and smoky flags. At

this point the line of battle melted almost away; it had become
an excited mass of men unable through the reaping fire to close
up, the ranks mowed down at almost every step. Suddenly a
shell tore my side. In the frenzy of excitement it seemed a
painless visitation. The nearer our approach, the easier seemed
the way! We were now under the glare of that mountain of fire,
and to cross the ditch did not seem out of the question.

I still followed close our State colors. The memorable
injuction of Gov. Andrew to us was ever ringing in my ears, that
those "colors had never been surrendered to any foe," and I had
determined to remain close to them as I saw the sacred emblem
swaying in the smoky breeze of fire in unaccomplished victory!
A still further advance brought us to the second obstruction . . .
in front of the ditch. The enemy's fire did not abate for this
crossing, and here it was I received another wound, a canister
ball in my foot, the direction of this blow demonstrating to me
afterward that we were in close proximity to the limit for the
depression of their artillery. It was becoming then a question of
hand grenades, of torpedoes, of bayonets amd musketry. As I
stood faltering with the shock of this wound, the advancing
column, passing by me and over me, with deafening shouts and
deafening curses filled the alternating spaces of deathly missiles
in the atmosphere.

The enemy, maddened by our contiguity, redoubled the
vigor of its fire. . . . Our heroic color-bearers, bearing the State
colors and the Stars and Stripes, had reached the ramparts with
some forty men led by Capt. Appleton, of Boston. To a Haiti
negro, long a citizen of this country, had been confided the
national colors of the regiment. Wounded unto death, this
dauntless negro, fired with a courage which had no bounds, had
planted his colors in the southeast bastion of Fort Wagner.
Surrounded by the color-guard, crippled but still living, un-
aided, and unsustained to any great extent by the white soldiers
of the storming column, he rallied for twenty minutes within
the precincts of the bastion of the rebel Hell! Vanquished,
overpowered, after a hand-to-hand fight with bayonets, these
trusted black soldiers of Massachusetts retired from the position
they could not hold.

All that was left of the Federal colors was the pole and a

few shreds, which now fittingly adorn the State House hall in Boston. . . . It is related that, wounded unto death, the life-blood pouring from his groin, this valorous color-sergeant. . . . on the parapet of Fort Wagner, held, through the storm of battle the colors of the Fifty-fourth, while a squad of rebel artillerymen clung to its folds in desperate contention for its capture.

From the fiery furnace of this encounter I had dragged myself . . . completely to the water's edge, skirting a distance . . . of thirty rods from the seamoat of the fortress. The situation . . . seemed settled as far as the movement against Fort Wagner was concerned. It was no longer a question to me that we were terribly beaten!

My own situation seemed perilous indeed, and as the roaring guns in front proclaimed an irrevocable defeat, I began to think of the best way to regain the rear. The only hope of safety was to crawl behind a ridge of sand. I might die there, before the life-blood ebbed from out me, under a sky that still was ours, and in the shelter of a solitude where attempted ignominy could not prevail at my death. It had been rumored that Jeff Davis had issued a manifesto, ordering the white officers of the 54th Massachusetts hung if captured alive.

I had forsworn for myself the possibility of any such comfortable process of extinction before going into this fight, and this supremely sacred determination probably saved my life. After dragging myself away along the beach for some distance, I found a knoll, under which I became less exposed to the still terrific fire. . . . Some ambulance men from my own regiment, with an empty stretcher, passed me while stampeding to the rear. They placed me on the stretcher; consciousness to me was fast playing itself out. Only one distinct recollection I now possess, and that was after being borne for a distance to the rear, and still under the mercy of Wagner's fitful guns, a round shot blew off the head of the stretcher-bearer in my rear, producing a horrible and instant death. We all fell down together, except the companion stretcher-bearer, who betook himself in a lively manner to the fastnesses of some secluded sand hole. . . .

A tender Providence had laid his hand on me, and, in some marvelous manner, I found myself within the tents of the

Sanitary Commission, nearly three miles away. This must have been in the early morning of the following day. . . .[64]

The circumstances which led to Wilkie's safe return home were even more marvelous. Wilkie, along with hundreds of other wounded and dying soldiers, was transported that evening to a field hospital in Port Royal Harbor, a hospital in the loosest sense of the word. The wounded lay in rows on the bare ground, covered by hastily constructed tents. Because medical supplies and personnel were so scarce, civilians volunteered their services as nurses, and those wounded soldiers who could walk cared for those who couldn't. Many soldiers died from infected, untreated wounds.

The army had no efficient system of notifying families of their son's, fathers', or husbands' injuries or death. Relatives often learned their whereabouts through letters dictated by the injured soldiers to volunteers or to soldiers well enough to write. Fathers often traveled to the sight of a battle to locate their sons, or to claim their bodies.

Henry James, Sr.'s, artificial leg made such a pilgrimage out of the question; however, Cabot Russell's father traveled to South Carolina. At first, it had been reported that Russell and Simpkins had been taken prisoner. Not until weeks later was it ascertained that Cabot had been killed, and his body and that of Simpkins thrown in the same pit with Shaw's, along with the bodies of black soldiers. The Confederate commander, General Hagood, was quoted as saying of Shaw: "He is buried with his niggers." This was later refuted; and Hagood insisted instead that he had said: "I shall bury him in the common trench with the Negroes that fell with him."[65] When it was suggested, after the war, that Shaw's body be exhumed and buried in a place of honor in New England, his parents insisted that it was already buried in the most honorable place possible: with the black men whom their son had led into battle. In addition, Shaw's parents made a donation to help to rebuild the town of Darien, which had been sacked by Shaw's men under the orders of Colonel Montgomery.

Cabot's father searched for his son for days and spotted Wilkie by accident among the wounded soldiers. He notified the James family immediately, telling them that he would continue to look for his son and would soon bring Wilkie home to Newport.

By early August, Russell gave up all hope of finding his son and brought Wilkie home on a stretcher. They traveled by boat as far as New York; the canister ball which had lodged in Wilkie's foot had to be removed on board. Wilkie barely survivied the journey; both wounds, the one in Wilkie's foot and the one in his side, close to his spine, were severely infected. Wilkie's stretcher had been deposited just inside the door of the James home, and the doctors determined that he was too ill even to be moved to a bedroom. Wilkie remained in the entry for days, unconscious, delirious, and near death, while the family watched and waited. Henry James, Jr., recalled the painful incident in his *Autobiography:*

> . . . the stretcher on which my younger brother was to lie for so many days before he could be moved, and on which he had lain during his boat journey from the South to New York and thence again to Newport, of lost Cabot Russell's stricken father, who, failing, up and down the searched field, in respect of his own irrecoverable boy—then dying, or dead, as afterwards appeared, well within the enemy's works—had with an admirable charity brought Wilkie back to a waiting home instead, and merged the parental ache in the next nearest devotion he could find. Vivid to me still is one's almost ashamed sense of this at the hurried disordered time, and of how it was impossible not to impute to his grave steady gentleness and judgement a full awareness of the difference it would have made for him, all the same, to be doing such things with a still more intimate pity. Unobliterated for me, in spite of vagueness, this quasi-twilight vision of the good bereft man, bereft . . . of his only son, as he sat erect and dry-eyed at the guarded feet of our relief; and so much doubtless partly because of the image that hovers to me across the years of Cabot Russell himself, my brother's so close comrade—dark-eyed, youthfully brown, heartily bright, actively handsome.[66]

William helped to nurse Wilkie, and the sight of his younger brother lying helpless inspired William to sketch Wilkie's face as he lay on the stretcher. Since Wilkie was not yet out of danger, perhaps William felt the need to capture and preserve a likeness.

The many friends of the Jameses sought information about Wilkie's condition, and Henry James, Sr., complied, as in the following letter to his friend Caroline Sturgis Tappan:

Wilkie had a bad day yesterday and kept me busy or I shouldn't have delayed answering your inquiries till today. He is very severely wounded both in the ankle and in the side—where he doesn't heal so fast as the doctors wish in consequence of the shell having made a pouch which collects matter and retards nature. They cut it open yesterday, and today he is better, or will be. The wound in the ankle was made by a canister ball an inch and a half in diameter, which lodged eight days in the foot and was finally dislodged by cutting down through the foot and taking it out at the sole. He is excessively weak, unable to do anything but lie passive, even to turn himself on his pillow. He will probably have a slow and tedious recovery—the doctors say of a year at least; but he knows nothing of this himself and speaks, so far as he does talk, of going back in the Fall. If you write please say nothing of this; he is so distressed at the thought of a long sickness. He is vastly attached to the negro-soldier cause; believes (I think) that the world has existed for it; and is sure that enormous results to civilization are coming out of it.[67]

Several days later, Wilkie's condition had improved somewhat, and Henry James, Sr., wrote to Elizabeth Peabody. The letter reflects his blind faith; it also reflects the anguish and suffering which Wilkie endured after he was injured:

Wilkie's wound in the side distresses him a little. . . . Otherwise he is getting on well. He said to me the other day, "Come now father, sit down here, take my hand in yours and preach me a sermon. "Very well," I said. "I'll take my text in the first verse of the 23rd Psalm—The Lord is my Shepherd and I shall not want," and was proceeding to prove to him by his own (to me) miraculous getting home to his mother's care after such grievous wounds at such a distance from home, that we were actually in the same relation of utter dependence to the Divine hand, than any silly sheep was to its shepherd, and that our best wisdom lay in becoming therefore as innocent and free of self-providence as sheep; when he interrupted me saying, "Ah father, it is easy preaching faith in God's care, but one night it was hard to practice it. I woke up lying in the sand under my tent, and slowly recalled all that had happened, my wounds, my fall, the two men that tried to drag me to the rear, their fall one after the other, my feeble crawling to the ambulance—when memory slept, and I here woke to find myself apparently forgotten of all the world, and sick and faint for loss of blood. As I lay ignorant of all that had happened meanwhile and wondering whether I should ever see my home again, I discerned . . . a poor Ohio man with his jaw shot away, who finding that I was near to him and unable to move, crept over on me and deluged me with his blood. At that I felt. . . ." Here he stopped too full to proceed, and I suppose he was going to say, that then he felt how hard it was to hope in God. But the story made me realize some of the horrors of this dreadful war.[68]

Henry James, Sr.'s, Swedenborgian beliefs remained intact, however, as can be seen in the conclusion of his letter of condolence to Robert Gould Shaw's father, Francis Shaw: "In the mystical creation, we are told that 'the evening and the morning were the first day,' and so on. This is because in Divine order all progress is from dark to bright, from evil to good, from low to high, and never contrariwise. And this is the reason why, though I feel for you the tenderest sympathy, I cannot help rejoicing for him even now with unspeakable joy, that the night is past, and the everlasting morning fairly begun."[69]

Wilkie's friends from Newport, Boston, and Concord continued to inquire about his health. Louisa May Alcott knitted an afghan and wrote a poem for him. Wilkie was extremely proud of this tribute, and when he died in 1883, the entire poem was quoted in his obituary in the *Milwaukee Sentinel*.

William helped to nurse Wilkie until September of 1863, when he left Newport to study in Cambridge. He wrote home almost immediately asking Alice about Wilkie, and he described his brother's condition to his cousin Kitty Prince: "I heard from home . . . that 'Wilky was improving daily.' I hope he is, poor fellow. His wound is a very large and bad one and he will be confined to his bed a long while. He bears like a man. He is the best abolitionist you ever saw, and makes a common one, as we are, feel very small and shabby."[70]

By the end of September, two months after Wilkie had been injured, his condition had improved considerably. Henry James, Sr., wrote the following description to Mrs. Cranch: "I am glad to be able to say that Wilky is a good deal better today. Yesterday and the day before he had dysenteric symptoms which alarmed us, but they have passed off and we feel reassured. His wounds improve daily and if there are no more fragments of bone to come out of his foot, he will probably be up and out of bed in a month or two. He is very good and patient, and he desires to be affectionately remembered to you and George."[71]

Family letters show that Wilkie was still recuperating in November of 1863. William wrote to his parents: "Please tell Wilky I received his letter last week and am delighted he is improving so well and is so patient."[72] Wilkie's patience, it seems, did not last much longer. Henry wrote that Wilkie "recovered with difficulty, but at last sufficiently, from his wounds . . . and made haste to rejoin his regiment in the field."[73] Apparently, Wilkie had returned too soon. He wrote to his parents on January 4, 1864, assuring them that he was "well and in good spirits";[74] however, soon after that letter was written, Wilkie was forced to return home for a second time. According to Emilio's history of the regiment, Wilkie resigned on January 30, 1864, as a result of his wounds, and did not return until December 14, 1864, when he was again mustered into service.

Wilkie's second period of recuperation at home is never mentioned in any of the James family correspondence or in Henry's *Autobiography,* although he wrote of Wilkie's injuries and arrival home in great detail. It is peculiar that such an incident has remained unexplored in one of America's most carefully and thoroughly researched families. It *is* known that Henry James, Jr., intentionally omitted mentioning the family's brief return to America in 1858, giving his nephew the following reason: "I've covered over the fact, so overcome am I by the sense of our poor father's impulsive journeyings to and fro and of the impression of aimless vacillation which the record might make upon the reader."[75] Perhaps Henry was worried about the impression Wilkie's premature return to active duty would make on the reader, in light of the fact that he and William had not enlisted at all, allegedly because of their health. Henry did note, however, that although Wilkie recovered satisfactorily, he was "ever afterwards considerably to limp."[76]

Wilkie's letters from the field resumed on December 20, 1864, and he assured his father about his health: "I am in excellent condition in regard to my wounds and I am astonishing myself in regards to my powers. We went some 26 miles yesterday and walked about three in thick mud, but I don't feel the worse for it in any way.[77]

And on December 22, 1864, Wilkie joked about his appearance: You would be amused and scandalized also I imagine if you could see my present costume. I am no longer the stout party on crutches of six months ago, but a meagre, sallow, highly moustached cavalier with more mud on his clothes than on his boots.[78]

On Christmas Day 1864, Wilkie wrote again to his parents, assuring them that his foot had never felt better. Although his letters to his family increased in frequency, Wilkie seemed to suffer none of the symptons of homesickness so prevalent among soldiers. He wrote: "It has been a curious Christmas day for us. We opened this morning early upon the Rebs. with our three-inch and twelve-inch guns and gave them the merriest Christmas wish we possibly could."[79]

Fort Wagner had fallen into Union hands on September 6, 1863 (with the help of Bob's Fifty-fifth Regiment), shortly after Wilkie was borne home on a stretcher. Now, a little more than a year after he was so gravely injured, Wilkie was fighting with his regiment to capture the city of Charleston.

Early in February of 1865, Wilkie reinjured his foot in a fall from his horse. There is no record of the nature or extent of the damage, but it was serious enough to prevent him from continuing in the field with his troops. As a result, Wilkie joined General Gillmore's staff as an aide de camp, and in February of 1865 he was promoted to captain. Of course, he notified his parents immediately of the change.

> I write in a great hurry to tell you that I have been placed on General Gillmore's staff as A.C.D. It is just the very thing for my foot under the present circumstances, and I may consider myself very fortunate to have got the place. I like the General very much so far; he is very kind and genial and very considerate. My duties will be principally those of carrying orders to Savannah, Morris Island, Fortress Monroe.[80]

On February 19, 1865, Wilkie wrote to his parents, "in haste and consummate joy" to tell them of the capture of Charleston.

"Charleston is ours," he wrote. "It surrendered to a high regiment yesterday at 9 a.m. We have just come up from Sumter where we have hoisted the American flag. Old Gillmore," he concluded, "is in fine feather."[81]

Correspondents from the *Boston Journal* and the *Tribune* carried accounts of the event; they were particularly interested in Wilkie's reaction because he had been so gravely injured trying to capture Wagner. The first correspondent gave this account:

> I saw a young officer, looking musingly and long toward Morris Island—sitting there, the old flag floating over his head, apparently unconscious of everything around him. He walked away at last—rather haltingly, for he was lame and wounded—still gazing toward Wagner. It was Lieut. James (a son of the distinguished author), who was wounded in that celebrated assault on Fort Wagner in which Shaw lost his life and gained his immortality. He is on Gen. Gillmore's staff now, his wound having unfitted him for active service in the field.

The second newspaper account was even more histrionic:

> Our flag was hoisted at Fort Sumter on Saturday last, by Capt. Bragg, a young officer of Gen. Gillmore's staff. Long may it wave there! Capt. James of the Massachusetts 54th, who is now aide to General Gillmore, was of the party. He was wounded in the assault on Wagner. He gazed at the ruins with satisfaction and pleasure, not unmixed with melancholy, for yonder, beneath the sands of Morris Island, his beloved commander was lying—his colonel, his general, his brother officer and fellow soldier.[82]

This was too much for William. He wrote to Alice that he had seen the newspaper accounts and concluded that Wilkie "must have been behaving in a very theatrical way. I made a caricature of him," wrote William, "brandishing his foot at Fort Wagner, which I sent him."[83] Wilkie, accustomed to his brother's good-natured taunts, cherished the sketch, and pasted it in a scrapbook which he kept all his life. It is a pen-and-ink drawing, and it is a wonderful contrast to William's sketch of Wilkie as he lay gravely wounded.

Actually, Wilkie perceived the victory over Charleston in a more pragmatic light. He wrote to his father several days later and described the capture as "valuable only in so far as its moral victory tends to strengthen the Union cause." Wilkie also described for his father the adverse effect the Emancipation Proclamation was having on Southerners:

> Governor Aiken of South Carolina came up to Headquarters today and called upon Gillmore, and they had a long talk together upon the situation of the South. He is a gradual emancipationist and says that the worst act of the President was the Emancipation Proclamation. That before that everyone in South Carolina was ready to come back again on gradual emancipation and would have done so if the Proclamation had not made them utterly crazy. . . .
>
> Just think of this immense slaveholder telling me as I drove him back to his house that the coat he had on had been turned three times and that the pants he had on were the only ones he possessed. He was so simple and touching in his narrative that I could not help offering him a pair of mine which he refused however.[84]

Things were not much better for the Northern troops. "We are starved out nearly as to rations," wrote Wilkie in February of 1865, "and have come down to hard bread and corn for a living. This is well enough however and I feel none the worse for it. A clean shirt and a piece of soap would be better than the most Falstaffian board. There is no telling what we may be called upon to do next. If Sherman fails we shall no doubt all be called off to him. His whole army hate negro troops and we have been insulted a good deal since here, but a good time is coming."[85]

Less than a week later, Wilkie's spirits were high; the Northern troops sensed that victory was near. "I never felt better in my life than I do now," he wrote to "Daddy and Mammy and Everybody Else": "The fact that I have been able to stand everything thus far and even then have extra steam on hand gives me no end of satisfaction. Beside this, the prestige of the whole army seems to be greater now than it ever was. We are just whipping these fellows clean out in every direction, and the war to us seems nearer to a satisfactory end than we ever expected it could be."[86]

Lincoln's assassination on April 14, 1865, was a particular blow to Wilkie. On April 27, he wrote a poignant, intimate letter describing his grief. The letter is marked "Private," and the postscript reads: "Please burn this Father and Mother when you read it, and don't let any one else see it as it is simply my own self talking to you two." The letter shows just how much Wilkie had been influenced by his father's Swedenborgian views, yet it also reflects strong strains of Calvinism, inextricably mixed with the Jameses' own extraordinary attitude toward death: an acceptance and confidence that events, however painful, are welcome in that they contribute to the greater good.

My heart is overflowing tonight with mingled sorrow and hope at the frightful calamity which has stricken down the magnanimous people of the North. I have never felt in all my born days before the same sentiment of grief and consternation that tonight almost completely possesses my soul. The effect of poor Lincoln's death has given a life-long lesson to those who watch it, and the effect that his death has made upon the army is truly very touching. Every man feels that his own well being has been trampled on, that his own honor has been violated. I never in all my life felt so inexpressibly small and sneaky and why I should feel so is more than I can explain. It is the reaction of the bluster we have been having here lately without doubt, with great men and women who came down here to claim his honors and monopolize the joys of his pure-minded and glorious counsels. It seems to me something like a romance this career of his, but a romance that never could again be imagined nor countenanced. We have permitted it this time because it will doubtless in the end do good, but such a thing can never happen again. I don't think that anything in any young man's life of the present day is calculated to give him more hope . . . than this occurrence. Excuse these expressions of my innermost heart, but if I have ever felt sad, it is tonight. We have been talking him over and over ever since we heard of his death, and such a crowd of heartbroken young men you would never see again. We have had meetings and subscriptions all over the Dept. to raise a monument immediately and I hope that his memory may in some degree impersonate himself for a little while longer. You no doubt see something a great deal higher and better than I do in this murder, yet I see something a good deal higher than I ever thought I should. I see God's wise Providence and justice ridding the sinner of a too pure-minded and clement judge, and putting over him a less worthy and more competent and timely one. He knew that Lincoln never would give the hell to these men that they have been preparing themselves for, and consequently arranged this aright. It is nearly 12 o'clock p.m. I ought to go to bed, but I feel for you and mother tonight the same feeling that I did when you were nursing me in my bed in the summer of 1863. Do write as often as possible. We are getting on splendidly here; Gillmore I must say I like exceedingly. Best of love to Aunt Kate and Harry and Alice.[87]

In August of 1865, four months after the Confederate surrender and one month after his twentieth birthday, Wilkie was mustered out of service. He had served admirably and well. His dedication to the black cause was evident. Even though his wounds had made him eligible for a medical discharge, he returned to his regiment anxiously. The black soldiers, under the command of young and brave idealists such as Wilkie, had proved beyond a doubt that they were as good as, and often better than, their white counterparts.

Wilkie had written home on the last day of 1864 to tell his parents how he felt about the year he had just passed in the army, but he could have been speaking about his entire military experience when he wrote:

This is the last day of the year and I feel upon the whole a good deal more satisfied in passing it here than anywhere else. The army with all its disagreeable associations has a wonderful way with it of making men respect themselves and each other, and in those two paths lie the highest good. For after all, when a man feels he is doing his best for an idea, he feels a great deal more satisfaction than if he is doing it for some material cause.[88]

3
SO EAGER AND ARDENT:
Bob's Civil War Service, 1863–1865

Only one of the letters written by Bob to his parents has survived, but Bob delivered an address in Concord, Massachusetts, in 1896, describing his three years' military service. This address, coupled with Henry's recollections in his *Autobiography,* is the only existing record of Bob's Civil War experience. It is possible that Bob's letters to his parents were included in the bundles of letters destroyed by Aunt Kate. It is also possible, however, that the letters were destroyed by Henry James, Sr., to protect Bob's privacy. Some of Henry James, Sr.'s, responses to Bob from this period have survived, and they indicate that Bob's letters to his parents contained confessions that his conduct "may not have been irreproachable."[1]

These letters will be discussed later, but there is no doubt that Bob behaved bravely as a soldier. Like Wilkie, he was wounded but refused a medical discharge, and, like Wilkie, he was promoted to captain for his valiant service. Under any circumstances, a soldier's self-doubt and inner turmoil would be understandable, but this is even more so in Bob's case, when one realizes that Bob, at only sixteen years of age, was enduring contempt from other white soldiers for leading inexperienced black men into battle. And in too many instances he was watching them die.

It is certain that Bob enlisted in part because he was bored and restless; Henry James, Sr., reminded Bob, in one of his letters, of "all the idleness of old times."[2] But Bob was also inspired by other, better reasons. He noted in his address the signs of war which he had observed in Concord as he traveled to and from the Sanborn School. He remembered "the jocund faces of that double rank of militia surmounted by the bear skin caps which stood there in April of 1861."[3] And while he was still a student, Bob saw the returning wounded, "the figures of legless or armless men who came back to the homestead."[4] In Newport, Bob, then only fifteen years old, had yet another view of the war, which he recorded for his Concord address: "One day a huge frigate steamed into that peaceful Newport harbor reminding those who looked that war was not far off how'er the sounds of it were muffled. This was the *San Jacinto,* and when the white haired Commodore Wilkes came ashore the citizens cheered him, for they knew the story of Mason and Slidell by heart. Then came, after a while, a hospital transport, her decks covered alas, with a bulk of wounded volunteers, steaming to the hospital further up the bay, where many of them died."[5]

Henry James, Jr., recalled in his *Autobiography* the family's reaction when Robertson enlisted on May 21, 1863:

> Bob, who had strained much at every tether, was so eager and ardent that it made for him a positive authority; but what most recurs to me of his start in the 45th, or of my baffled vision of it, is the marvel of our not having all just wept, more than anything else, either for his being so absurdly young or his being so absurdly strenuous—we might have had our choice of pretexts and protests. It seemed so short a time since he had been *l'ingénieux petit* Robertson of the domestic schoolroom, pairing with our small sister as I paired with Wilky. We didn't in the least weep, however—we smiled as over the interest of children at its highest bloom, and that my parents, with their consistent tenderness, should have found their surrender of their latest born so workable is doubtless a proof that we were all lifted together as on a wave that might bear us where it would. Our ingenious Robertson was but seventeen years old, but I suspect his ingenuity of having, in so good a cause, anticipated his next birthday by a few months.[6]

Actually, Bob was sixteen, and the minimum age for enlistment was seventeen. Bob was somewhat reticent about his precocious enlistment in his Concord address: "Perhaps owing to a juvenile intractability which was sympathetic with the times," he explained, "and at an age so adolescent as to make any reference to it a matter of much embarrassment, I found myself commissioned as a Second Lieutenant."[7]

Robertson, like Wilkie, was initially assigned to a conventional all-white regiment, the Forty-fifth Massachusetts. In the spring of 1863, while Wilkie was sailing toward South Carolina, Bob was ordered to help quell the draft riots which erupted in Boston, primarily as a result of the three-hundred-dollar commutation clause. Bob described the events of the week-long riots in his address.

Dock Square . . . held a mob which for three days spread terror in the city and hunted down any man in certain localities of it wearing the uniform of our army. This feeling was not wholly confined to the North End, for I can remember carrying a message for General R. A. Pierce . . . which brought me in contact with the draft rioters on the Tremont Street Mall of the Common itself, and I was glad to escape from their jibes and threats. For many hours, a dozen of us, including the General, were shut up in a room over Read's Gun Store in Dock Square, the mob having gutted it and armed itself with its contents. There we waited for reinforcements from the Armory to disperse the roughs who held the Square below. Baltimore and New York rowdies were arriving by every train to swell the panic here. During those hours, the life of a black soldier in certain streets . . . was not worth five minutes' purchase. Dark must these hours have seemed indeed to our loyal citizens whose fathers and brothers were surrendering without question their lives at the front while the foreign rabble was running down the cringing blacks and hanging them to lamp posts as was done in New York City.

It was little otherwise in Boston. One night during that memorable week I was patrolling North Street with a brother officer sent . . . to report upon the state of civil order in that locality. In default of any of my own, the Commonwealth had supplied a horse many sizes too large. . . . My friend and I had been felicitating ourselves that the slums had relapsed into a state of torpor induced by the events of the day, when almost without warning we found ourselves ambuscaded by the enemy. Ere one might ejaculate Jack Robinson the cursing rowdies were upon us, my Trojan horse surrounded and apparently captured and my friend's in the same predicament. Seeing him turn to draw his sabre (for he was a cavalry officer) it was borne in upon me that it was justifiable, and . . . I punctually . . . covered the individual whose hand was upon the bits of the horse with a navy revolver, constructed very much upon the same heroic scale as was the black charger I was astride of. I never have been quite able to account for the denouement of the affair. The impression lingers of the men and women with their base faces, the rum shops on either side . . . , the snarls and obscene maledictions as of Jackalls thwarted of their meat, then the detonnation of the fire arm. The human barricades divided before the plunging horses and quite without expecting it we were borne beyond the reach of the crowd behind.[8]

Soon after the draft riots, Bob began his service with the Fifty-fifth Massachusetts Regiment, traveling to the camp in Readville to begin training as an officer, just as Wilkie had done. Bob, at sixteen, was probably the youngest soldier, much less officer, at the camp. He recalled the treatment he and the black recruits received: "After this interval of years, it is difficult to realize the contempt which was shown these humble blacks . . . a feeling which also extended to the white men who well nigh forfeited all social recognition in consenting to officer them."[9]

The Fifty-fifth departed for Newbern, North Carolina, in mid-July 1863, about the same time that Wilkie was wounded. They arrived on Morris Island, near Charleston Harbor, on August 14, 1863, less than two weeks after the Fifty-fourth had endured its crushing defeat trying to capture Fort Wagner. Reports of the Fifty-fourth's valor had spread throughout the Union, but so had the rumors and incriminations that the Fifty-fourth had been ordered to lead a strategically impossible and poorly planned and executed military maneuver. In 1896, when Bob delivered his address in Concord, he was still convinced that Wilkie's regiment had been needlessly sacrificed, and he quoted an unnamed army officer who had been present during the attack on Fort Wagner:

On the parapet of this work, sleeping in common earth, lie many brave men, victims of a plan in which regular approaches were overlooked, weak points neglected, a proper hour disregarded, to whom reinforcements were not sent, nor a pathway leveled for them with artillery; nor finally was the commanding General [Gillmore] as all eyewitnesses agree, where he could either know or direct their advance, their management, or their retreat. In vain . . . did these brave soldiers stumble from one impediment to another, groping from ditch to parapet, falling by scores beneath the murderous fire of the foe. All along the line, the slain covered the ground, monuments of folly and woe.[10]

It is impossible to determine exactly when Bob learned of Wilkie's near-fatal injuries, but the news deeply affected him. A letter which he wrote over forty years later to his daughter, who was visiting the South, shows that he had never forgotten the tragic battle in which Wilkie was almost killed. He wrote to his daughter: "What I would like you to do is to write me just the impression which Charleston Harbor makes on you. As I remember it, I can think only of the red ruin of Sumter in the Channel, the sand pit of Morris Island and the Fort Wagner Eminence of buried valor. How I wish I was there with you and your mother to show you where . . . Wilkie's maimed body was snatched from the rebels."[11]

The Fifty-fifth, along with other regiments, remained on Morris Island for months. Their primary duty was to construct, out of sandbags, an island, between their position and James Island, on which they would mount a gun. Emilio described the contraption:

The famous battery known as the "Swamp Angel" . . . was situated in the marsh between Morris and James Islands. It was constructed upon a foundation of timber, with sandbags filled upon Morris Island and taken out in boats. A two-hundred-pounder Parrott gun was lightered out to the work at night with great difficulty. Its fire reached Charleston, a distance of 8,800 yards. This gun burst after the first few discharges. Later, two mortars were mounted in the work in place of the gun.[12]

Bob described the agony of the undertaking, given the severe heat and the constant firing from enemy guns. "There is an undiversified dullness about this story," he wrote:

there is no advancing and retreating, only the dull monotonous roar of guns, the weaving of gabions and firing the death volley over the body of the latest victim. . . . As time wore on we settled into a dull apathy of expecting nothing to eat and a willingness to be very dirty indeed. The intense heat . . . came on and we still stood in the same shirts with which we were invested at the time of our departure from North Carolina six weeks previously. With the advent of vermin a Regiment ceases to think of itself with self-respect. The men feel that they are reverting to the animal state. There they were, herded like so many sheep in the shambles, ten thousand of them on what was in reality only named an island by courtesy, for it was but a sand spit in the sea. Ten thousand men festering in shelter tents not much larger than a pocket handkerchief under a torrid sun. The flies of a whole continent had congregated there to harass the emaciated creatures who were dying by scores in the field hospitals. In Gordon's Division, the one in which the 55th Mass. was placed, there were ten regiments. In no one of them at the time in question were there more than 200 men fit for duty, and in most not to exceed ninety. When it is considered that these regiments had left the North some of them but lately with their full complement of 1,000 soldiers each, some idea may be formed of the havoc which war and disease had wrought. At nightfall, the details of men required in the Swamp Angel or in the approaches to Wagner would begin their hazardous labor. The Swamp Angel was situated about a mile and a half from the island where the men were camped. It was approached by a single plank set upon trestles in the mud. Upon this, the men had to balance themselves as best they might, each with his burden of sand carried on the shoulder, and underfoot, upon the board, was left by the retreating tide a treacherous deposit of a slippery ooze. As a fatigue party would approach the spot where the Angel was to be mounted, the Rebel gunners opposite would let fly their murderous twelve-pounder Napoleon guns. Of course, these parties worked in the dark, but so accurate was the range obtained that daylight could hardly have helped them in their aim. There were many stories told in those days about the obstacles which had to be overcome by the despairing Engineer officer who had charge of the work. There was one to the effect that, thoroughly discouraged, he at last reported to Gillmore, who had assured him that nothing he might ask for would be withheld, that he must be furnished with a detail of 50 men, twenty-five feet long, to work in mud twenty-feet deep or else the work must be abandoned.

There was not much to choose between this service and that in the parallels in our approach to Wagner, save that in the latter men could find cover at times from the bursting of the rebel shells. It was a monotonous, joyless pursuit.[13]

Bob remembered, too, the summer days when "the water in the shallow wells actually stank" and swarmed with rats, and he suffered from dysentery in September of 1863.[14]

The regiment's diet was atrocious. One of the company's commanders, Charles B. Fox, whose duty it was to inspect all meat for maggots, wrote the following description for his wife's amusement of the beans the regiment ate: ". . . some beans which we finally decided must have been preserved by Noah in the Ark as a relic of other days in some way came into the possession of Uncle Sam. At any rate, they were soaked all night and then boiled five hours, and at the end of that time could not be crushed except by the application of a hard substance and a great deal of force. . . . We ordered them boiled two hours longer"[15]

Given such conditions, it is no wonder that the men, particularly the officers, grew more and more resentful of the North's lack of volunteers and the government's too-lenient draft laws, which permitted draftees to be excused for reasons of health. Even more galling to the officers and men of all-black regiments was the still unresolved issue of pay for the black soldiers. Given the brutal climate and duties which the black soldiers were forced to endure, their officers were growing more and more fearful that, unless the inequitable pay conditions were resolved, their men would revolt. The black soldiers in the Fifty-fourth had given their lives in far greater numbers than their white counterparts, and now the black soldiers in the Fifty-fifth were performing exceedingly hard manual labor while being fired upon; yet the government continued to pay them less.

The problem was not limited to Wilkie's and Bob's regiments. The number of black soldiers was growing daily. By July of 1864, Congress, desperate for men, declared that black recruits could be used by each state to satisfy draft quotas. These more recent recruits, however, did not have the support of ardent abolitionists such as Governor Andrew, who proposed to make up the difference in pay with money from the Massachusetts treasury. (The men refused the governor's offer, insisting on what was due them from the federal government.) Nor were these later black recruits always commanded by commissioned officers sympathetic to their cause of emancipation and equality. The issue of pay was just one of many inequities which black soldiers faced. Their plight is described in *A Documentary History of Emancipation:* "Organized into separate black regiments, paid at a lower rate than white soldiers, denied the opportunity to become commissioned officers, often ill used by commanders whose mode of discipline resembled that of slavemasters, and frequently assigned to menial duties rather than battlefield roles, black soldiers learned forcefully of the continued inequities of American life."[16]

Bob chafed at the treatment his men were receiving. He discussed the issue of pay and morale in the one extant letter to his parents. It was written early in 1864, while he and his men were en route to Florida.

The men seem to be in better spirits than they have been in for some time past. They had begun to grumble a great deal about getting no pay. We have been cautioned to do everything that can conduce their comfort, and make them happy under the disheartening usage they are receiving from the Govt. It was reported that the 54th had refused to do duty until paid, but it was merely a rumor. It would be one of the most frightful things that could possibly occur, and there may be danger of it if their pay is kept back much longer. Nine months of trying service, without a cent of pay, and starving families at home. If there ever were martyrs to a good cause these are the arch martyrs. I would be overjoyed if the men could only get that which belongs to them; it is disgraceful, the way in which the Govt. is treating them.

We hear that the 34th and 3rd U.S. have started from Jacksonville on expedition. Pay or no pay, the men will fight when the time comes. It was flattering to notice the way in which we were cheered by the white troops on leaving this morning. It did the men as much good as the pay will. They have rather an original argument about not taking the $7.00 a month. They say that he who refuses is not so much of a "nigger in the world's eye as he was before, but he who takes it makes himself three times more of a nigger."[17]

The issue of equal payment was not resolved until June of 1864, and even then there were arbitrary terms and conditions. The entire matter, which lasted almost as long as the war itself, was an example of government ineptitude and capriciousness which disgusted both the black soldiers and many of their officers. Bob was disgusted by the government's behavior, and for the rest of his life he remained suspicious of and often hostile to most forms of bureaucracy, particularly the federal government.

The mutiny which everyone feared did occur on several occasions, once in Bob's regiment. He described the inevitable reaction of the black soldiers after they "had waited patiently for months for their just and lawful due":

Month succeeded month of non-payment. The demeanor of the men grew more sullen every day. Once before roll call in the morning it broke the bounds of order and we found that the non-commissioned officers had assembled a small number of the men upon the beach with the intent of making a general defiance. The movement was intended to be a concerted one among all the men but miscarried. Then a private detailed for picket duty refused to fall in. His lieutenant commanded him to do so, but the man forcibly resisted. He was tried by court martial, convicted and shot on the beach in presence of the troops.

Bob remembered the morning of the execution, and the soldier,

as he stood on the beach in the early morning light of that Southern dawn. Friendless, awaiting the last touch of infamy which could be placed upon him by a Government claiming to be based on the equality of all men—not a quiver of the lip denoted the fear of death. I doubt not that in a light which was not mortal his bandaged eyes already gazed on those realities of freedom which are not of earth. . . . In the face of this travesty on fairness, when the smoke of that death volley rolled away, without a murmur even, his comrades—those of his own kindred and color, returned to their unpaid duties as soldiers. That act of unquestioning loyalty and obedience could not have been duplicated with white troops.[18]

Bob, who had been promoted to first lieutenant, remained on Morris Island with his regiment throughout the summer of 1863, preparing for the final siege on Fort Wagner. Finally, after weeks of unending fatigue work and constant shelling on the fort, General Gillmore gave the order to mount a final attack on September 7, 1863. Bob described the siege in his Concord address, and the suffering of the Confederate soldiers who had withstood the summer-long Union offensive:

Formed in column by Regiment, a staff officer presently brings the order to our Colonel that black troops shall again have the honor of filling that ditch with their dead. All . . . preparations have been consummated in perfect silence. It is a solemn moment, waiting there as if for the crack of doom, for a good many months of familiarity with the rebel stronghold has made it certain that only by burrowing from the earth's center upward can it be possessed by us. And now one of the unique weapons of our War was brought into requisition, a calcium light. As we stood there waiting for the command to advance, a shaft of pallid light was cast upon that plain in front . . . . It was among the possibilities that Beauregard, suspecting the process which had been made with the sunken passage, had ordered an evacuation by the garrison of the fort. To determine this, two scouts volunteered to pick their way across that torpedo-studded plain, that waste of sand which in the spectral light was indeed the abomination of desolation. So, in this wan surrounding, these two men crawled belly-wise as far as the ditch of the hateful fort. Then in they both went, only one emerging after a while on to the parapet. . . . Seldom are so many hopes and fears centered upon the issue of one man's coming and going. . . . He is on the crest of the parapet at last, and over he goes into the mysteries of secessiondom beyond—but only for a minute, in which the hearts of three or four thousand men seem as if in concert to stop their beating. The calcium light . . . flickers as if to say the play is o'er, and then redoubles its energy. We strain our eyes, and there the lone figure of the man stands. Over his head his cap is waving. A great cry—as the rushing of many waters, goes up from the long-baffled army, and the fleet responds to it in a hoarse cannonade muffled by the fury of the wind. Fort Wagner at length is known to be evacuated. You would not thank me to tell you of the revolting spectacle within that charnel house. It was a mal-odorous spot. The bomb proofs were foul with the long occupancy of men who never knew what it was to enjoy an hour of unbroken rest. In them we found a pitiful legacy of corpses in various stages of decomposition, and so hurriedly had the garrison departed that the wounded of the past few days had been abandoned where they lay. So ended a siege the like of which has seldom been met with in military annals.[19]

In February of 1864, the Fifty-fifth, along with several other regiments, including the Fifty-fourth, was ordered on an expedition to Florida. (Wilkie was not with his regiment; he had returned home for his second period of recuperation.) Emilio explained the reason for the move: "General Gillmore had resolved upon an expedition to Florida. . . . President Lincoln . . . desired to make Florida a loyal state. Gillmore's purposes were to secure an outlet for cotton, lumber, turpentine, and other products, cut off a source of the enemy's commissary supplies, obtain recruits for the colored regiments he was authorized to form, and inaugurate measures to restore Florida to her allegiance."[20]

Bob was less sanguine and diplomatic in his description of the purpose of the mission:

It was no surprise . . . to find ourselves aboard transports once more, sailing up the Saint John's River in Florida. . . . It had been a cherished hobby of either Mr. Lincoln or Mr. Stanton that supplies of cattle which the rebels were procuring from the pasture lands of Florida should be cut off. It seems incredible that these gentlemen should have attached any importance to such supplies if any there was. . . . Be this as it may, the War Department had ordered that a cordon of military posts be established . . . across the head of the peninsula. General

Truman Seymour, a Regular Officer of seasoned courage and experience had been entrusted with this work. He was a plucky determined man, but many knew full well the fatuity of his mission. He protested without avail against it, showing very reasonably that although there might be no force to oppose him in Florida when he should enter upon the business, after permitting him to penetrate into the wilderness of the interior it would be the simplest thing in the world for Beauregard to hurry a lot of troops down by rail from Charleston and Savannah and so crush the Union forces that there should not be enough of them left to swear by. There is one obstacle, however, against which even a veteran officer has to surrender, and that is the one of official ignorance in high places, and it was this obstacle before which poor Seymour fell.[21]

The battle of Olustee (near Jacksonville, Florida), on February 20, 1864, was another debacle for the Union army; and many of the same accusations of ineptness were made against those commanders who had disregarded all warnings that the Union soldiers would certainly be trapped. Again, black soldiers bore the brunt of the attack; the Fifty-fourth Regiment, among others, was left exposed, and the Fifty-fifth was called upon to cover the Fifty-Fourth's retreat. Bob described the carnage in his Concord address:

> Exhausted as was our black regiment, it was still necessary to cover the retreat of our men as best we might. During the night I occupied with the men under my command a strong stockade which protected the only road upon which the stricken forces could defile in their retreat. . . . Of that well organized body of five thousand men which had gone into the fight at Olustee, in the morning 2,200 did not return.[22]

It was during this retreat that Bob became too ill to continue to serve with his regiment. Henry James, Jr., in describing his brother's service during the war, noted that while Bob's regiment "was engaged in Seymour's raid on Florida he suffered a serious sunstroke, with such consequences that he was recommended for a discharge; of which he declined to avail himself, obtaining instead a position on General Ames's staff and enjoying thus for six months the relief of being mounted."[23]

Bob served as an aide de camp on the staff of General Ames in Virginia and Florida. He recovered sufficiently, however, to return to his regiment in time to participate in the siege of Charleston. Henry quoted "from memory" a passage from one of Bob's letters describing his valor during the siege: " 'It was when the line wavered and I saw Gen'l Hartwell's horse on my right rear up with a shell exploding under him that I rammed my spurs into my own beast, who, maddened with pain, carried me on through the line, throwing me down, and over the Rebel works some distance ahead of our troops.' For this action he was breveted Captain."[24]

At about this time, Bob *was* promoted to captain; however, according to his Concord address, it was not he but a soldier named Dewhurst whose mare had accidentally balked and surged forward. "On such slender threads," Robertson observed, "as the balking of a horse . . . is suspended the fate of battles."[25] Henry's crediting Bob with the deed may simply have been an error; however, Henry frequently used his *Autobiography* to portray his family in the way *he* wanted them to be seen.

In March of 1865, Bob travled to Columbia, South Carolina, with General Hartwell and his troops. Soon after Bob's arduous journey, Wilkie, who had returned to his regiment at Hilton Head, South Carolina, was able to visit Bob, and he wrote to his family to describe Bob's condition.

> I drove out to the entrenchments today to see B., and found him with Hartwell . . . smoking their long pipes on the verandah of a neat country cottage with a beautiful garden in front of them and the birds chirping and rambling around. Bob looks remarkably well and seemed very nice indeed. He speaks very highly of Hartwell, and the latter the same of him. They seem settled in remarkable comfort at Charleston and to be taking life easy after their 180 mile march through South Carolina.[26]

Two days later, Wilkie sent his parents yet another comforting report of Bob's situation: "I wrote you in my last letter about my visit to Bob. I never enjoyed seeing the child so much before. He is really very much of a man and upon my word I believe that he is the coming one of the family. He looks remarkably well and seems to be happy and contented."[27]

It is possible that Wilkie's pleasant descriptions of Bob to his parents were not as guileless as they seem. For the past year, Bob had been complaining of his restlessness and unhappiness in his letters to his parents, and Wilkie, who had been home recovering for the second time, had almost certainly read them. One suspects that Wilkie was trying to assauge his parents' fears about Bob's circumstances. Wilkie's favorable reports, however, probably did not assure his parents, for in late April of 1865, shortly before Bob returned home, Henry James, Sr.'s, letters to Bob still contained advice for Bob's doubts about his self-worth, his drinking, his relationship with God, and his behavior with women.

The scarcity of Bob's Civil War letters makes it difficult to establish the seriousness of his personal crisis, or when it actually began. Those family letters which do exist reflect a preoccupation with Wilkie's injuries. If Bob is mentioned, it is only to say, almost parenthetically, that compared with Wilkie, Bob is well. Another possible explanation for the lack of news concerning Bob is that the construction of the "Swamp Angel" during his stay on Morris Island was a secret military operation, and perhaps Bob had advised his parents to remain silent about his activities. However, in the few letters extant from Henry James, Sr., to such family friends as Mrs. Cranch, Elizabeth Peabody, and Samuel Ward, his reticence concerning Bob is understandable for another reason. It was acceptable for a parent to discuss the physical ailments of his children, and Henry James, Sr., even discussed Alice's nervous ailments at length in his letters. Based on the responses of Henry James, Sr., to Bob, however, one can determine that Bob was making painful confessions to his parents concerning his moral behavior, not a topic to be discussed casually in letters to friends.

Bob's problems probably began during his six-months' service as an aide de camp, when he had more time and freedom than he had had in the field. He could simply have been suffering guilt over his involvement with alcohol and women, an involvement not uncommon among soldiers. However, it is possible that Bob, who was sensitive, intelligent, and restless, was experiencing an identity crisis similar to the ones which his father, Henry, and William had suffered. William and Henry eventually gained substantial control over their nervous ailments, partly as a result of traveling and study financed by their parents, but also as a result of their fierce determination to overcome their problems. Bob, however, was never able to

settle into a profession which suited his artistic, sensitive temperament, and his letters often reflected a misanthropic state of mind. He
eventually came to resent the fact that he had carried first the
burdens of a soldier and later those of a family without ever having
had time to develop his own interests and talents.

The letters which Henry James, Sr., wrote to Bob, both while
he was serving in the Civil War and later when he lived in Florida
and Milwaukee, show that Bob relied heavily on his father's appro-
bation and advice, despite the fact that it seemed to do little good.
Shortly after Bob returned to service with the Fifty-fifth Regiment,
Henry James, Sr., responded to a plea from Bob for advice in a letter
of over fifteen hundred words. It read, in part:

My dear Bobbins,
    Mama and I have each got a letter this morning, and I lost
no time in doing my best to contribute to your "peace of mind"
as you say.
    You are beginning you think to feel homesick and have a
better appreciation of its comforts and order than you had
before, etc. All that is very good to hear, and several of your
preceding letters say the same thing in other ways. In short your
good angels are reviving in your bosom certain affections which
the world has somewhat dimmed in your active career. And
under this influence you naturally think there is nothing like
giving full play to these affections.
    But after all my dear Bob you are the object of a greater
pride and a far more lively affection on the part of your family
where you now are than if you were at home. You are now
performing a great service—the greatest any one can perform
towards your family, your friends and your country; and although it seems to you for the moment preferable to be at home
and surrounded by its comforts (as they now look to you) you
may depend upon it, it is a temptation which your manhood is
called upon to resist. Whatever temptations you have where you
are, you would have much worse ones at home, where you
would not be a month without being back again at all the
idleness of old times. I know very well that it seems to you quite
otherwise, while the temptation to forsake your place is so
strong upon you.
    At the back of this strong desire you persuade yourself and

promise yourself that you will be all that is amiable and excellent, but it is all an illusion. You don't perceive it, but it is a mere impulse of your natural versatility disguising itself under these affectionate feelings and taking its own supreme will. Don't believe any of its persuasions. I know all about it, for I have been through the experience often myself, and have been duped to the point of utter shame by it more than once. I know perfectly well that if you should yield to the weakness it prompts, you would regret all your days having done so, provided of course your aspiration towards a manly character be genuine.

A certain tone recently about your letters suggests to me, my dear Bob, that your conduct may not have been irreproachable of late in your own eyes, and that the softer feelings which are now germinating in your bosom are merely the effort which your better nature is making to restore you to self respect, and prevent you from being unduly cast down. . . . Now you have probably been doing something of late which your conscience disapproves. I don't seek and don't care to know what it is, but I want you to understand one thing, which is, that you probably have a *morbid* conscience on the subject, and should resist it if it becomes tyrannical.

The letter concluded:

Cheer up then my dear boy, and be a man, where you stand. Keep yourself from vices that are in vogue about you, and be firm and punctual in the performance of your functions; this is all you want to evince you an infinitely better manhood than you could acquire at home in a hundred years. The manhood you want is now being Divinely provided you in the career of duty; and you will bless God all your days if you do not weakly renounce it. I can see you are under a great temptation, but it is that and nothing else. Resist it like a man, and it will flee from you.[28]

The letter was signed: "Your affectionate and anxious Papa."

Six letters written by Henry James, Sr., to Bob during the Civil War exist; they all contain admonitions for Bob to remain with his regiment and instruction in Swedenborgian philosophy. Apparently, Bob asked for such instruction, since Henry James, Sr., in one of his letters, promised to recommend "a suitable book for a beginner of Swedenborg."[29] Aware that some of his letters were dry and long, Henry James, Sr., once stopped abruptly in the middle of a convoluted explanation, afraid that Bob would suffer from "intellectual indigestion."[30]

In a letter dated August 31, 1864, Henry James, Sr., advised Bob again, far more sternly, to remain with his regiment.

> My dear Bob
>   I had not closed my letter before your letter of the 21st to Mama and another to Willy arrived.
>   In the former your weakness gets apparently to a head . . . as I feared it might. I hope you will not be so insane. I conjure you to be a man and force yourself like a man to do your whole duty. At this moment of all others when the rebellion is caving in for want of men, and Government is calling every one to the field, it will be considered and will be very dishonorable in you to resist.

The letter concludes with an admonition for Bob to remain "manfully at your tracks."[31]

Another letter, written in September of 1864, assures Bob: "Don't be troubled; you were never so well off as you are now when your opinion of yourself is at the lowest," since according to Swedenborgian philosophy,

> the man who never does evil will never be apt to feel himself any too much the equal of his fellows, will be apt indeed to be proud and highminded, and to exclude Divine things from his bosom. It is only the repentant bosom that is really softened to the access of the highest things, and there is nothing accordingly so full of hope and joy to me as to see my children giving way to humiliation. You mistake if you suppose any of the boys have a perfectly good conscience; they all sin and all repent just as you do; though their sins perhaps being of not so conventional or public a quality as yours, their repentance is not quite so profound.

This same letter contains more instruction in Swedenborg, a comparison of a professional church with a true living church, and an analogy between Bob and the prodigal son: "Our three boys at home as you say are very good boys, and we appreciate their goodness very highly, but don't you remember the parable of the Prodigal Son, how the fatted calf is killed, and music and dancing is inaugurated, not to celebrate the virtue that never falters, but that which having faltered, picks itself up again?"

The missive ends in this way: "I close by repeating how joyful your letter has made me—made Mama and me both. We have killed and eaten the fatted calf of our hearts over it, and our souls are full of music and dancing. Keep up your courage then darling child—keep steady and all will be more than well with you."[32]

Although Bob had not been present to partake of the feast, his spirits did seem to improve. The next letter extant contains no stern remonstrances, only a rather gentle reminder to "keep up your spirits meanwhile dear Bobbins; be sure that we all love you most tenderly at home here, and will be prepared to welcome you by and by with true joy when you return with your duty manfully done."[33]

In his last letter to Bob during the Civil War, Henry James, Sr., advised Bob, after a discussion of the differences between appearance and reality and other philosophical matters, to

> avoid all impure intercourse with the other sex; I mean all intercourse with impure people. And in your intercourse with pure women study to do nothing and say nothing and feel nothing but what would elevate them in their own self respect and the respect of their kind. You will soon find someone responsive to your spirit, who will give yourself in chaste marriage to you, and your life will take a new start.

In the same letter, dated April 28, 1865, Henry James, Sr., predicted that peace was near, and he passed along advice from a family friend who wished him "to tell Bob and Wilky to stay with their regiments as they will be permanent."[34]

It is difficult to comprehend why Henry James, Sr., would recommend any such thing to Bob, given the pain, temptation, and guilt which Bob had endured as a soldier. Furthermore, a letter written by Alice James many years later indicates that Bob's propensity for alcohol had manifested itself when he was in the army. Henry James, Sr., was probably aware of this, since Bob confessed, it seems, everything to him. Henry James, Sr., himself had struggled with an addiction to alcohol when he was a college student, and one wonders why he would advise Bob to remain in an occupation which had triggered such severe problems.

Perhaps Henry James, Sr.'s, advice reflects the changes which had taken place in the James household from the time Wilkie and Bob left, almost three years earlier. When they enlisted, their father was pleased with the arrangement. William and Henry, for whatever reasons, did not want to enlist, yet the army was the very thing for Wilkie and Bob, who were bored and restless scholars and perfectly robust. In 1863, Alice had still been able to function normally, even though she was beginning to experience the nervous symptoms which would eventually leave her dependent on her family for support.

In June of 1865, however, as Wilkie and Bob prepared to return home, Henry James, Sr., must have realized that with the return of his two youngest sons he would again have all five children at home, unemployed and dependent upon him for financial support. William was studying in Cambridge and would continue to live at home until his marriage in 1878. Henry remained at home—more accurately, in his room—reading and writing. His and William's trips to Europe were financed by their parents, and although he was soon able to support himself through his literary earnings, Henry did not leave home permanently until 1875, when he moved to England. Alice's friends were beginning to be married, and Henry James, Sr., congratulating Ralph Waldo Emerson on the engagement of his daughter, could only hope "my poor little bird will find as tender a nest."[35] If Henry James, Sr., could convince Wilkie and Bob to remain with their regiments, he could at least be assured of the ability of two of his children to support themselves.

In fact, Bob did ask to be considered for a permanent position. The request was approved by Generals Gillmore and Hartwell, under both of whom Bob had served, Hartwell noting that Bob had served "faithfully and efficiently."[36] It is not clear if no position was available or Bob changed his mind, but on June 25, 1865, he was honorably discharged.

Bob concluded his Concord address by nothing that in the

spring of 1865, the hearts of the soldiers "turned Northward, turned to the peaceful humanities of New England firesides and innocencies of civil life."[37] Bob found no such peace on his return home. He could not even find a job, much less a profession which would permanently satisfy him, and he soon began a search which would, in effect, consume him for the rest of his life. He found, from time to time, satisfaction in his wife and children, or solace in the study of his father's philosophy, and he exhibited talent both as a writer and as a painter. His life was for the most part, however, from the end of the Civil War until his death, a series of earnest but vague comings and goings which led to nothing but further disappointment.

4
PATIENCE AND PHILANTHROPHY:
The Florida Enterprise, 1866–1871

Bob arrived home in July of 1865, Wilkie in August. The Jameses had moved from Newport to Boston in 1864, and this pleased Wilkie, since he was that much closer to his friends from Concord and Cambridge. Wilkie had not lost his good nature and sociability, but Bob, who at fourteen years of age had wanted his father to set him up in a drygoods store, was as restless as ever. He began immediately to search for a job, along with thousands of other returning soldiers and a recent influx of immigrants. The economy, which was contracting after the Civil War, did not help Bob's prospects. At nineteen years of age, he could speak fluent French and possessed the ability to lead men into battle, odd qualifications for employment in the Boston area.

Henry James, Sr., confronted with such a practical dilemma, turned to a family friend, John Murray Forbes, for help. Forbes, an ardent abolitionist, was one of the richest and most influential men in the country, his fortune having grown with the railroads. Henry James, Sr., thanked Forbes for his help on November 4, 1865.

My dear Sir:
    I am as much obliged to you as Bob himself is, for your kind thought of that urchin in his hour of need; for I myself am so destitute of all business tact and connections, that I don't know which way to turn to find my boys pasture. I counsel Bob to give up anxiety and trust to Providence who will provide for him as He does for the lilies and ravens; but Bob says the lilies and ravens are content with board and lodging, while he wants in addition . . . other things, some occupation of his time and

faculties, which will come only by seeking and not by waiting. And meanwhile he keeps up such a bobbing, beating the bush from Maine to Georgia that I can't myself help the hope that he will ere long find what he is in pursuit of. However this may be, I shall gratefully remember yours and Mrs. Forbes' good will to both of my boys—Wilky and Bob.[1]

Specifically, Henry James, Sr., was thanking Forbes for securing a job for Bob with the railroad. The position, however, was not near Boston but in Burlington, Iowa, a rather desolate outpost at the time and an unfortunate location for a nineteen-year-old who had recently suffered so severely from homesickness.

It was probably at this time that Forbes discussed with Wilkie the prospect of buying land in Florida and using freedmen to raise cotton. Thousands of Northerners were scurrying to buy land in the South, and Forbes was one of many Northern businessmen to see the possible advantages of such an enterprise. Lawrence N. Powell, in his book *New Masters: Northern Planters during the Civil War and Reconstruction,* noted them: it was an opportunity to buy confiscated Southern land cheaply; it would provide raw cotton for the many cloth manufacturers in New England; and for abolitionists such as Forbes it was an opportunity to prove that former slaves, if trained and treated properly, could function as responsible laborers. Governor Andrew, a close friend of Forbes, had recently formed the American Land Company and Agency and raised a subscription with which to finance Northern men in the purchase and cultivation of Southern land. Northerners such as Forbes and Andrew were convinced that the only hope for former slaves, and for the South itself, depended "on the emigration of the Yankees and Yankee energy."[2] Most important, Wilkie's status as a former soldier was extremely useful, since men who had served in the Union army were required to pay only one-fourth of the purchase price immediately and the balance in three years.

Most Jamesian biographers have implied that Wilkie's and Bob's Florida venture was an isolated experiment, supported only by their father's idealism and money, and that their intention was to further the cause of the blacks for whom the had recently fought. Actually, they were far from alone in their hopes of becoming successful cotton planters. Powell estimated that "anywhere from twenty thou-

sand to fifty thousand Northerners tried their hands at planting."³
Bob did not join Wilkie in Florida until several months after Wilkie
arrived there, and his primary purpose in going then was to escape
from the backbreaking work, the cold, and the loneliness of his
railroad job. Of course, Wilkie, and later Bob, was inspired to an
enormous degree to help the freedmen; Powell, in his book, used
them as an example of the idealism of some of the soldiers who
headed south. However, they were also embarked upon a hard-
headed business venture. Profit was not their only motive, but it was
an essential one if they were to survive. Surprisingly, according to
Powell, only five percent of the Northerners who went south had
ever been farmers; however inexperienced, they were optimistic that
they could succeed, despite the almost certain resentment of the
defeated Southerners whose land had been taken from them.

Bob departed for Burlington in early December 1865, and
Wilkie left for Florida in February of 1866, accompanied by another
former Union officer, Henry B. Scott, and four other men, all
former Union soldiers. There were two Bryans, Stephen and Syd-
ney, and there were a Jenkins and a Dennis, whose first names are
not mentioned in land deeds or letters.

Wilkie and Bob had been home for only six months. During
that time, they did not see William, who was traveling in Brazil to
study under Prof. Louis Agassiz, at the expense of his father and
with a contribution from Aunt Kate. Henry Jr. and Alice were both
at home, with no plans of leaving. These facts would not be lost on
Bob four months later, when he too wished to come home.

In April of 1866, Bob wrote to his parents complaining of the
heavy work, the lack of art and culture, and the separation from
family and friends which he was enduring in Iowa, and proposed
that he be permitted to return to Boston to study architecture. Bob's
proposal was not unreasonable when one remembers the efforts and
expenditures which Henry James, Sr., had made for his older sons.
He had, in 1860, brought his entire family back to America so that
William could study painting; he had financed William's trip to
Brazil; he had agreed to finance Henry while he established himself
as a writer; he would finance trips to Europe for both Henry and
William to cure them of symptoms ranging from backache to
melancholy. In addition, he invested in cure after expensive cure for
Alice, including a trip to Europe. Yet Bob, who had served for fifteen

months as a soldier and was supporting himself doing manual labor for the railroad, was denied the opportunity to train for a profession. Mrs. James explained the reasons for the decision in a letter to Wilkie in Florida.

> Do you ever write to Bob or hear from him? He has been getting unsettled of late. His desire now is to become an architect, and he wrote some weeks ago to Father wishing to come home and apply himself seriously to the study of architecture at once. He has been writing all winter long very long and very nice letters, suggesting how he was starved for pictures, and how he enjoyed every crumb in this way that fell in his path. Willy sent him a lot of photographs which he says he spends most of his leisure time in copying. Father wrote him reminding him of his versatility and telling him that even were his tastes ever so matured and pronounced, he could do nothing at present, as we were going to leave Boston for six months and could give him no home. He has borne the disappointment thus far very well, but has not given up the idea. The truth is that Bob has some artistic taste and not a little sensibility to beauty in nature and art, and having been cut off from his ordinary enjoyments in that way (and being heartily tired of his work which grows heavier as the summer comes on), he exaggerates his enjoyments of these things into a controlling taste, and wants to give every thing else up for it.
>
> Willy talked to Mr. Van Brunt who is a very popular and successful man just now about the matter. He says that one must study diligently, going through a great deal of drudgery for three years, after that time he will receive moderate returns for his work, but it can never be money making except for the few. Mr. Van Brunt is said to be one of the few.
>
> How will Bob ever stand three years persevering study? And how will he ever be contented with moderate going? I should think cotton planting at 25 or even 15 per cent would suit his genius much better.[4]

Mrs. James protested too much. Her argument reflects the favoritism which later led Bob to complain that he had felt abandoned. The Jameses had been willing to finance William's study of art, certainly a profession which could never be money-making "except for the few." When Henry went to Cambridge to study at Harvard, his parents paid for a room for him, in addition to tuition; they did the same for William when he studied at the medical school. Mrs. James implored Wilkie, in another letter, to pay them a visit at the summer house they rented in Swampscott, about fifteen miles from Boston, yet in Bob's case they "could give him no home." Mrs. James's ulterior motives are clear. Bob had been kept home as a companion for Alice when William, Henry, and Wilkie were sent off to day school and boarding school; later, Bob had been sent to the Sanborn School to provide companionship for Wilkie. Now, Mrs. James was determined to have Bob join Wilkie in Florida, since farming "would suit his genius much better." It is impossible to determine how she reached such a conclusion, since Bob had never worked on a farm and since he hated his outdoor work in Iowa. Actually, Wilkie and his partner, Scott, had begun to experience difficulties in working together, and Mrs. James was aware of this. Bob would, according to her plan, replace Scott, be company for Wilkie, and earn a living. Mrs. James got her wish. Bob did join Wilkie in Florida, but he remained for less than two years.

The family's initial attitude toward the Florida venture was described by Alice to her friend Mrs. Frances "Fanny" Rollins Morse:

> Wilkie has gone down to Florida with a Colonel Harry Scott to raise cotton. It is rather a serious undertaking, but we feel pretty sure it will succeed. Mr. John Forbes is very much interested in it and has raised a great deal of money for them. They are going to buy at first some three thousand acres, part of which they are going to cultivate themselves and sell the rest to other Northern men who want to go down and try the thing on a smaller scale. Their object is to make a settlement of Northern men in Florida in which way they will be doing the country a great deal of good. I only hope, I am sure, that they won't have a dreadfully hard time.[5]

Alice's next letter to Fanny Morse was even more optimistic; she noted that Wilkie was having "no trouble with the 'natives,' they on the contrary have been almost universally friendly to them." Alice also mentioned at this time yet another reason why Wilkie and thousands of other soldiers had decided to attempt cotton raising. She noted that it was "a very hard life and a very adventurous one, but then it is infinitely better than plodding on in some dingy office in State Street."[6]

Wilkie purchased land near Waldo, Florida, in Alachua County, approximately ten miles north of Gainesville. Land records show that Wilkie bought, between July of 1866 and January of 1869, over forty thousand dollars' worth of land. All of the parcels, which were adjacent to each other, constituted a large tract, which Wilkie and Scott named the Gordon Colony, after Scott's brother-in-law, Gen. George Gordon, a United States marshal from Massachusetts. Their intention was to sell off parcels of land to other Northerners to form a community of cotton-growing plantations.

It is difficult to determine exactly whose money Wilkie used to make these land purchases. Alice mentioned to Fanny Morse money raised by Forbes, but Wilkie, in another letter to his parents, mentioned traveling to Jacksonville to purchase land for Forbes and a Mr. Griswold; this was in addition to the land he purchased in Alachua County. In another letter, Wilkie used the word "subscribers." In a letter from Mrs. James, interest due Aunt Kate is mentioned, indicating that Catherine Walsh also invested in the enterprise. However, in the letters which have survived, Wilkie refers primarily to his father's investments. At the end of 1867, Forbes withdrew any further support of cotton raising in Florida; thus it is certain that after that date Wilkie was backed only by Henry James, Sr.

Initially, Wilkie's plan seemed to work. He and Scott soon became involved not only in running the farm but in local matters as well. They began negotiations to buy a mill which already existed on their land, and they made plans to organize a school "for whites and blacks," expecting to "have a large class."[7] They applied to the postmaster to have a post office instituted. "One of us is to be appointed Justice of the Peace," Wilkie informed his father late in March of 1866, "and gradually we are shaping ourselves into a community of thrifty, loyal, and prosperous Floridians."[8]

Wilkie was as happy in Florida as he had been as a soldier. He concluded his letter to his father with the following confidence:

I grow more and more interested every day in our enterprise and congratulate myself heartily on having entered on it. The familiarity which one acquires from working constantly with Nature and overcoming . . . her manifold and different problems opens one's eyes very sensibly to important truths. I have never in all my life before been able to reason more clearly and with less difficulty than I do now. The fact is no man has begun life until he has systematized his duties and doing this you are much more apt to choose the shortest and best road than you are to choose any other.[9]

Henry James, Sr., was pleased with Wilkie's progress. After receiving several reports from Wilkie, he responded in part:

I can't resist . . . telling you how vastly delighted we have been with your letters, and the genial account they give of your adventurous life. Everything is as it should be. Be patient and manly and upright, and your experiment will turn out not only a giant success in the lowest or pecuniary point of view, but a great blessing to your own future career, and to the country itself: for everything is now dependent in our future peace and comfort, upon the issue of just such experiments. They are worth more than all the charity in the world. We are full of love and pride in you.[10]

From the start, Wilkie seemed compelled to assure his father of a good return on his investment, and he was often too optimistic over his potential profits. After less than a month in Florida, he sanguinely predicted: "I think that we shall declare to our subscribers a dividend of 35% on this year's crop."[11] In April of 1866, he wrote to his father: "I don't think that you will miss the mark too much if you calculate on an addition of $2,500 to your next year's income. That is taking cotton at its present price, and very possibly, by that time its price may double."[12] (In fact, when it came time for Wilkie to sell his first crop, the price had dropped.)

Wilkie was also too sanguine about the Southerners' acceptance of the Northerners and their use of former slaves as paid employees. In addition, some of the black soldiers who had fought for the

Union were working for their former officers on plantations throughout the South. Federal troops had been stationed in the Southern states to insure the safety of blacks, and to guarantee their rights under the Fourteenth Amendment. The Ku Klux Klan grew rapidly during 1866, and over five thousand blacks were murdered in the South by whites during 1865 and 1866. Yet Wilkie was filled with hope and courage as he described the situation to his father in the spring of 1866:

> Things still look promising down here. There is a rumor here today that our troops are to be removed. If so, so be it, I don't think we shall suffer, but I doubt whether the poor negro will get much good from it. We can hold our own, I am certain of this. We have made some friends among the best men in our county, and although I don't think it would be safe for one or two of us to be here alone, I think that six of us together will be able to make out. Sometimes I feel blue and feel as if we were going to fail, but after sober reflection a good angel generally comes to the rescue and sets me all right again. The difficulties after all we encounter are simply those that all men who having responsibilities weighing upon them are always doomed to encounter. . . . We came down and settled in a region where many of the inhabitants have never seen a Yankee, where the population though sparse was ignorant, rude, and lawless. None of them had faith in negro labor, all of them in fact jeered at the thought of any man being able to keep them one week together. We started a farm, got together our hands, got all our supplies and stock and have yet to see the time when a cross or unsympathetic word reaches us from an inhabitant. Our hands began to work, and in two months got through an immense deal of labor. We gave a great impetus to labor immediately, for in less than a month most of the planters about us were hiring negroes themselves and starting their own farms again. Our seed has all been planted, our corn came up a week ago, and our cotton made its appearance yesterday and is doing well. We are at the mercy of the elements, frost and fire and secession may injure us, but we have fully vindicated the principle we started on, that the freed negro under decent and just treatment can be worked to profit to employer and employee.[13]

Wilkie's concern over the welfare of his black employees is evident in almost every one of his letters. "If you can send us some books to read," he wrote to his parents, "also some slates, pencils and some more school books, we shall be exceedingly grateful. Go to the Bible Society and get some Bibles for us also. We want to give our negroes an insight into eternity as well. The Bible Society will supply you with as many Bibles as you desire."[14]

Within four months of Wilkie's arrival, one of his black employees, a former soldier, became involved in a lawsuit, and Wilkie described the circumstances to his father. Again, his concern for his black employees overrode any concern he had for his relationship with local Southern farmers:

> We have just begun a law suit for one of our men against Mr. Washington Sparkman. A man named Simon has a pistol in his possession which Sparkman swears is his. . . . We are satisfied that Simon is right and intend to establish the precedence in practice as well as in theory that colored people shall have the right to bear arms—the old law to the contrary notwithstanding. That law is now played out and utterly unconstitutional. The Attorney General of the State in a recent proclamation has proclaimed it so, and the constitutional amendment which the State Senate passed 8 months ago has made it so. And if any miserable pettyfogging Cracker Lawyer wishes to test the strength of human progress, he now has his chance. It will be just as hard now to return to those old games as it was to break up the Union.[15]

In June of 1866, Wilkie returned to Boston on business, and Alice explained to Fanny Morse Bob's decision to return to Florida with Wilkie. Alice did not mention, of course, that Bob was going to Florida primarily because his parents had refused to permit him to remain at home to study architecture:

> We have been very much excited lately by the unexpected arrival of one of the infants from Florida and the other from Burlington. Wilky came on business and could only make us a very short visit—took Bob back with him for whom he had made an opening. It is very nice having them here together

especially as Bob dislikes the West so much and fairly revels in the Southern climate. Wilky was looking well and seemed so encouraged by their prospects that it was delightful to see him. He has wonderful plans for our going down South and spending next winter with them on "our plantation."[16]

Wilkie assured his parents, in his first letter to them after he had returned to Florida, that Bob seemed "willing to work hard, and is very enthusiastic and pleasant. In fact, I don't anticipate anything but the most pleasant relations with him."[17] Wilkie was almost certainly responding to warnings from his parents that Bob's behavior would be troublesome. Wilkie also assured his parents that Bob had recovered from the asthmatic symptoms that he experienced upon his arrival in Florida. Mrs. James, in her next letter, attributed Bob's asthma to "the sudden change to extreme heat,"[18] but given the correlation between major decisions and psychosomatic symptoms in the James family, it seems more likely that Bob's asthma was sparked by his decision to join Wilkie.

In fact, Bob did not write home for three weeks, and his mother finally wrote to him asking why. One suspects that Mrs. James was conscious of Bob's resentment:

> My faithless Bob,
>   It is just three weeks today since you left us, and not one single word from you has reached us—you in whom we confided to give us the earliest and fattest and most satisfactory of letters—I should say: of course Bob has written more than once and his letters have miscarried—but two from Wilky have come promptly and why not Bob's?
>   Wilky said you were suffering from short breathing but were better—the sudden change to extreme heat, was doubtless the cause of your oppression—but I should like very much to hear more about it from yourself.

In addition, Henry James, Sr. added a postscript: "Why don't you write darling Bobbins? I am truly disappointed not to have heard before this. All the more sure am I to get something worth waiting for when it does come."[19]

Four days later, Mrs. James began her letter to Wilkie with the following query:

> My darling Wilk,
> I wrote to Bob by the last steamer 4 days ago, to ask what was the matter with him that we had not received one word from him since he left. Is he sick? or out of spirits? that he has lost his inspiration for writing letters.[20]

Her prodding had the desired effect; Bob did finally write less than two weeks later. Unfortunately, none of his letters from Florida has survived. He must have expressed satisfaction with his situation, however, since Mrs. James, in her next letter to Wilkie, wrote that she had received his and Bob's letters, and was "delighted to hear that all was so prosperous, and that you are both so happy. Nothing on earth can make us so happy as to know that Bob and you are a mutual help and comfort to each other." She couldn't resist referring again, however, to Bob's laxity in writing: "Bob's letter was an especial pleasure as we had waited so long for it." The remainder of her letter was less pointed, and she gave an amusing account of the family's reaction to the death of a pet bird which Bob had given to his parents:

> Our dear little Bob will charm us no more with his song. He expired the other morning while we were watching him and praying for his deliverance, for it was truly painful to witness his sad condition. Willy made a surgical examination of his brain, which according to Father's theory was the seat of his trouble, and found it had started to ossify. We miss him for his own sake, and also for the sake of the Donor, whose song too has sometimes charmed us, but will I trust often charm us again.[21]

Wilkie had been experiencing difficulty in working with his partner, Henry Scott, almost from the start of their venture. Mrs. James, concerned with the potential financial losses if the enterprise did not succeed, recommended patience. "Scott's economy and your liberality of spending may produce a little jarring sometimes," she wrote to Wilkie, "but will work well in the end."[22]

Wilkie did agree to endure working with Scott, but Bob, after less than a month, had had enough of Scott's demanding and frugal nature. One of the other men who had originally settled with Wilkie, Colonel Jenkins, also decided that he wanted "rather to get away from Scott," and he joined Bob in a move to one of the other farms which Wilkie had purchased nearby. Wilkie explained the shifts in living arrangements to his father, along with a detailed account of Scott's behavior:

> The trouble with Scott is that he is so small and so unimpressionable. He has no magnanimity whatever and in fact no excellence whatever in his character. . . . He is excessively small and close in pecuniary matters and although this in the long run may rebound to my benefit, I should tenfold rather associate with the other extreme, in point of view of common decency and comfort. I do not let it disturb me much to all appearances, but really it wears terribly on me, and has been doing so for the last 8 months. I put up with it, and *shall* do so as long as I have a dollar of responsibility on my shoulders.

Wilkie was careful to agree with his mother's view that Scott's smallness in money matters "may rebound to my benefit," but it is obvious that Wilkie was struggling to make a bad situation bearable. He and Scott had purchased the land with borrowed money; it would not do to have his mother think that he was not trying his best to make the project succeed. In fact, he concluded his letter, written on his twenty-first birthday, in this way: "Don't feel uneasy or anxious about this. My 21st birthday has arrived, and I think I can accomplish as much now, having arrived at manhood, as I have done in former times in childhood. Our crops are looking admirably and every thing promises well; the town is filling up and never in my life did I feel so interested and contented with my vocation as I do now. Much love to all."23

In another letter, Wilkie informed his father that the case of Simon, the black man who had been accused of stealing a pistol, had resulted in a mistrial, and this satisfied Wilkie: "To think that the jury could be found in this county who would not . . . render a verdict adverse to the negro in a case between him and one of their own color, is a notable sign of the times."

However, Wilkie concluded his letter by noting, rather casually, the reaction of the local Southerners: "The people about us are wanting very much to sell out and get out of the way, they feel our atmosphere and it depresses them."[24] Wilkie still did not seem to realize the depth of resentment being engendered by his and the other planters' presence, or if he did, he did not want to alarm his parents.

By the end of July 1866, Wilkie's letters were as optimistic as ever, but several matters were referred to which would eventually prove to be disastrous. Wilkie mentioned a mortgage; Henry James, Sr., had agreed to lend Colonel Jenkins ten thousand dollars in order to buy one of the farms which Wilkie had originally purchased, thus pouring even more capital into an unproved venture. Wilkie was unable to send his father the mortgage documents because the county clerk was not sober enough to record it, an indication of the type of men with whom Wilkie had to associate.

Henry James, Sr., continued to recommend patience to Wilkie, quoting Solomon: "Greater is he who ruleth his own spirit, than he who taketh a city."[25] In his closing remarks, Henry James, Sr., sent his love to Bob, along with "some literature" and a promise to send Bob a copy of George Eliot's *Felix Holt*, which Henry Jr. had recently reviewed for the *Atlantic*. Bob was still craving literary stimulation, much as he had while he was with the railroad in Iowa.

The case of Simon, Wilkie's hired man, was still dragging on, but the circumstances were growing ugly and threatening. Sparkman, the plaintiff, had bribed two black men into giving false testimony, and Wilkie began to realize his true circumstances. He wrote to his father of the local Southerners: "It only goes to caution us against placing too much confidence in their protestations of Friendship. I believe most sincerely that they are all prodigious scoundrels and that they are all as cowardly as they are rascally."[26]

Yet nothing could diminish Wilkie's enthusiasm, and on August 9, 1866, he sent his father the following note: "I enclose you some of our first cotton picked from the plant about an hour ago. We begin to pick tomorrow, and I think this week we shall have some 3 or 4,000 pounds picked. This is not ginned yet."[27]

Wilkie wrote to his father again, less than a week later, about his first cotton crop: "It is gratifying to see our cotton coming in after all our labors. The staple is a remarkably fine one, and all that remains to be done this year is to pick it, gin it, back it, and sent it to market."[28]

Sending it to market was something Wilkie was unprepared for, however. Although he was convinced that his cotton was worth a dollar a pound, he was able to sell it for only sixty cents; his only other option was to not sell the cotton at all.

Throughout 1866, the entire country was divided over the issue of Reconstruction. President Johnson's plan was to pardon all Southern whites except the Confederate leaders, as opposed to Lincoln's plan, which had stipulated that only Southerners who took an oath of allegiance to the Union could be pardoned. In addition, under Johnson's administration, "black codes," state laws severely limiting the rights of blacks in the South, were passed. Johnson's plan provided blacks with no role in the process of Reconstruction but stipulated that former slave owners would form their own state governments. When Congress reconvened in December of 1866, its radical Republican members, led by Charles Sumner of Massachusetts and Thaddeus Stevens of Philadelphia, refused to seat the Southerners who had been elected. Early in 1867, Congress passed its own Reconstruction acts, abolishing the state governments formed in the South under Johnson's plan.

Wilkie and his fellow Northern planters watched these events with great concern. He was aware of the potential for violence against him and his black laborers. But Wilkie's concerns were not only political, for his problems with Scott had intensified, forcing him to make the decision to terminate their partnership. Bob was no longer with Wilkie, having moved to another farm, and Wilkie, feeling isolated and lonely, confided his convictions and plans to his brother William in one of the longest letters he wrote while he was in Florida. Wilkie described his commitment to the enterprise and to the freedmen:

> Equal suffrage based on educational qualifications to every man white and black should be forced now upon the south. Ten years from now, they will thank us for it; they talk about a war of races now if such a policy were adopted. Now is the only time it can be adopted. Ten years from now the negro will demand it, and then their beloved theory of a war of races will be forced upon them. The only way to kill this negro prejudice is to do it

ourselves. The more the negro progresses, the greater it will become. They are working hard to better themselves. No colored man, woman, or child in this State is without his spelling book, and nearly all our negroes (and there are better than 30 and 40) know by this time how to spell easy words. The whites remain about as they always will: ignorant, depraved and licentious. The blacks jog on for the most part in their same peaceable shambling way. Some of them are wide awake to their condition, but the masses of them bow and scrape in their humility before the Almighty Anglo-Saxon. One cannot help loving the southern negro. Their innocence is very touching. Day after day they are cuffed and kicked by their masters and yet, firmly convinced all of them that such treatment is no longer fair and legal, they cannot get vindictiveness enough within them to resent it.

I consider it a great privilege to be able now to lead these people right, and certainly the only way it can be done is to do it "upon the line" we are trying. One northern man of sound views can exert more influence for good than anything else. Our settlement is well known throughout the whole of East Florida They call us Yankee town and in case of trouble we can depend upon the majority of the colored men in this section of the state. I apprehend no trouble whatever unless the south gets so much encouragement from Johnson as to warrant some outbreak. That would not begin here at any rate, and in the meantime we could make ample preparations for defense. Our rear is open to Jacksonville and our eastern flank to the St. Johns River. Our armory is good and we could arm some 30 or 40 negroes, but come what may, we have faith enough in the Northern people to make our dislodgement here only the forerunner of a much more stable and secure one. No sensible man can see anything but perfect madness in a crushed people still trying to fight the infallible logic of all history.[29]

Henry James, Sr., idealistic as ever, continued to send messages of support and love to his sons: "All my joy . . . is in thinking of my dear children. The affectionate delight I feel in you and Bob, in the principle you display and the practical energy it produces, is something unspeakable, and keeps my soul matted with gratitude to the

Lord for all his goodness. I love you unutterably and bless you both every moment. I am especially charmed with your self control with respect to Scott. Keep on, all will go right."[30]

Bob could not "keep on," however. After less than four months in Florida, he decided to return home for a visit. As Alice explained to Fanny Morse, "he needs a little rest after his hard work."[31] But it is clear that Bob was not happy in Florida, for understandable reasons. He had consistently indicated his desire and preference for an exposure to art and literature, always asking that books, prints, and newspapers be sent to him. The rough and hostile temperament of the Southerners must have distressed him severely. More important, Bob had been able to deduce in four months the true state of affairs in Florida, and he realized that unless more Northerners came to cultivate the land which Wilkie had purchased, they would never survive. Mrs. James had gotten her wish, that Wilkie and Bob, together in Florida, would be "a mutual help and comfort to each other," but there would not be the "25 or even 15 per cent" profit which she had written about to William.

At the suggestion of Edward Atkinson, a prominent and successful Boston businessman and investor, Bob wrote a letter to the *Boston Advertiser* praising the advantages of investing in Southern cotton raising. The letter appeared on October 30, 1866, but it did not have the desired effect. Political and economic considerations kept investors away, and even Forbes began to have doubts about the wisdom of his decision to invest in Southern land. By 1867, he decided to pull out of the enterprise altogether.

Henry James, Sr., retained his enthusiasm, however, writing to Wilkie in February of 1867:

> My darling Wilkums:
> Don't be discouraged. Things will all turn out right if we will be patient, prudent, and hopeful. It is the universal law, and no one who is ever to be good for anything can evade it, that our real life must flourish out of disappointment to an unreal one. Your hopes were a little extravagant about the pecuniary returns to be enjoyed at first from the Florida investment; but they might have been worse, so far as one now sees, and you have only to hold on manfully and find your hopes justified in the end.[32]

Given the events which had occurred during the remainder of 1866, Henry James, Sr.'s, expectations at the beginning of 1867 are somewhat startling.

Soon after Bob returned to Florida, he wrote to his parents and to Mrs. Forbes asking that a subscription be raised and clothes be collected to help the families of "Union men who were murdered during the war by rebel scouts." He wrote:

> If you could see the condition in which these poor creatures are living your heart would bleed for them. They have large families of young children entirely dependent on them for support, and they have to trudge for miles over a sandy road to get a night's shelter, or to beg and borrow a little corn or bacon. The malignant feeling of whites down here is still so intense against Union men, and particularly deserters, that the relatives of these people turn them from their doors, and will allow them to starve.[33]

Mrs. Forbes raised $275.00 for Bob to distribute; Henry James, Sr. added $25.00 of his own money.

When Wilkie returned after his visit north, he discovered that in his absence local Southerners had instigated his black employees into demanding higher wages. As a result, Bob and Scott were forced to travel to South Carolina in an attempt to hire former slaves there and bring them back to Florida, a situation which would only exacerbate the hostility against the Gordon colony. Bob and Scott returned, without hands, and Wilkie began, for the first time, to express doubts to his parents about his ability to succeed: "Bob returned this afternoon from his trip after hands, having been gone three weeks and a half. He did not bring one with him, and consequently he and I sit in our room this chilly night together, thinking more than ever of our dearest family in Cambridge, and wishing that the same roof was to cover us all again tonight. Bob feels despondent of course, but I have made a vow not to feel so."[34]

Wilkie also informed his father that Jenkins was still unable to make any payments on his loan from Henry James, Sr.; within six months Wilkie would be forced to foreclose the mortgage.

Mrs. James sounded very much like her husband when she responded to Wilkie in the matter of his help holding out for higher wages: ". . . need we wonder that wearing the chain, they should have the souls of slaves. Nothing but freedom with education will raise them up, and that will be slow work. In the meantime, astuteness to understand them, and patience and philanthropy to bear with them, will have much to do with successful cotton growing."[35]

The letters to and from home also reflected a lighter side. Some of Wilkie's friends from Newport had visited him in Florida, and when he complained of the added burden of preparing meals to his mother, she sent him a "little cook book for cooking eggs, you will find the simple way of boiling and scrambling the best." Wilkie's friends had given a report of his condition to his parents, and Mrs. James sternly admonished Wilkie about his smoking: ". . . stop now before you go further, and moderate this pernicious habit, make a rule for yourself about it, and show yourself man enough to muster a bad habit before it has permanently injured your health."[36]

By the end of March of 1867, Wilkie's mood had improved considerably. Although other Northern planters throughout the South were returning home, unable or unwilling to endure another year of poor crops (many of them had had their entire crops destroyed by insects) and Southern hostility, Wilkie and the other men in his party were determined to learn from their past mistakes and remain in Florida. The uncertainty of Wilkie's living and working arrangements had been resolved by his moving in with Bob while Scott worked alone on the original farm. The other settlers were also managing better.

On March 18, 1867, Mrs. James asked Wilkie: "Did you get more hands . . . as you hoped?"[37] but Wilkie's response is missing. One can only assume that he did, judging by the optimistic tone of his next letter. He detailed for his family a "perilous" trip he had taken to Jacksonville, but his description was as much for their amusement as for any other reason, a definite sign that he was feeling better about himself and his prospects.

My dearest Father,

Your letter of March 11th was received today on my return from Jacksonville after one of the most perilous trips I ever had. I started last Monday and not making any connection at Baldwin, took the train for Fernandina with a view to take the steamer there from Jacksonville. The train smacked up within 8 miles of Fernandina and all the passengers were obliged to walk and crawl into town. Tuesday the steamer had not arrived from Savannah owing to the . . . storm, and on Wednesday after it had arrived, the storm had increased with such violence that there was no possibility of our crossing the bar at the mouth of the Saint Johns River. Wednesday noon, while I was walking over to Col. Gourand's mill, I slipped through the bridge which was made of two planks and Captain Kent whose arm I had pulled over with me, and down we went a distance of some 5 or 6 feet into the swamp below. This however did not injure our bones, but did injure my appearance decidedly. The swamp consisted of about two feet of the blackest mud I ever saw, and as I acted in the capacity of flooring for Kent who fell on top of me, of course no particle of my face nor clothing was without a smear of mud.[38]

Wilkie rarely mentioned Bob in his letters. When he did, however, Mr. and Mrs. James could not have been pleased, since his description of Bob must have reminded them of the symptoms of self-doubt and morbid introspection which had so plagued Bob during the Civil War. "I have the greatest respect for Bob's temperament," wrote Wilkie.

full as it is with distrust of himself and consequent unhappiness. I have thoroughly discussed our danger. He is sometimes exceedingly happy and much more hopeful than me, but as a general thing he has a distrust in his own morality. By that I mean he has a distrust in his own power of controlling his bad impulses. He is the most thoroughly manly fellow I ever knew. He has a discussion with a man, and hurts his feelings, and is so disgusted and despondent with his temperament that he groans for hours under it.[39]

When Wilkie wrote the above letter in the summer of 1867, the crops were "doing finely," and he was able to get away for a visit home, where he spent several days with his old friends in Newport. Mrs. James worried about Bob, alone in Florida during Wilkie's visit home, and she wrote him a long and encouraging letter, telling him that Wilkie "often says if Bob were only here how perfectly delightful it would be." Such letters did not comfort Bob, however; he was far too astute to agree with his parents that hope and patience would save the enterprise. None of Bob's letters from Florida has survived, but an indication exists of his attempts to warn his parents that their hopes for financial profits were too high. In the letter quoted above, Mrs. James wrote to Bob:

> Wilky read me your last letter in which you fear that Father is too sanguine about your profits the coming year. Do not be too anxious on our account. So long dear Bob as we feel and know that Wilk and you are conscientiously and cheerfully doing your best to make the thing go we will be contented whatever the result may be.
>
> It was too large a sum of money to invest in so uncertain an enterprise, but it looked so inviting and was done for the best— and I do not doubt that by industry and patience you will be able to get out of it safely in a very few years.[40]

Wilkie returned to Florida in late August 1867, intending to run for election as a delegate to the convention being held in Florida. Under the new Reconstruction Act passed by Congress, the voters of each state which had seceded would elect a convention, which in turn would adopt a new state constitution. Only then could the states be readmitted to the Union. The election in Florida would not take place until May of 1868, but Wilkie had heard that efforts were being made in his district to nominate another man in his place, and he therefore returned to Florida earlier than he had intended. Wilkie's devotion to the fair treatment of blacks, the major difference between his position and that of the Southern candidates, was clear. Mrs. James quoted his feelings in a letter to William:

> Wilk ['s] . . . last letters are cheerful as usual—Wilky and Dennis are candidates as delegates to the convention. Dennis will decline but Wilk means to go if elected. He writes very well about it—he says his youth, inexperience, and ignorance disqualify him, but if there is the smallest chance of his keeping out a disloyal man he ought to go. He says, "I represent a principle

which is far deeper than the Seven wise men of old, and the establishment of this principle is indispensable to the future welfare of the state."[41]

When the convention occurred, Wilkie must have realized that he did not have enough support to win, for he threw his votes to two other delegates. According to a newspaper article which Wilkie saved in his scrapbook, "The Convention gave him three rousing cheers."[42]

Wilkie probably found the following letter from his father when he arrived back in Florida. It indicates how far the relationship between Scott and the Jameses had deteriorated; and it reflects the concern Henry James, Sr., felt over the battle being waged between the Northern moderates and the radical Republicans in Congress. No longer was Henry James, Sr., simply concerned over the philosophical and moral differences between two warring factions; the largest financial investment he had ever made was contingent upon the outcome of such political battles.

> My darling Wilkums,
>   I send you herewith all the letters that have come for you.
> . . . There is one . . . of Scott which I mistook for one of Bob
> and opened it. I recommend to you to hold Scott to a very
> straight path; it is evident from Bob's letter that he is very
> tricky. If he objects to your paying for the horse and buggy out
> of his interest due me, then postpone your payment until your
> interest will permit you to pay him. Be sure of this, and don't let
> any fear of him drive you to act timidly. . . . Johnson is behaving
> very badly. . . . I have no doubt myself that it requires all his
> stupidity and obstinacy to force the North into doing its duty
> by the South, and that at last it will be effectually done.[43]

While Wilkie was en route to Florida, Mrs. James received a letter from Bob which alarmed her. She wrote immediately to Wilkie, describing Bob's mood, and as usual sought Wilkie's opinion of Bob's condition. "It is almost a year now since Bob was at home," she concluded in her letter, "and he must want brightening up very much; at any rate we want the brightening up of seeing him as soon as he can leave. I want him when he comes to stay until he is tired of us, so don't let him come until he can make a visit of several months."[44]

Bob's symptoms were the same as those which he had suffered during the war, and Mrs. James's belief that a visit of several months would brighten him up was ill supported by previous experience. Bob had never been able to stay at home for more than a week or two without sinking into moods of irritability and depression. He had tested his parents beyond endurance when he remained at home in 1862 rather than return to the Sanborn School, and he had been unable to endure the customary idleness of the James home when he returned from the Civil War. This time it would be no different.

Mrs. James termed Bob's coming home a visit, but in fact, when Bob did arrive home, the decision was made that he not return to Florida at all. Less than a week after his return, Bob visited the office of Edward W. Kinsley, a wool dealer in Boston, in an attempt to interest him or his associates in purchasing plantations in the South. Bob did not find Kinsley in, so he left a letter describing "the security and profit" of such an investment, "Mr. Johnson and the Rebs notwithstanding."[45]

Bob's motives in paying such visits and writing such letters are pitifully clear. He was desperately attempting to find buyers for at least part of the eight thousand acres of land which Henry James, Sr., owned. Scott was not keeping up with his payments to Henry James, Sr., and neither was Jenkins, and Wilkie was barely making enough on his crops to cover his own expenses.

Bob had no success. Too many Northerners had already returned home, unable to succeed at raising cotton and unable to sell their land at any price. Word of massive crop failure had spread, though Wilkie had been luckier than most. In addition, too many Northerners had attempted to become delegates to the states' conventions, intensifying the bitterness of the Southerners toward the Yankee carpetbaggers who had come to make a quick killing.

Predictably, Bob's chronic symptoms reappeared within one week of his arrival home. Mrs. James wrote to Wilkie: "Bob seems very much as usual. He complains very much of his throat, and seems at times rather depressed by it."[46]

Less than a month after Bob had left Wilkie, Wilkie began to manifest such severe symptoms of malaria that he too had to return home in order to recover in the cooler, drier climate. Mrs. James explained in a letter to William the "rather stirring time" these events were causing:

> Wilky came home about a week ago sick with intermittent fever. He broke down with the fever about a day after Bob left, and I presume intense anxiety and depression on account of their affairs was the reason why it took such serious hold of him, for his mind was in such an excited state that it was thought necessary he should be got home as soon as possible. We did not imagine he had been so ill, and were therefore extremely surprised to see him. He looks very much altered, very thin and sallow, and his mind evidently shaken. He has had two agues since he got home, but I am in hopes good nursing and this tonic air will soon bring him all right. The crops have been an almost total failure this year; incessant rains and caterpillars have done the business. They have done better than their neighbors, their land lying higher, but neither Scott, Jenkins, or the boys will be able to pay us anything. If the boys pay Aunt Kate and Bryan's interest it is all that they will do. Scott has not paid one cent; and has proved himself not only incompetent, but unreliable.
>
> Bob you know came home about a month ago to stay. He commenced *at once* a most vigorous inquiry after work which he kept up day and night but found nothing nor any hope of anything (for he met constantly people with greater advantages and poorer patience than himself who have been engaged in the same fruitless pursuit for months), so having an offer . . . of the same place at Burlington he had before, he decided at once to take it, and went off the day before yesterday. I am very doubtful about the wisdom of his going to live in so severe a climate, on acct. of his catarrhal trouble which seems to trouble him very much—but there seems no help for it. He is perfectly wretched at home, and makes us all very uncomfortable—so we fitted him once more and bade him God speed. Poor Wilk will have to struggle on alone in Florida which if he could only keep his health will not be a bad thing for him. Bob was a sore trial to him on account of his temperament, and he thinks he will be happier without him. It will be a severe discipline to Wilk that

dreary life there, but will make more of a man of him than the
life here would.[47]

Bob's "catarrhal trouble" may have been a recurrence of his asthma.
One must keep in mind the correlation between Bob's search for a
profession and such symptoms. He was ill during the Civil War
when he wanted to leave the army and return home; he was ill when
he first arrived in Florida after his parents refused his request to
study architecture. Now, as he prepared to return to a job he had
abhorred in 1866 in Iowa, his catarrhal trouble reoccurred.

Wilkie was well enough to return to Florida on November 24,
1867, after recuperating at home for two weeks. He had convinced
himself that his crops had failed primarily because Scott had insisted
on buying pine land rather than oak land. Thus, Wilkie decided to
purchase land in Serenola, about twenty miles north of his other
land holdings, using capital supplied by his father. Never was there a
clearer case of throwing good money after bad, and one suspects that
decisions such as these, as much as anything else, had convinced Bob
not to return to Florida. He had tried to warn his parents of their
overly optimistic estimations of success. Henry James, Sr., had not
received one cent of his initial investment back, much less profit, and
yet he was willing to purchase more land, even when it was
impossible to sell the land he already owned.

Further expansion at this time was extremely risky if not
outright foolish. Wilkie must have been aware of the conditions
which existed in the South at the end of 1867. Powell described the
situation which all cotton growers faced at that time: ". . . the fall of
cotton prices to a low of fourteen cents a pound in 1867 was a grave
blow to men who discovered that incidental expenses were greater
than they had counted on. . . . In 1867, selling one's cotton did not
even pay the expense of raising it."[48]

Wilkie's insistence on blaming Scott for the troubles they had
encountered was illogical, given these circumstances. However,
Wilkie refused to give up; he believed that his pride and manhood
were in question. The worse conditions grew, the harder Wilkie
worked, but against enormous disadvantages. His first letter written
from Serenola indicates his single-minded determination to salvage
the Florida enterprise.

My dear Mother,

Your letter came to me yesterday, while I was very busy with engines and machinery on the one hand, and a drunken overseer on the other. The latter trouble was worse from the fact that a white underling in this country, when one has occasion to reprimand him, assumes invariably the attitude of the high toned injured innocent and talks of pistols and the like. All one can do is to answer in the same way, and to keep as stiff an upper lip as is consistent with one's disliking of bowie knives and revolvers. The trouble terminated last night by an apology from that dignitary, and a promise that he would drink no more while in my employ. I should have kicked him off the place immediately if he had not been and is now a most invaluable working man.

I have had rather a varied experience of ups and downs since my return this last time to Florida. The experience has been more trying than ever, principally from the fact that I have now more to do than ever, and consequently come into contact more with new men and more men. Weather it all I have to do, and weather it all I have done; after all, I am conscious perhaps of being the stronger man for it.

I often wonder though at myself as to how in the devil a man so fond of ease and smoothness has been able to weather it as well. My determination has been though not to think ahead at all, and not to fret, but to meet difficulties only as they came and to get over them and forget them as soon as possible.[49]

Wilkie concluded his letter with an explanation of the terms of a potential sale of the Jenkins property, outlining the financial benefits for Henry James, Sr.; a later letter, however, indicates that the sale never materialized.

Little was said of Bob, but it is clear that he was unhappy in Iowa. Mrs. James mailed one of his letters from Iowa to Wilkie (it has not survived) and commented: "The tack Bob has taken in this matter is very funny, and puzzles me. It does not seem like him, but it indicates extreme annoyance with himself. Father begged him in his letter to give him a minute account of his catarrhal symptoms . . . but he ignores the whole subject."[50]

In April of 1868, Edward Emerson visited Wilkie in Florida. This must have pleased Wilkie very much, but the pleasure of the visit was probably lessened by Wilkie's concern for his crops. He explained the circumstances to his parents: "For two weeks after our cotton and corn were fairly planted, we had no rain, and we feared that the seed would rot in the ground and consequently require a complete replanting again; on Sunday, however, a heavy rain storm blew up from the South, and gave us two days of splendid rain and caused everything to open magnificently and now we breathe freely again."

In the same letter, Wilkie confessed his real reasons for remaining in Florida. Although he was painfully homesick, the idea of returning a failure was unthinkable to him. He disguised his homesickness with tongue-in-cheek flattery of his family, but his conflict was real and intense all the same.

> I am pretty lonely and secluded and often think of you and Mother and all the family with intense longing, and wonder whether the day will soon come when I can with honor and satisfaction to myself and with profit to the family, live once more in your midst free from all the many smallnesses and wretchednesses arising out of this chaotic condition of southern society: where I can get sympathy and instruction in what pertains to all things heady and hearty by turning to my father, and a constant example of joy and affection and saintliness by turning to my mother, in all things that pertain to holy living and holy thinking, the constant fellowship of such minds as Aunt Kate's, Harry's, and Alice's, (especially the latter) and this all by merely asking for it. Do write soon. I have not had a letter from home in two weeks, and am getting pretty mad. Let me hear all about Bob and Willy, and let me hear from Father in answer to my two last business letters.[51]

On October 17, 1868, Wilkie wrote a seven-page letter to his father informing him of the possibility of several planters from South Carolina purchasing the 4,250-acre farm which Jenkins had bought with the ten thousand dollars lent to him by Henry James, Sr., and which Wilkie had repossessed. Wilkie was hoping to get $8.00 an acre, almost double the $4.50 per acre which he had paid.

But the sale of the Jenkins land never materialized, and Wilkie's remaining letters from Florida contain little other than news of Southern hostility, hard work, and disappointment. Despite this, Wilkie assured his family that there was no cause for alarm. He concluded one of his letters by stating: "I think every thing will come out right in the end. If you can be patient at home, I feel in my bones that I shall eventually succeed down here."[52]

Wilkie's optimism was unwarranted. Conditions in the South were deteriorating almost daily: the Ku Klux Klan was growing in strength, and even the army regiments sent into the South by Grant had had little effect in stopping the sporadic and violent attacks on blacks and on white sympathizers. Wilkie described for his parents only one of hundreds of incidents which occurred in November of 1868, during an election, when violent attacks increased in order to frighten the blacks and keep them from voting. Under the circumstances, Wilkie's sang-froid is amazing.

My darling Father and Mother,
I have been so awfully busy during the last week that I have hardly had a chance to sit down, much less write a letter. The elections came off here quietly on the 3rd and the news has not yet reached us of the result, although many wild rumors are afloat, and there is a good deal of excitement. The only atrocity was committed the day before the election at Gordon within 2 miles of my place. A party of 5 white men mounted rode up to a negro cabin and murdered the negro within. It was the most cold-blooded murder I have ever heard of. They shot at him through the cracks of his house and tore down his roof, threw a light-wood knot on fire into his room, and tried to smoke him out. He came out finally exhausted to deliver himself up, and they put eight holes through his body with their rifles. It has caused great excitement among the negroes in Gordon and for two or three days all work was suspended and they were gathered together in large mobs armed with knives and guns swearing very loud upon all white men.
I went down as soon as possible and found that they were quieting down and were very susceptible to counsel and advice. The men have all been suspected and the case is being closely investigated. All we can say is that it is horrible; but as long as

we are here, we must fight out the beastly nuisance and join hands with negroes to do it if we can't with whites. I apprehend no further difficulty though whatever, and we have every reason to congratulate ourselves that so fiery an ordeal has been passed with so little bloodshed.[53]

Southern hostility toward Northerners was becoming more overt daily. For the first time, Wilkie personally felt the effects of this hatred, and he confided to his parents that his life was in danger. His position only reinforced his determination to remain in Florida, an admirable but impractical decision under the circumstances.

My dear Father,

I have been rebaptized in the faith of my father of late, and it has come through trouble and anguish. The fact is, affairs here have assumed such a change, that I no longer feel that safety which I once felt, and to tell the plain truth I feel that any moment, I may be called upon to give up my life for the faith of the principle I professed when I was a soldier in the open field. I was insulted grossly in Gainesville the other day, and if the man who insulted me had not been a crippled drunkard, I should have knocked him down. It is well perhaps that I did not. Dennis wrote me from Gordon the other day that he could hardly hold out any longer; that a body of armed men five in number were prowling nightly around the plantation to take his life, that these threats were openly made and that at any moment he might be killed. Today, one of the best friends I thought I had in the whole county called upon me and informed me that hereafter I was his enemy. He had recently learned that I was an officer of the 54th Mass. and that hereafter all our intercourse must cease. If this man who represents the intelligence, the culture, and the refinement of the South, as he certainly does, and who has one of the warmest hearts I ever knew feels that it is a matter of principle to wake up old issues we had thought were settled by the war, then all I can say is that it becomes me to stand as firmly as I did in 1863 and to give up everything else in so doing.

Do not understand me now as backing out of this enterprise. On the contrary, I say I have been rebaptized in my faith, and that if all goes with me, my example if it is a worthy one remains behind to attest the strength of my convictions. I am still hopeful though that good sense will eventually prevail. My political opinions which have been growing more conservative of late upon the subject of these detestable and unstable carpet-bag governments are not budged one iota by such occurrences as these. On the contrary I regard these as the effect of just such causes. There is not much virtue compatible with a government administered by greedy office-seekers, who have already taxed the state beyond its material power of production. . . .

I am more determined than ever to stick to this, and this I consider my duty, clearly laid out and defined to me. Do not read this letter to a soul. Remember this request I make most religiously of you. So few people who are not on the spot can appreciate my position, that I do not wish to have it even thought over by curious outsiders who rant and rage about matters they cannot even be made to think of with coolness and consideration.[54]

As he had done during the Civil War, Wilkie took the occasion of New Year's Eve as an opportunity to confide his innermost feelings to his parents at the end of 1868:

My darling Father and Mother,
On this eve of the New Year, I sit down to tell you by pen, ink and paper how much I love you all, and how constantly my thoughts are with you and the dearly beloved ones at home. If I only had in my staunch body full of strength and health half the delicate and moral force which either one of your afflicted brethren and inmates of Quincy Street possess, I could not only be a great comfort to myself but I could be of great material comfort to all of you. I never appreciated home so much as I do now, and I never knew until this new year what it contained of upright, innocent, unprejudiced, unbiased human nature. This feeling with me is as deep as the soul, and is brought about by the daily rubbing I have to experience with the world down here. The fact is that I am going through daily with a series of adventures which are softening every day my moral side, and opening my eyes constantly to the obliquity of those poor

creatures who have been born and bred under influences less auspicious than my own. Here one sees it daily in the most flagrant way, and to see it is to have fought perhaps the hardest fight against it. White men and negroes alike, whether they came from Massachusetts or South Carolina are all bent upon getting the best of each other, and for the last two months since I have had so much to do, in the care of two plantations, I have had a chance to get my fill of the diabolical atmosphere which keeps alive men of this class. Politically and privately, all men, with but few exceptions down here, are working for but one object, namely, that of cheating every one else in order to add a few dollars to their own possessions. It is enough gain though, to have become fully and constantly fortified against this at the loss of one's own faith in honesty and justice.

I am all alone tonight with a pelting rain outside to remind me of the next two months of rain to come. January and February are our wet months here.[55]

Wilkie's emotional strain is evident. As he sat alone with nothing to anticipate but two months of rain, he described the terms which he had set out for himself: an incomprehensible and illogical coupling of a Calvinist approval of material success with his father's belief that one's moral worth was far more important than his financial worth.

Wilkie's reference to the "afflicted brethren and inmates of Quincy Street" is accurate, however. His mother's letters to him contained constant references to the infirmities of William, Alice, Henry, and Henry James Sr. Wilkie, however, had inherited the Walsh constitution; like his mother and Aunt Kate, he suffered none of the psychosomatic symptoms which so plagued the others, and all three were usually flourishing in the midst of the "afflicted brethren." Mrs. James and Aunt Kate nursed their less robust counterparts, but Wilkie was determined to do nothing less than support them. He continued the above letter with the promise: "I shall relax no effort to succeed this year, and I do hope and pray that such will be the result."

Each spring, Wilkie's faith in the Florida venture was rejuvenated, and despite the overwhelming evidence to the contrary, he was convinced that 1869 would be different from the past three years. He wrote to his sister on April 28, more confident than ever:

My darling Alice,

Your letter was received last night, and I was delighted to hear from you. I had just returned from a trip to Gordon, whither I had been for the last week, watching the "chopping out" process with my cotton, and came back full of hope and feeling happier than I have in some time. . . .

Everything is looking remarkably well. I never had before so little trouble with my niggers, nor my crops as clean. I defy the caterpillars to injure me much this year, I am so far advanced in my cotton as to be able to get ahead of any serious loss from accidental visitations such as caterpillars or rust. My hands have been working steadily since the first of January and although they have been more expensive to me than they would have been under a later start, the difference will tell in the end. . . .

I shall be North I hope by the 10th of May.[56]

Wilkie did arrive home for a much-needed rest in May of 1869, intending to return in September. His aim was to avoid spending July and August in Florida, since the climate aggravated his malarial symptoms. However, his vacation was ruined when he received the following response to an inquiry he made regarding the condition of his crops. Savage and Haile, his cotton brokers, informed him:

We regret we cannot remove the impression conveyed in our last respects as to the ravages of the caterpillars on your place and that of your neighbor. . . .

Still, there is no necessity for your return at so early a period, on the contrary it is wholly unnecessary, so far as your plantation interests are concerned, and we may add in our poor opinion rather imprudent for sanitary reasons.

We have not heard from Gordon for some days but all other accounts from the neighborhood of Newmansville are far more favorable than the destruction here would lead us to expect, and we sincerely hope that Gordon at least may escape.[57]

Though Wilkie returned to Florida late in 1869, it is difficult to ascertain the exact date of his return, or of anything else, for that matter. No letters exist either from or to Wilkie while he was in Florida after his letter to Alice, written in the spring of 1869. The last extant letter from Mr. and Mrs. James to Wilkie is dated April

12, 1868. It is known that other letters were written, but it is possible that Wilkie chose to destroy them if their contents made him look foolish or obstinate in his refusal to leave Florida.

Wilkie remained in Florida until early 1871, though Mr. and Mrs. James must certainly have implored him to abandon the project when they received news from him of failing crops, or when they learned in November of 1868 that his life was in danger. One intriguing reference to Wilkie has survived from this period in a letter from Henry Jr. to William, written on March 8, 1870: "I should like extremely to get a line out of Wilky; but fate seems adverse. I very much wish by the way, that someone would let me know *who and what* is William Robeson, his partner."[58]

The family did not respond to Henry's request for more information, or if they did, the letter has not survived. Land records show that Wilkie, acting with a power of attorney from his father, transferred one-half interest in one thousand acres of land to William R. Robeson for eight thousand dollars in January of 1870. In February of 1881, after Wilkie had settled in Milwaukee, he transferred the other half-interest in the property to Robeson for a token payment of one dollar, indicating that mortgage terms or some other agreed-upon form of payment had been satisfied.

In addition to the land transactions with Robeson, Wilkie also sold two other parcels of land during this time for a total of twenty-five hundred dollars, indicating that he had attempted to liquidate his father's holdings during the last year he remained in Florida. However, even after Wilkie settled in Milwaukee, the Jameses still owned at least four taxable parcels of land in Florida.

Whatever transpired, it is known that the Florida enterprise, both in its length and in its losses, caused consternation in the James home, and letters written by Mr. and Mrs. James after Wilkie settled in Milwaukee indicate that they had, because of the Florida venture, lost confidence in his ability to support himself.

One can surmise how disquieting Wilkie's last year in Florida must have been to lead Henry James, Jr., to describe the Florida enterprise many years later in his *Autobiography* as "the vain experiment" which "dragged on for our anxiety and curiosity, and finally to our great discomfiture."[59]

Henry James, Sr. (Kindness of Henry Vaux.)

Mary Walsh visiting Wilkie and Robertson, 1872. (Kindness of Henry Vaux.)

Garth Wilkinson James, known as
Wilkie. (Kindness of Henry Vaux.)

Robertson James as a soldier.
(Kindness of Henry Vaux.)

Sketch of Wilkie "hard at work reading" made by William James. (By permission of the Houghton Library, Harvard University.)

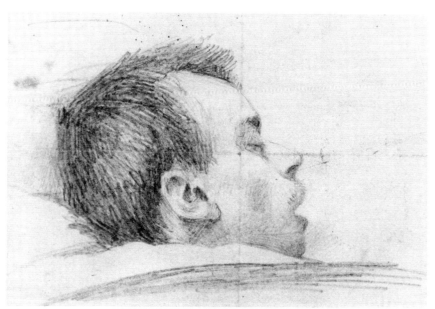

Sketch of Wilkie as he lay wounded, made by William James. (By permission of the Houghton Library, Harvard University.)

Sketch of Wilkie "brandishing his wound" at Ford Wagner, made by
William James. (Kindness of David James.)

Portrait of Robertson James made by John La Farge. (Kindness of Mrs. Slater Brown.)

Wilkie James in Milwaukee, ca. 1873. (Kindness of Mrs. Slater Brown.)

Mary Holton James, wife of Robertson James, wearing the cross Henry sent to her as a wedding present. (Kindness of Mrs. Slater Brown.)

Robertson James ca. 1865. (Kindness of Henry Vaux.)

Henry James. (Kindness of Henry Vaux.)

Alice James. (Kindness of Henry Vaux.)

William James. (Kindness of Henry Vaux.)

Robertson James sketching the Minot House in Concord, Massachusetts, ca. 1902. (By permission of the Concord Free Public Library.)

Sketch by Robertson James of The Concord Manse, residence of Nathaniel Hawthorne. (Kindness of George Vaux.)

A former slave, employed by Wilkie and Bob, learning to read. Sketch by Robertson James. (Kindness of Henry Vaux.)

Robertson James, ca. 1882. (Kindness of Henry Vaux.)

Robertson James at the sanatorium in
Dansville, New York, 1898. (Kindness of
Mrs. Slater Brown.)

Henry James with his nephew, Robertson's son Ned James.
(Kindness of Henry Vaux.)

5
A QUARREL WITH DESTINY:
Milwaukee, 1868–1882

"As to this RR place of yours now," William wrote to Bob in January of 1868, "I don't rightly understand whether you have taken it temporarily, or whether you propose to make it the starting point of your career."[1] William's confusion over Bob's return to the railroad was understandable. Bob had joined Wilkie in Florida in 1866 in order to escape from the railroad, yet less than two years later he was returning to the same position, which he had abhorred. Even Mrs. James doubted the wisdom of Bob's return to Iowa, to "so severe a climate," although she must have been relieved to see him depart, since she had written to William in November of 1867: "He is perfectly wretched at home and makes us all very uncomfortable."[2]

In September of 1868, Bob transferred to Milwaukee, Wisconsin, where he continued to work as a clerk for the St. Paul Railway, after refusing an offer to work in Galveston, Texas. Mrs. James was relieved that Bob decided not to accept the position in Texas. "Upon a moment's reflection," she had explained to Henry Jr., "it seems to me a wholly unsuitable place for Bob—when one remembers his peculiar and troublesome temperament, how dependent he is on his social surroundings for his happiness, it frightens me to think of his living among the kind of people that he will be likely to find there."[3]

Soon after Bob arrived in Milwaukee, he wrote to Alice describing the social scene, a rather different one from that he had been accustomed to in New England. The distance between houses was great, and Bob noted that "when people go to make a call at such a distance it seems to follow that the matter must be aggravated still further by staying twice as long as ordinarily would be the case." But Bob also noted that the daughter of the house was "a pretty and nice girl."⁴ It is likely that marriage, or at least female companionship, was on Bob's mind. At twenty-one, he was lonely, in a strange and new environment (Wilkie had not yet moved to Milwaukee), and Henry James, Sr., often extolled to Bob the virtues of a good wife to offset emotional and moral difficulties.

Henry James, Sr., was not pleased, however, when Bob announced that he had become secretly engaged to one of his cousins. It is not clear when or where this took place, but perhaps the relationship began when Bob returned east for a visit in the summer of 1868. In any event, in November of 1869, William wrote a long and stern letter to Bob, preaching the virtues of self-control and admonishing Bob about the consequences of a consanguineous union.

Two letters from William, dated November 14, 1869, and July 25, 1870, are the only references to this episode which exist. William's reference to the subject of consanguineous marriages and the mention of the young woman's name as Kitty have led biographers to assume that Bob had become secretly engaged to his cousin Kitty Temple, the sister of Minny Temple, whom Henry and William greatly admired. However, Kitty Temple had married Richard Emmett in 1867, two years before this incident, and in August of 1869 she had her first child. Bob probably had become engaged to another cousin Kitty, whose full name was Catherine Barber Van Buren, the daughter of Ellen King James, Henry James, Sr.'s, sister, and of Smith Thompson Van Buren, son of Pres. Martin Van Buren. If this is the Kitty to whom the letters refer, Bob was secretly engaged to his first cousin, the granddaughter of a United States president.

The effect Bob's behavior was having on his relationship with his family is evident in one of Mrs. James's letters to him. Apparently, Bob had decided to tell his family of the engagement but then changed his mind. Mrs. James wrote: "Such mysterious telegrams are flying about the country in these days, and letters to be returned unopened that we are at our wits end to grasp what it all means. If you have a secret to tell, why not tell us outright at once, the women part of the family at least, who know so well how to keep a secret. The men of course are not to be trusted and would be sure to blab."⁵

Apparently, the family believed that the matter was settled

favorably, for nothing more was said in the few letters from William to Bob which exist from this period. It is telling, however, that William's letters to Bob are filled with advice and concern over Bob's poor health, for it is probable that Bob's symptoms were a reaction to the emotional turmoil he was suffering as a result of the relationship.

Sometime between May and July of 1870, Bob returned east again and visited his cousin Kitty in New Haven, Connecticut, so, the relationship was far from over. Bob wrote to his father defending the engagement, and William wrote to Bob that he was unable to agree with Bob's "glorious flushes of excitement during which one says—'let the truth, the internal good unrelated to consequences prevail.' "

William repeated the same arguments against the engagement which he had written two months earlier, but he sympathized with Bob over Henry James, Sr.'s, position: "I have had and have now the utmost sympathy with you and hope you will never fail to count upon it. If you have felt any lack of it in Father, it does not much surprise me, for his religious optimism has I think a tendency to make him think too lightly of anyone's temporal troubles, even to neglecting to look closely into them at all." William could advise nothing less than the "keeping up of a true and courageous spirit."[6]

Apparently, Bob did so in this instance, but it took its toll. Nothing more was ever said about the affair, but his health remained bad. In August of 1871, William wrote to Bob: "It grieves me extremely to hear of your eyes being so bad. . . . I suppose the trouble is the old one with the lids for which I advise ice."[7]

Conditions did not improve. On June 22, 1872, William tried to assuage Bob's fears about impotence and nocturnal ejaculations.

. . . it would probably do you much good to unburden your mind about it. Your case as you describe it belongs to the most trifling class, amenable to treatment in some form; and if continuing in spite of medical treatment, ready to cease when sexual intercourse begins regularly. I don't think you need be in the least degree anxious about impotence. That is an effect of a totally different class of cases from yours, and moreover very uncommon.[8]

Bob's symptoms continued, but at about this time a Miss Holton begins to be mentioned in family letters. It is not known exactly when Bob met Mary L. Holton, a pretty, petite, twenty-three-year-old native of Milwaukee and the daughter of one of the city's most successful settlers. The engagement was a brief, informal one, and they were married on November 18, 1872.

Two months before the wedding, Mary Holton visited the Jameses in Cambridge, without Bob, and William wrote to Bob to congratulate him on his good fortune. "Having seen Miss Holton . . . I think you are to be congratulated in having been able to gain the confidence and affection of such a fine and charming person as she seems in every respect to be. We are certainly most fortunate, and in your good fortune we are all sharers."[9] The postscript to William's letter, however, indicates that Bob's eye troubles persisted; the prospect of marriage had not improved his health.

William wrote regularly to Bob during this difficult period, long letters containing not only diagnoses and prescriptions but also messages of support and love. "I love you my dear old Bob, more than words can express," William wrote toward the end of a six-page letter.[10] Bob, in turn, lent support to William, who was suffering through a stormy relationship with his future wife, Alice Howe Gibbens. When William did finally become engaged to her, he wrote to Bob to thank him for his support and confidence.

Wilkie had left Florida and returned to Cambridge in early 1871, with no employment prospects. He reestablished contact with his old friends and accepted an invitation from John Murray Forbes to travel by railroad from Boston to California. Ralph Waldo Emerson's health had not been good; and his good friend Forbes (who was also Edith Emerson's father-in-law) organized the excursion as a respite for Emerson. James Bradley Thayer, a Harvard law professor who was of the group, wrote a book entitled *A Western Journey with Mr. Emerson,* but he so feared playing the "part of a mere Boswell" that he wrote little more than pleasing descriptions of the scenery and recollections of Emerson's conversations.[11] Thayer does mention that there were twelve members of the party; however, he was so reticent that one cannot ascertain who the twelve people were. Gay Wilson Allen named nine of the travelers in his biography of Emerson: John Murray Forbes and his wife; their daughter Alice; Mrs. George Russell; William Forbes and his wife, Edith Emerson

Forbes; Emerson and Thayer; and Wilkie. Wilkie's good friend Edward Emerson did not take the trip. He had probably intended to go along, but illness, which was later diagnosed as smallpox, prevented him.

After arriving in Chicago, the group boarded the *Huron,* a car leased from George Pullman, after whom the Pullman car was named. The group traveled from Chicago to Burlington, crossed the Missouri River at Council Bluffs, and went through Nebraska and the Territory of Wyoming and up through the Rocky Mountains. They saw antelopes, but no buffalo, and made a twenty-four-hour detour to Salt Lake City, where they met Brigham Young. In the Yosemite Valley, Emerson's party was entertained by the naturalist John Muir. The men, on horseback, lined up side by side, but they were still narrower than one of the sequoias. In San Francisco, the group toured Chinatown, and on May 19, 1871, they started home via Lake Tahoe. They arrived in Boston on May 30.

Wilkie did not travel all the way to Boston; he left the group at Chicago and traveled first to Burlington to look into the prospect of employment with the railroad, and then to Milwaukee to visit Bob. According to a letter from Mrs. James to Henry, Bob had spoken to one of his supervisors about a possible position for Wilkie. This pleased Mrs. James since Wilkie and Bob would again provide companionship and support for each other and would each be self-supporting, something which Henry and William still hadn't achieved.

Henry James, Sr., wrote a strange letter to Wilkie at this time, containing a strong indication—an indication which would often be echoed by Mrs. James—that the family had lost confidence in Wilkie's ability to handle his own affairs. The letter suggests how costly and painful Wilkie's Florida failure had been to his parents. Wilkie had been offered a position with the railroad in which he would be handling money, probably as a payroll clerk, and Henry James, Sr., was concerned. He wrote on June 4, 1871:

> Your manhood is going to be tasked in this new (or *any* new) occupation, my dear boy, a little differently from what it has been hitherto; but I have no fear, and no one else has any, that it will not stand the test. There is no possible harm can come to one's manhood but by the . . . desire to grow rich rapidly; which

leads young men to become disgusted with such employments as they have, and which are barely renumerative, to seek wealth by speculation; or else tempts them to misuse funds belonging to other people. You have too much conscience of course even to feel the latter temptation; but the former will try you, and if you hold out there, you are safe for ever. How we all sympathize with you and feel for your new fortunes from the very bottom of our hearts, I despair of telling you even if I should try. But the sympathy is acute and constant. Every one of the family sends a special message of love to you—Mother, Willy, Harry and Alice; and you may count securely upon never being forgotten for a moment.[12]

Wilkie moved permanently to Milwaukee in the fall to begin work with the Chicago, Milwaukee and St. Paul Railway, the same railroad by which Bob was employed. Little is known of Wilkie's and Bob's activities at this particular time, but later letters indicate that Wilkie, like Bob, disliked his railroad job. Henry James, Sr., and Mrs. James visited the boys in Milwaukee in June of 1872, and at that time Bob, despite his developing relationship with Mary Holton, expressed for the first of many times a strong desire to leave Milwaukee. He was also beginning to manifest the same symptoms of self-doubt which had plagued him during the Civil War.

Henry James, Sr., concerned over Bob's mood, wrote to his son from a railroad station on his way home to offer him refuge in Boston. "I forgot to ask you when you were telling me your recent temptation to go away from Milwaukee," he wrote, "why under the sun you didn't think of coming home at once?"[13] Obviously, Bob's state of mind was not a good one for a man who was to be married in less than six months.

Despite the sincerity of Henry James, Sr.'s, invitation, Bob did not accept. Bob never had, and never would, find the promised refuge and solace at home. Each time he returned to his parents' house, his irritability increased. Henry James, Sr., tried to comfort him, assuring him that he was "passing through a crisis in [his] spiritual history known as rejuvenation . . . ," but the crisis, in effect, never passed.[14]

Bob and Mary Holton began to make wedding plans, and when Wilkie arrived in Milwaukee, Mary introduced him to her friend

Caroline Cary. Wilkie and Miss Cary, who was nicknamed Carrie, were attracted to each other almost immediately, and Mrs. James in Cambridge wanted more information from Wilkie and Bob about these two young women. As she obtained it, she passed it on to Henry and Alice, who were in Europe in the summer of 1872. "You want to hear I know all I can tell you about Miss Cary," she wrote:

> Wilky sent another photograph which is more pleasing—a side face. She answered our letter very promptly although Wilky said it would cost her a great effort as she was not given to letter writing. Her letter was simply a very frank and womanly expression of her strong affection for Wilky, and of the supreme happiness she felt in his love for her. Wilky, I should judge, is very much in love, and Bob says in a letter this morning: "Wilky seems very happy, I think Miss Cary ought to make him so, she will make you all so by and by." These girls are neither of them I should judge at all intellectual. Miss Cary is probably a person of more sentiment and stronger affections than Mary Holton. She will ask more from Wilky in a sentimental way than Mary will from Bob—and this is just right—how she is on the practical side I have not found out—perhaps one of these days they might join their resources and live together, and let little Mary manage for them all, for I imagine she would be equal to an emergency, so great a little power is she.[15]

Mrs. James had taken a liking to Mary Holton; she particularly admired Mary's practicality. Mary was not "at all intellectual," nor did she strive to be. She had graduated from the Milwaukee Female College, a proper finishing school for the daughter of Edward Holton, one of Milwaukee's most famous and successful citizens. Edward Holton had begun his career at the age of twelve as a clerk in New England. By the time he was twenty, he was general manager of a steamship company in Buffalo, New York, and in 1840 he migrated west and began a general store in Milwaukee before Milwaukee was even a city. In 1853, he was nominated for governor of Wisconsin on a prohibitionist and abolitionist ticket, but he lost the election. By the time Bob met his daughter, Mary, he was one of the richest and most influential men in Wisconsin. Today, in Milwaukee, there is still a Holton Street and a Holton Street Bridge, named after him. Bob was marrying into a formidable clan, some of whose descendants would take greater pride in being Holtons than in being Jameses. (It is interesting to note that the financial success of both Bob's and Wilkie's fathers-in-law, through cunning and hard work, strongly resembles that of William James of Albany.)

Bob soon developed a dislike for his powerful father-in-law, whom he accused of meddling and manipulation. Eventually, Henry James, Sr., came to understand Bob's position. After a visit by Mr. and Mrs. Holton to Cambridge, Henry James, Sr., employed one (or two) of his wittiest metaphors to describe Mr. Holton: "Mrs. H. is a very sweet good woman. . . . But she has got the most empty-hearted coxcomb for a husband that ever woman had. He is an animated town clock, and if he could only get a position where every one would be content to listen to him 24 times a day, his happiness would be complete. He did nothing but orate and gesticulate with arms borrowed from a windmill all the time he was here."[16]

There was from the start between the Jameses and the Holtons a mutual if unexpressed disapproval. The Holtons were, after all, tradespeople from the West, and Mrs. James once expressed her relief that Mary was "not too Western in her manner."[17] And the Jameses were, in the eyes of Mary's relatives, effete Easterners who had never had to earn their own living.

The situation was worse, and more blatant, with the Cary family. Wilkie's future father-in-law, Joseph Cary, had emigrated to Milwaukee from Litchfield, New York, in 1836, at the age of twenty-nine. Like Edward Holton (and William James of Albany), he had little formal education, but he was exceedingly enterprising and resourceful. He was soon the owner of one of the most successful men's clothing stores in Milwaukee, and he made some wise real estate investments. He was humorless and thrifty, and although he, like Edward Holton, was described in the *History of Milwaukee,* an indication of prominence, he never achieved the power or conspicuousness which Holton enjoyed. Joseph Cary was uninterested in philanthrophy of any sort. He was aloof and self-reliant, and his home life, after his wife died and left him with four children, was colorless.

When Mr. and Mrs. James finally met Carrie, a few days after she and Wilkie were married in 1873, they took an instant dislike to her; they were, in fact, offended by her. But during the summer of

1872, Mrs. James had nothing to go on but letters from Bob and Wilkie, so she demanded from Wilkie more information about his financée than he had already supplied. Wilkie resented his mother's inquisitiveness, but he responded as best he could under the circumstances. Wilkie's description of his future in-laws could not have calmed Mrs. James's misgivings that Wilkie was acting precipitately.

My dearest Mother,

Your letter arrived yesterday and I was glad to hear from you and shall be only too glad to answer all your questions about Miss Cary.

I should have done so voluntarily if you had given me a little while longer to do so, but the sensation of love to me, the true love which fills my bosom for this pure lovely girl is so deep and so strange, that it becomes daily and daily a less familiar subject to my mind, and simply fills me with an inward contentedness and acquiescence so great as to make the relative subside into comparative obscurity and privacy so far as any approach at analysis is concerned. We are different in disposition and temperament, as different as we can be. She is exceedingly reserved and unimpassioned and never betrays an emotion or feeling on any subject scarcely, but the outward lack of it is only the sign of an inward fullness which cannot be computed. I know this instinctively and I feel it all the time so deeply that I cannot help liking it and respecting it. She has had no mother since she was 8 years old; ever since she had been able she has been the head of her father's house, directing it and managing it for him.

She is the centre of the family, and although they are all rather undemonstrative in their feelings it is evident that she cements them altogether. There is in her a capacity for improvement greater than any woman I ever knew, and when one thinks of the deadening influences she has all her life been under, it is wonderful to think what she has made of herself in the way of simple womanly trueness and purity and gracefulness.

Her father worships her and I suppose will never consent to her leaving him, but will live with us when we are married. He is very old and infirm, and he really requires her care more or less.

He is one of the first settlers here and his house now stands on what was 25 years ago a wilderness. He is a good simple and very straightforward man with as little imagination as can be. He is rather cold and undemonstrative and has no occupation save of sitting on his piazza and reading the papers and looking at the thermometer and opening and closing the window-blinds. Her brothers are three in number, one of whom lives in Iowa and is in business there. I have never seen him. The oldest one here is an insurance man and a very good fellow but rather uninteresting. The third and the youngest is the brightest of the family, but inclined to the lazy and dissipated rather.[18]

In August of 1872, Wilkie wrote to Alice and Henry Jr., thanking them for their "letters to your new sister that is to be." Referring to his parents' visit to Milwaukee, Wilkie wrote in the same letter: "Mother and Father's visit here was a great success. We enjoyed it immensely, and I don't think I ever knew their full value to us till then. They saw Mary Holton but they did not see Miss Cary. At that time I did not know myself what was in store for me, and of course very little was said to them about the matter, except inferentially by my friends."[19]

Wilkie had not been as guileless as he tried to appear in neglecting to introduce Carrie to his parents. He certainly must have anticipated their disapproval; the awkwardness of his letter to his mother describing Carrie attests to that.

Wilkie's engagement would prove to be longer than he and Carrie had anticipated, and until his position with the railroad improved, he simply could not afford to get married.

Bob's wedding plans were proceeding, however, and Mary Holton and her father visited the Jameses in Cambridge in September. Mrs. James's description of Mr. Holton to Henry Jr. in Europe does not exist, but it must have been interesting, for Henry responded with a reference to "the Holtonian visit," writing "we . . . are most curious to behold the remarkable Holton *pere*."[20]

Mary and Bob were married at Highland Home, her parents' residence. The Holton family had kept a family journal from the time of Edward Holton's arrival in Milwaukee in 1845, and the entry for November 18, 1872, describes a simple and graceful ceremony: "Mary was married to Robertson James at Half past eleven this morning. The day was very pleasant and the house made cheerful with beautiful flowers and handsome presents. She was married in her traveling dress of navy blue with no ornaments but a few natural flowers. About fifty guests were present. The ceremony was performed by Rev. Mr. Ladd in a simple and beautiful manner."[21]

Mary and Bob traveled to Cambridge to visit the Jameses after their wedding. Henry James, Sr., seems to have found the entire affair rather piquant, and he described it for Henry:

> My darling Harry,
>   We have had Bob and his little dame on hand now for a week, and sent them back yesterday . . . to Milwaukee. . . . There seems to be a genuine and even lively affection on both sides, especially on the husband's, and the providence which has knit the tie is I think palpable even to sense. Bob is the most subjective and self conscious of creatures, sensitive, shy, suspicious, moody, cloudy, rainy, freezing if need be; and his wife has absolutely no "innards," but is altogether in her senses, so that her influence over Bob *must* be to rescue him from his natural tendencies. She is as pretty and tempting as a summer rose . . . She is a little creature you like to pet. Alice caresses her all the while as she would a child; and Willy was charmed with her. She is in no way responsive; takes everything as her due, is a peer of all the world; and don't know the beginning of a life beyond sense. Bob was grim, self-inverted, thoughtful, speculative, religious, manly; and impressed us with a sense of a very profound mental experience. Willy was very much struck with him, and his own intellectual convictions (if I mistake not) very much deepened by his intercourse with him. I think his wife who has no glean of sympathy with his subjective states—yet draws him out of those so effectually by her personal attractions, that she can't help proving the very best helpmate for him you can imagine. We are all immeasurably—not satisfied, but encouraged, hopeful, delighted.[22]

Henry had sensed all along Bob's immaturity, and he wrote rather presciently of his brother's marriage: "I hope he knows what he is about."[23] Bob had written to his father in October of 1872, recalling his parents' visit the summer before, and the letter reflects his sentimental and childish reverence for his father's beliefs. His attitude about Mary and his hopes that she would share his devotion to Swedenborg's philosophy did not seem promising, coming from a young man less than one month before his marriage.

> Every morning I go to you in thought and imagine the delight I should have were I near enough to hear you talk. . . . I never turn a page of any book of yours now or of Swedenborg—but immediately some glorious intonation of the love and wisdom of God and our great destiny flashed up like some dazzling sunlight in the bottom of the sea. . . . Sometimes I feel sorry that I daren't mention this speechless bliss to Mary. Once or twice we have talked it over but I could see her attention was only given to it from courtesy. I never knew a mind that questioned less than hers.[24]

Henry James, Sr., was not at all alarmed by this letter. He was probably delighted with Bob's spiritual development, and he had once told Bob that he had married Mrs. James for her moral, not her intellectual, worth. More important, Henry James, Sr., was probably convinced that marriage would provide a cure for Bob's various problems and temptations, and he wrote to Bob:

> I let angel and devil chase each other about the empty chambers of my mind as they will; and remain myself a looker on, knowing very well that the drama is of world wide concern, and will be played out to the glory of God and the welfare of man without pretending to join in.
>
> I should be however sometime terribly tossed and wrenched between the combatants, if I were not a married man; that is if I were not able when the celestial powers were in *force* to lavish my infinite and exquisite interior tenderness and peace upon my wife and children, and when they were in *flight* to run to the bosom of your mother, the home of all truth and purity, and deafen my ears to everything, but her spotless worth till the pitiless inflowing infamy had spent itself.[25]

Bob and Mary were, in fact, exceedingly happy during the first three years of their marriage, despite Bob's dissatisfaction with his railroad job. Bob had inadvertently found the cure for his varied and painful symptoms, a cure which had eluded him, his brothers, and a large part of the neurasthenic population of the nineteenth century: hard physical exercise. Bob had been transferred from Milwaukee to Prairie du Chien, a small town on the Mississippi River in Wisconsin, to take charge of the railroad outpost there, and his work was physically demanding. But shortly after he and Mary had moved, Bob wrote to his father: "We have been filling two ice houses, and this has kept me on the river lately, and at other times the work is out of doors—and I feel like a giant and full of health. . . ."[26]

On the first anniversary of her marriage, Mary gave birth to a nine-pound baby boy, and everyone was jubilant. Alice reported to her friend Fanny Morse: "You will be glad to hear that we have excellent news from our dear little baby and its dear little mother. The baby weighed nine pounds when it was born, which is doing pretty well for Prairie du Chien, I think, don't you?[27]
Henry James, Jr., was equally delighted with the arrival of his first nephew. He wrote to his parents:

> Your news of Bob and his Baby is most exhilarating and father's extracts from B's letters extremely beautiful. I long to see the wondrous child and pull its cheeks and pinch its legs. (I mean Baby's—not Bob's.) I await with anxiety its baptism. If it should be Henry no. 3, I shall feel queer, so sandwiched between infancy and maturity. You and mother must be in a terrible state to behold it. It's a pity it can't be sent on by express, to spend alternate weeks at Cambridge and at home."[28]

Mrs. James did not share Henry's dread of having a "Henry no. 3." She reported to Henry in December of 1873: "The boy's name is not yet announced, Mary has the naming, and her conjugal sentiment it would seem is not strong enough to make her understand Rob's (for I presume he leaves her perfectly free) strong desire in the matter or she would decide at once. The little fellow from all accounts gives promise in strength and beauty of doing credit to his name whatever it may be."[29]

Mary Holton's sentiment was perfectly strong and clear: she christened her son Edward Holton James. The baby was nicknamed Ned, and the Jameses loved him none the less for his namesake.

Although the distance from Cambridge to Milwaukee made it difficult, the Jameses showered their first grandchild with gifts and messages of love. And Mrs. James kindly relieved Bob's conscience in the matter of the naming. She wrote:

> Your decision upon the name was very wise I think (under the circumstances). The Holtons attach so much more importance to the matter than we do, that it is well they should be gratified, and you showed great tact and affection, in relieving Mary of any responsibility in the matter. So rest assured we shall dote on the little fellow just as foolishly, and spoil him as heartily if he is an Edward, as if he was a Henry, although between ourselves if he were to turn out a philosopher Henry James would seem more harmonious.

Mrs. James couldn't resist giving some stern maternal advice, however; she had certainly had enough experience in the matter: "Don't let the little tyrant begin so soon to rule his mother; she wants above all things her night's rest—so if he has such broad shoulders and deep chest, *let him bawl a good bit,* that is if you are sure his stomach is full, and there is no pin running in him. . . . As Mary is nursing that great boy, who will grow heavier and make more demands upon her every day, give her all the relief you possibly can."[30]

Mrs. James doted on her grandson, and some of her happiest letters to Bob date from this period. She wrote in February of 1874:

> We have heard of . . . the baby through Wilky, who says . . . all babies look alike to him, and that he feels quite incompetent to describe his peculiar beauties, as I desired him to do, but we have had his praises loudly sounded from another quarter. Yesterday father received a letter from Mr. Holton evidently inspired by a strong personal pride in his promising little offshoot, and in a friendly feeling to us in wishing us to be made a partaker of the pleasure. He really gave us a more satisfactory picture of the boy than we have had at all, to our great pride and delight. He says his skin in the fairest, "his eyes as blue as the best blue in the vault of heaven, and his head is shaped like your own, he is an outright James without doubt."[31]

Edward Holton's influence on Mary and Bob was evident from the start. In deciding whether or not to accept the railroad position at Prairie du Chien (about eight hours by railroad from Milwaukee), Bob wrote to his father: "Mr. Holton recommends it and Mary is willing to go."[32] But for the time being at least, Bob was happy, and his parents were relieved.

Mary was pleased too with the Roman cross which Henry, Jr. sent to her, and the letter which accompanied it. "Ever since your marriage," Henry wrote to his new sister-in-law, "I have been wanting to send you some little token that I thanked you heartily for becoming my sister-in-law. . . . Here is a little Roman cross which I hope will help you to think of me sometimes until the day comes when we may know each other and I can speak for myself."[33]

While Bob thrived in his new marriage and his good health, Wilkie began to be depressed with his tedious office job and the low salary which prevented him from getting married. Aunt Kate wrote to Henry Jr.: "Wilky [is] making a four day visit, and was looking well, but a little depressed with monotonous work in a close office."[34]

Mrs. James described Wilkie's predicament far more severely. She wrote to Henry: "This is a crisis in Wilky's life when he is brought face to face for the first time with the fact that he has got to stand on his feet, and provide for himself, and that too under the deepest sense of his own infirmities and temptations. But he will come out all right."[35]

Two positions were offered to Wilkie, and he chose the one at Watertown, about a hour and a half from Milwaukee. Mrs. James reported to Henry that the position was an immense improvement over the one which Wilkie had had; it was out-of-doors, as opposed to the close office work which Wilkie so loathed.

Henry was anxious to see a photograph of his future sister-in-law, and on February 28, 1873, Mrs. James wrote to Henry: "I will enclose a photo of Carrie which Wilkie thinks the best likeness of her. Tell me what you think of it. I think it a great deal more pleasing than the other."[36] After receiving this letter from his mother, Henry wrote to Alice: ". . . Mother tells me she encloses a new photo-graph—and, as usual, the enclosed treasure is not enclosed. Do have it sent in the next letter."[37]

Mrs. James responded: "I said in postscript to my letter I believed that upon reflection I thought I ought not to send it, because it was the only good one we have of her, and when asked by our friends about her, we want to show her to the best advantage. Wilky sent us one enlarged from this one, but it had made her look coarse, and being in a black dress is not pleasing."

This flurry of correspondence dealing with Carrie's photograph is intriguing, for although pictures of every other member of the James family exist in one collection or another, not one picture of Carrie James has survived, nor have any of her letters.

Mrs. James's opinion of Carrie had not improved, and she continued the letter to Henry by saying of her future daughter-in-law: "Poor Wilky, he says very little about her of late, but to mention her name. I am afraid she is not a strong helpful woman and does not keep up his courage."[38]

A few months later, Wilkie's situation brightened somewhat: he was promoted and transferred back to Milwaukee, and he and Carrie quickly set a date for their wedding. Mrs. James was far from certain that Wilkie could support himself, much less a wife, but her attitude toward Carrie softened somewhat when she learned of Wilkie's prospective living arrangements. She wrote to Henry Jr.: "Did Alice tell you of the munificence of Old Cary? He has given Carrie the house in which they live, in which she was born, all comfortably and fully furnished. He will live with them. Carrie has I believe a small property of her own, and upon this basis with Wilky's salary, and Milwaukee prices and style of doing things, they ought to be able to live."[39]

Wilkie and Carrie were married on November 12, 1873, and Bob provided the only, and rather humorous, description of their wedding: "Wilkie got married all right. Caroline was loaded down with many presents and good wishes. Owing to the number of guests I didn't have much time to converse with the happy pair. I saw three men packing Wilky's valise, and two more exploring his quarters for his bridal suspenders at the last minute."[40]

Mary and Bob had what may have been their first serious argument at this time. Mary was in her final month of pregnancy, and she did not feel that Bob should leave her alone in Prairie du Chien while he attended Wilkie's wedding in Milwaukee. The issue was serious enough for Bob to mention it in a letter to his father, and Henry James, Sr., agreed unequivocally with Mary. He wrote immediately to Bob: "Remember what tenderness is her due always, but now in a most especial manner. Let every influence around her be sweet and peaceful. Of course I am no law for you, but if I were her husband, I should never leave her in her present condition to go to Wilky's wedding, as her labour might chance in my absence, and the wedding could go on just as well without as with me."[41]

Bob attended Wilkie's wedding, but he did arrive home in time for the birth of his son, which occurred six days later. Mary, however, never forgave him for leaving her at such a time, and in a datebook she kept, she noted for November 12: "Wilkie married and Bob goes to wedding."[42] She was obviously hurt enough by Bob's insensitivity to make a permanent note of it.

Wilkie and Carrie traveled to Cambridge directly after their wedding, just as Mary and Bob had done. But the Jameses' response to Caroline Eames Cary James was far different from their response to Mary. Henry James, Sr., described Carrie with dismay to William and Henry, who were together in Europe at the time.

I must communicate all I can for your future profit and guidance about your new sister. . . . [She] is a somewhat plain young lady, of less than your mother's height, fair complexion, light brown hair, very slender person, self-possessed, even nonchalant in manners, though her manners are ladylike also and easy, dresses to the top of the mode, five thousand dollar's (literally) pendant from her ears in the shape of two magnificient diamonds, a thousand or two upon her fingers, with no conversation either in *esse* or *posse,* a good disposition I should think where every thing goes smoothly, but an extremely firm not to say obstinate will when things go against it. She is polite when addresssed, is not without a certain neatness of repartee when bantered, in every way inoffensive in fact as to any *positive* tendencies and yet does not in the least conciliate your affections or your prognostications. I can't for the life of me imagine why Wilky fell in love with her. He *is* in love apparently, deeply so with an utter unconsciousness of its seeming a strange state of things to outsiders. . . . Wilkie . . . must perceive that we do not take to the bride as warmly as we might; and yet he is so content with her perfections that perhaps he does not the least suspect our disappointment. We are assiduous to hide our feelings of course, and put on a mask of gaiety even when we are at bottom

the gravest; and we hope therefore that he does not positively
know our hearts . . . feted little. . . . Last night Mother gave a
party. All Wilky's old friends . . . amounting to some 90 persons
invited, 60 of which came; and it was a beautiful entertainment
truly. Such flowers! Such meats and drinks! But mother will tell
you all about this herself.[43]

Mrs. James did not dwell on the festivities; rather, she echoed her
husband's sentiments: "There is one great consolation in it, that he
[Wilkie] seemed to have no shadow of misgiving himself, about his
having drawn a prize— and let us hope that it may turn out that we
have made the mistake, not he."[44]

Mrs. James's attitude could not have improved when she
learned that Carrie's father was not giving his house to Wilkie and
Carrie after all. She wrote to Bob of the matter one month after the
wedding:

It seems (did Wilky tell you?) that boasted gift of the house to
Carrie was never made. Nothing was ever said about it, and a
few days before the marriage, Wilky felt bound to speak to Mr.
Cary about it. It seemed that some serious objection had been
made by the boys, for Mr. Cary said to avoid family dissention,
he had determined not to do it. Carrie it seems was very much
annoyed, as well she might be, for she had told some of her
friends, and Wilky said if it had not been for this gift he never
would have married. . . . Carrie does not strike one at all as a
person fit to be the wife of a poor man—Perhaps it was her
diamonds, and her fine clothes that helped to give one this
impression, there seemed such a lamentable want of harmony
between these things and the meagre subsistence Wilky's
present means can offer her—I truly hope he has been frank
with her, and that she has taken the step with her eyes wide
open.[45]

Carrie's diamonds had, it seems, put a chill into everyone.
Henry wrote to his father upon receipt of his parents' descriptions of
Carrie: "I am sorry Wilky's wife is not more interesting to those who
are fond of him: but that matters little, so long as practically she

proves a help and not a hindrance. I devoutly trust she may, in spite of her diamonds. I had dreamed of offering her the tribute of some modest Roman toy; but the diamonds put me out of countenance, and I think I shall let it slide."[46]

Mrs. James's dislike of Carrie persisted, and she wrote to William describing Wilkie's situation early in 1874: "Wilky sends good news of his housekeeping. His result is that he can live more cheaply as a married man than a single one! Very like Wilky, who never looks accurately or rationally at anything when money is concerned. Poor fellow! He writes *more affectionately* to me, a good sign that his wife has not weaned his love from his mother."[47]

William wrote to Wilkie soon after Wilkie's wedding, and under the circumstances his tact was admirable. After congratulating Wilkie he wrote: "I'm very sorry I was not at home to enjoy your visit with the rest of them. But I suppose you'd rather hear me talk of Harry and myself than about you."[48]

Wilkie had been waiting for an opportunity to leave the railroad, and in April of 1874, he and another man went into business for themselves. Mrs. James described the venture to Henry:

Wilky's fortunes seem to be brightening; that is if he is prudent and all things work well. He is about to leave the RR altogether and to enter a business for the making of iron chains and bolts. He told us of his plans when he was home. It seems that more than a year ago, he borrowed $5,000 and put it into the firm. The business was started by a young man, son of the Whaling who is one of the kings of the Milwaukee and St. Paul Railway.

According to Wilky, this Whaling is a man of unusual business capacity and bound to succeed. He has great advantages in making contracts for work with RR's through his father. They are having a remarkably good start, in spite of the panic which crippled them for a few months. Wilky is so sanguine that one can place no reliance upon his judgement, and little upon his prudence, but he has to do the routine work which will make things much safer—and Bob who I feared would be very much opposed to the move says in a letter this morning that he thinks with prudence Wilky's prospects are fair.[49]

(Wilkie borrowed the five thousand dollars from his father-in-law, Joseph Cary, using as collateral one of the parcels of land in Florida.)

In describing Bob, Mrs. James wrote to Henry that "the news from the West is good."⁵⁰ But for the first time in two years there were signs of trouble, although Mrs. James didn't recognize them immediately. Bob mentioned some problems with his eyes, and he was again craving spiritual guidance and comfort, a sure sign that trouble was beginning. He was growing restless in the isolation of Prairie du Chien, and Mary, who was often left alone with her infant son, missed her parents, her sisters, and her friends in Milwaukee. William tried to help, but he confessed to Bob that his development was more philosophical than theological, and his own crisis "did not deal with my personal relations to God as yours seem to have done." He next offered him nothing less than the philosophy which would help him survive, and which would make him famous. "I worked through it," wrote William, "into the faith in free will."⁵¹

Even Henry James, Sr., was beginning to recognize Bob's crippling dependence on religion, and as gently as he could, he tried to steer Bob toward self-reliance: "It is not by praying, however impossible it be not to pray, that our life advances; but simply by forbearing not to do the vile things we are prompted to do, and feeling that we have all Divine power on our side when we thus forbear." He knew that Bob was again suffering "temptation and trial," although things seemed relatively smooth on the surface, and as a postscript to the above letter, he wrote: "It would kill me if one of my boys, especially you, turned out an unkind husband, or a base man. Take a look at the goodness of God every day, and see how great our hope is, if you only keep from evil. What is poverty? What is any hardship under the sun, so long as we keep our hope fixed on the Lord."⁵²

Carrie and Wilkie were expecting their first child in October of 1874, and Mrs. James seems to have softened somewhat in her opinion of Carrie. She wrote to Bob:

I have been very glad to hear of her being so well throughout her pregnancy, and trust all will go well with her to the end. I think Carrie has been improving since her marriage. Her last letters have shown much more sensibility, and less reserve than at first, indeed in the last one there was a decided touch of sentiment, and strong expression of her sense of Wilky's tenderness and devotion to her. It was very delightful to me to see it.[53]

On October 4, 1874, Carrie James gave birth to a son, whom she and Wilkie named Joseph Cary James, after Carrie's father. Henry James, Jr., must have been relieved that there was still no Henry no. 3, but the naming could not have made Mrs. James happy. Not until William's first son was born in 1879 was there finally a Henry James III.

Soon after the birth of Wilkie's son, the Jameses traveled to Milwaukee and then to Prairie de Chien to see their two grandchildren. William had visited Milwaukee that June, at which time he warned Bob against the use of tobacco and coffee. He had probably noticed Bob's symptoms of restiveness, and this, in part, may have caused Mr. and Mrs. James to make the arduous journey.

Henry James, Sr., with his customary generosity, had offered to pay for a nurse to ease Mary's burdens. Now he offered to give Bob the necessary money to buy a farm. Almost immediately, Bob found one to his and Mary's liking at Whitewater, Wisconsin.

Mary Holton James noted in her datebook that Henry James, Sr., sent them a total of seven thousand dollars, and Aunt Kate a thousand dollars. Bob had finally freed himself of the railroad, but he certainly had not found a place of more diversions. The work on the farm was brutal, long, and monotonous, and Mary wrote to her parents in February, a very cold month in Wisconsin: "For the last two days Rob has been hauling hay into the barn."[54]

William's letter to Bob in July of 1875, six months after the purchase of the farm, indicates that Bob was having trouble. The farm, like the move to Prairie du Chien, had not provided a permanent solution: "I hope you will never drink a drop of anything but water again. I wish you could give up tobacco, for I'm sure that with your temperament it is pure poison. The additional advice to care little how you *feel,* provided your feelings don't succeed in making you do something evil, contains all I can communicate in the line of cheap beneficence."[55]

The years Mary and Bob spent on their farm in Whitewater were difficult ones. On August 18, 1875, Mary had given birth to her second child, a girl, whom they named Mary Walsh James, after Mrs. James, whose maiden name was Walsh. Mary's notations in her datebook reflect the painful time she and Bob endured: "Hard time with servants; Water in cellar and no good water to use; First symptoms of liquor; Hard times with young baby; Neddie's first attack of asthma."[56]

Early in 1876, Bob and Mary decided to give up the farm, and on June 20, 1876, Mary noted in her datebook: "Bob goes to Milwaukee to see about getting RR work."[57] Bob was again considering returning to a job which he abhorred, and the result was all too predictable. Mary's next entry reads: "Rob goes to Boston after a bad spree in Chicago. When he returns we leave Whitewater . . . and go to Milwaukee. Remain at Father's while Rob seeks employment. Gets a little newspaper work. August . . . we go to board at Mrs. Thompson's so Rob can do night work on Daily News. Robbed here and return to Father's."[58]

The Jameses were alarmed at the above proceedings, but there was little they could do. Aunt Kate sent a check for a hundred dollars to offset Mary and Bob's losses in their robbery.

As a stopgap measure, Edward Holton decided to employ Bob to look after his affairs, which would provide Bob with a sorely needed income while he looked for permanent work. It must have hurt Bob deeply, however, to take what was, in effect, charity from his father-in-law, from whom he wanted nothing but total independence.

Both Henry and William wrote sympathetically to Bob, but neither of them was able to offer much else than advice. "I have wished I could in any way help you, but feel too much my impotence," William wrote. "it is all I can do to paddle my own canoe. My 'dying words' to you are, 'outward acts, not feelings!' "[59] Henry wrote from England that he had learned of Bob's "having arranged to look after Mr. Holton's affairs." He was pleased that Bob would again be living with Mary and his children; and he wrote:

> . . . I hope very much to hear that you are making it work. Don't let your periodical mania for change, which is simply a temptation of the devil attack you, or rather if it does attack you, don't on any account let it get the better of you, for if it does the devil will get possession of you altogether. Reflect well the good side of your situation, the security, the out-of-door life, the union with your family, that this arrangement assures you, and make

up your mind to get used to it, and give in to it, even when it
bores you most. Excuse my preaching. . . . I have a horror that
you have again tormented yourself into a quarrel with destiny,
at a moment when destiny is offering you easy liberal terms.[60]

Henry James, Sr., offered his share of advice also. The best of all
possible solutions was, he decided, for Bob to come home with his
wife and children. After the failure of the Prairie du Chien position,
he had written to Bob:

> It is simply indispensable in my opinion that you fix yourself
> within the bounds of civilized and cultivated life, where you can
> have intercourse with home once a year at all events, and oftener
> if need be. The thing is necessary to my happiness. I can't stand
> this tremendous separation from you, and must urge a closing
> of it upon my own account and mother's as well as yours. . . .
> You can find with a little loss of time (which is of no account,
> since you and Mary and baby would be our most welcome
> guests in the meanwhile) some activity nearer the East, where
> we might go to you, and you and Mary might come to us
> frequently, and this wretched *literary* intercourse be exchanged
> for a more living word. At all events we must move heaven and
> earth till we get the change effected.[61]

Heaven and earth was one thing, but moving Mary from her mother
and father was another. Mary was devoted to her parents; she relied
totally on her father for advice, and Edward Holton wanted his
daughter and his grandchildren near him.

Edward Holton wanted his daughter in Milwaukee. Henry
James, Sr., wanted his son closer to Boston. Bob wanted, more than
anything else, a more satisfying, intellectually stimulating profession.
Bob's luck, moreover, had not been good. Perhaps he could have
shown more endurance with his railroad job, but letters which he
wrote many years later indicate that he was forced to remain silent
while he witnessed corrupt practices by his employers, a situation
which no son of Henry James, Sr., especially Bob, could have easily
endured. When he finally did find a newspaper job which satisfied
him, his house was burglarized and Mary refused to remain alone
while Bob worked nights as an editor. As for Bob's alcoholism, it

certainly exacerbated his problems, but it had not caused them. Matters did not improve, and in October of 1877, Bob returned to the railroad. However, he then abruptly decided to travel to Colorado with his son. He hoped that the climate would relieve Ned's asthma, but his principal motive was to escape from his in-laws and to look for literary work of some sort. Bob carried with him excellent references from the railroad and from the newspaper where he had briefly worked, but he found nothing and soon returned home. Mary's entry in her notebook on Christmas Day 1877 reads that it was "a bad day with liquor."[62]

Mrs. James was less than supportive of Bob's attempt to find work in Colorado, and she wrote:

> It was a very great relief to get your yesterday's letter, for of course we had been made very anxious in hearing of your recent (as it seems to me crazy) doings in giving up one means of support, without any definite prospect of another.
>
> We are only too happy that the Colorado scheme did not succeed and that your little home in Milwaukee was not again to be broken up.

In the same letter, Mrs. James described Henry's success, writing: "Harry's recent things seem to be making him famous on both sides of the water. The English papers are full of favourable criticism and flattering predictions. Harper's have published *Daisy Miller* in their half-hour series, and it is having an immense run both here and New York."[63] Certainly Bob must have been happy for his brother, but such news could not have made him feel good about his own prospects, and one must question Mrs. James's timing, if not her sensitivity, in sending such news along to Bob at that time.

In May of 1878, William and Alice Gibbens set a July date for their wedding, and William notified Bob's wife of the good news:

> You may remember my writing to you a couple of years ago that I had seen at a party the evening before, 'the future Mrs. W.J.' I have now the pleasure to announce, not that she is already that, but that she has succeeded in overcoming her natural reluctance to contemplate it at a future possibility, and is in short 'engaged' to me since last Friday. Her name is Miss Alice Gibbens. . . .

Bob, who has had an inkling of this and of the thorns of my path will be glad to hear that they are all plucked and nothing but the roses remain.[64]

Neither Bob nor Wilkie attended William's wedding. But two years later, when Bob returned to Boston, unable to endure Milwaukee and unable to control his alcoholism, his new sister-in-law offered him support and friendship and continued to do so until his death.

At this time, Bob temporarily abandoned his studies of Swedenborg. He and Mary began to attend an Episcopal church, and early in 1880 they were confirmed.

Bob had returned to work for the railroad shortly after his return from Colorado, but in December of 1880, he fought with his supervisor. Shortly after that, Mary noted in her datebook that Bob had "hard feelings toward Father [Holton] refuses to let him have anything to do with the children."[65]

By the beginning of 1881, the situation had become intolerable. "Rob drinks much and is very cross," Mary wrote. "Wilkie and Mr. Conway helped me. Rob left with William for Boston, close the house. Move the furniture and go to Highland Home."[66] William, despite his own problems and responsibilities, had traveled to Milwaukee to take Bob home with him. This was the first of many times when William helped his brother, and William's wife would write to Henry in 1892 that William had taken care of Bob for so long that "he had gotten the hang of it."[67]

Soon after Bob arrived in Boston, Mrs. James wrote to Wilkie to describe Bob's condition, which was obviously a nervous breakdown:

> I presume you often find yourself wondering how we are getting along with the belligerent young man we have in the house. When B. first came home, he did nothing but justify himself, assert himself, and abuse other people. He was puffed up, and conceited to the last degree, and took apparently his separation from his family very coolly. Then after two or three weeks came a period of great nervousness and depression. He could not live without them, and he would telegraph Mary to come on immediately without a moment's delay. This we told

him could not be done. Would father or I write to her and ask her to send him one word showing she had not given him up altogether? Father did write, begging her to state fully all her grounds of complaint against Bob, and write a letter that could be shown to Bob. She did write and it was indeed a revelation. Instead of being the childish immature person who would not make up her mind about anything, which Bob had represented her, she showed herself to be a strong decided dignified woman, who had exercised more forbearance than I could believe was possible with such a selfish tyrannical turbulent spirit as Bob's. She told all she had had to bear throughout their married life. But she did it with moderation, while she held back nothing. The letter was shown him. It produced at first violent nervous paroxysms, but by degree deep humiliation, and I think that he has seen himself since in a totally new light. For days he could hardly hold up his head; and I trust it is working the peaceable fruits of righteousness in his heart. He is much less restless than he was, doesn't talk so much about what he is going to do. He does not seem at all well; complains of violent indigestion and many distressing nervous feelings in his head and of his back. He takes too little exercise, sitting over his drawing most of the time. If he could combine with his drawing, some out of door work, I think he would be well, and happier. He gets great encouragement to go on with his drawing. He has an unusually correct eye, and great facility, and could easily fit himself to teach it. This would change the whole atmosphere of his life, and I think it would soothe and humanize his temper. If a situation could be found for him here, that is at the East, it would on many accounts be the best thing for him.

I do not know whether it would suit Neddie, and Bob complains very much of his catarrhal trouble here—but to live within reach of us, where we could keep a check upon him, and be a comfort to Mary, would be most desirable.[68]

Because everyone was concerned with Bob's condition, few comments were made about Wilkie's situation. Henry wrote to William shortly after he received a letter from Wilkie: "Poor Wilkie gives a sorry account of his present business and says he means to leave it and look for a clerkship. . . . He seems to have a rude career."[69]

Wilkie declared bankruptcy in 1877. His liabilities were estimated at seventy-four thousand dollars against assets of eighty-one
thousand dollars. These assets, however, were in the form of real
estate, shops, bridge material, and bills receivable, assest which were
not quickly or fully liquidated. After Wilkie's bankruptcy proceedings were completed, his total debt was twenty thousand dollars, not
the eighty thousand reported by some biographers. Twenty thousand dollars was still an enormous sum, however, and of course
Wilkie was unable to pay it.

Most of Wilkie's creditors were suppliers. A newspaper article
which appeared in one of Milwaukee's newspapers, however, listed
as creditors, among others, Wilkie's father-in-law, Henry James, Sr.,
and Bob. Wilkie's loan from his father-in-law was secured with one
of the parcels of Florida land, and in satisfaction of this debt, Wilkie
transferred the land into Carrie's name. Although Wilkie's declaration of bankruptcy protected him from most of his debts, Bob had
co-signed an unsecured note for fiften hundred dollars and was
therefore obligated to pay it. Henry James, Sr., also suffered a loss as
a result of Wilkie's failure. Mrs. James explained the circumstances in
a letter to Bob: "The half of my patrimony is in the Del. and Hud.,
which has of late justified the hopes of its best friends, and risen as
high as 85—from 35—at which Father sold to meet Wilky's note,
leaving himself merely a fragment."[70]

These details give some indication of just how entangled
Wilkie's finances had become, though it would not become known
until after his death that he had also borrowed money using his life
insurance policy as collateral.

One other reference to Wilkie's situation was made by Aunt
Kate: "I feel very much for Wilky and his family. His last letters have
been hopeless about getting anything to do. How desperate the
times are."[71] Specifically, Aunt Kate was referring to the secondary
depression, which began in 1874 and which had an enormous
impact on businesses such as Wilkie's. His business required an
expensive inventory, and as building and expansion slowed or
stopped, Wilkie was left with a huge supply of iron and other
supplies. Unable to pay his own suppliers and employees, Wilkie and
other proprietors of small businesses had no option but to declare
bankruptcy.

From the scant information available, it seems that Wilkie had
entered into the business in partnership with a man named Whaling,

who was able to use his influence to obtain lucrative contracts. However, bankruptcy records indicate that in 1877 Wilkie's partner was named Soulerin, so Whaling had probably sold his share. The lack of references to and information about Wilkie's business failure in the existing family letters is in itself evidence of a serious problem. It is possible that the family had agreed to be reticent on the subject in order to avoid the embarrassment or discomfort of having it widely known that Henry James, Sr., had lent Wilkie even more money after having lost a great deal through the Florida enterprise. This would account for the general and evasive tone adopted by Henry in a description he gave of Wilkie to a family friend: "He is not particularly successful, as success is measured in this country; but he is always rotund and good natured and delightful."[72]

The economic conditions of the late 1870s certainly had a devastating effect on Wilkie's business, but one wonders how much of Wilkie's failure must be blamed on his own lack of financial talent, knowledge, or experience. Every reference to Wilkie which exists accentuates his genial, gentle nature, his kindness, his affability. One suspects that such descriptions, while altogether true, were also an attempt to compensate for Wilkie's shortcomings, shortcomings which were both painful and expensive for him and the family.

Even before Wilkie's business failure, Wilkie's deteriorating health was mentioned frequently. In many letters, there were references to his rheumatism as a result of his foot wound; Aunt Kate recommended Blair's Pills and clover tea. From time to time, Wilkie was forced to either remain in bed or use crutches. In 1876, Wilkie mentioned in a letter to Henry Jr. the possibility of amputation. Henry was greatly alarmed, and wrote to William: "I have just got a letter from Wilky, speaking sadly of his foot. Is it true that there is peril of his losing it? What a strange and sad consummation. I depend upon its being his loose way of talking."[73] William's response has not survived, but Wilkie's foot did trouble him a good deal, and toward the end of his life he was in constant pain. In addition, Wilkie was developing kidney and heart problems which would eventually lead him to seek the diagnosis of specialists, first in Milwaukee and later in Boston.

On Christmas Eve 1875, Wilkie's second child, a daughter, was born. She was named Alice James, after Wilkie's sister.

Wilkie's father-in-law, Joseph Cary, who had resided with

Wilkie and Carrie for their entire married life, died on March 18, 1880. Carrie and her three brothers were the sole and equal inheritors of his estate. There is no record of Joseph Cary's financial worth, but his real estate holdings were extremely valuable, since they were located in the heart of Milwaukee's growing business district. Soon after Cary's death, Carrie's three brothers, abiding by prior arrangement, transferred the house and its contents to Carrie. Wilkie and Carrie remained in the house with their two children, and despite Carrie's inheritance (predominantly real estate which could not be liquidated without her brother's agreement), their style of living seemed to remain very much the same.

In the spring of 1880, a year before Bob's breakdown and return to Cambridge, he and Wilkie attended an enormous reunion of Civil War veterans. Many former soldiers had settled in the West after the war, and they converged in Milwaukee, over seven thousand of them, not including their families. They resided with old comrades, in the homes of Milwaukee residents, and in camps set up for the occasion. There was an enormous procession; many men wore their old uniforms and carried regimental flags. Bob and Wilkie probably took part in the planning of the event, since they were both active members of the Military Order of the Loyal Legion, Wisconsin Commandery. It must have been a good time for Wilkie and Bob, who had suffered so many disappointments since the war. It was in November of that year when Wilkie wrote and delivered the address detailing his service with the Fifty-fourth Massachusetts Regiment. The address was published in the *Milwaukee Sentinel* in December of 1883.

Bob remained in Cambridge with his parents and Alice throughout 1881. The family's letters from this period are filled with advice and concern, and with pleasure when Bob seemed to be managing well.

There were attempts to bring about a reconciliation between Bob and Mary when it seemed that Bob was ready. Henry James, Sr., assumed the role of peacemaker, and he wrote to Mary that, after a month, Bob had conceded that it was his violent temper which was to blame for their marital discord. However, suggested Henry James, Sr., to his daughter-in-law, perhaps Mary's father had "interfered to influence [Mary's] judgements in regard to the truth of his [Bob's] complaints of being overworked, etc." The letter continued with a plea that Mary take "one decisive step in vindication of [her] own mental independence" from her father's judgment, by writing to Bob of the matter. Henry James, Sr., concluded that Bob was contrite, lonely, longing for word that Mary loved him, and willing to place himself in her counsel.[74] But Mary was furious that anyone should even imply that her father had interfered, and Henry James, Sr., quickly apologized in his next letter. Matters continued in this way with dismal regularity.

Aunt Kate was practically subversive in her encouragement of Mary's decision to live with her parents. "It must have been a great comfort to you to have your father's house to go to, and a mother's heart and sympathy when one is in trouble is the greatest consolation," she wrote to Mary in March of 1881.[75]

Bob's varied symptoms had returned with a vengeance: letters mention headaches, vertigo, rheumatism, loss of appetite and sleep. He spent his days drawing and painting with a Harvard professor named Moore, who recognized Bob's talent. Bob greatly admired William's wife, Alice, and he spent time with William and Alice in their home. Much to Bob's pleasure, he had time to converse with William's freinds; he had sorely missed stimulating conversation while he was in Milwaukee, and he was a good conversationalist. William enjoyed his company, and Henry remembered Bob's "aptitude for admirable talk," in his *Autobiography* as "[the most] charged with natural life, perception, humor and colour, that I have perhaps ever known. There were times when Bob's spoken overflow struck me as the equivalent, for fine animation, of William's espistolary."[76]

Mrs. James kept Mary well informed of Bob's condition and was as optimistic as possible under the circumstances, but early in the summer of 1881 Bob arrived at the James house drunk and abusive after a visit to see his Uncle Robertson in Stamford, Connecticut. Bob exhibited symptoms which Mrs. James described as "apoplectic," and she begged Mary to travel to Cambridge; she was convinced that Bob could not improve until he and Mary tried the "experiment" of living together again.

Bob's attack had been severe enough for him to commit himself to the Arlington Asylum, not far from Cambridge. Mary was alarmed, and she heeded Mrs. James's request to travel to Cambridge to join Bob, who had been released from the asylum. However, Mary's parents soon joined her in Cambridge, and Henry James, Sr., reported the disastrous proceedings to William in the same letter in which he described Mr. Holton as a coxcomb, a town clock, and a windmill. He began with a description of the heat and humidity they were having to endure, and "In the midst of it," he wrote, "the whole Holton party came down upon us. Add to this . . . Mother was sick and I nearly as much so. Add to this again, Bob had been so demoralized by the unsuspected return of Mary upon his hands, as to shake off almost entirely the decent quietness of behavior he had lately attained to, and to menace us with a visitation of all his old insolence. But thank heaven, it is all over without damage."[77]

Bob finally did return to the West. Information from this period is sketchy, but one of Aunt Kate's letters to Mary says of Bob's whereabouts: "I have been waiting to hear something more definite to send him a Christmas present. Now I learn that he is twenty miles from you on your father's new farm."[78] Bob was again working for his father-in-law, a situation which had failed in the past.

Henry James, Jr., returned to America from England in 1881 after a six-year absence, and he sent both Bob and Wilkie money. Bob's letter of appreciation has not survived, but Henry responded to it by assuring Bob that in addition to the initial $250, "an equal sum is at your disposal as often as you need it."[79] Wilkie's thank-you letter reflects enormous gratitude, but it also reflects the extent to which his health had deteriorated.

Mr dear Harry,

I am in receipt of your letter today and hasten to acknowledge it and to give you a fraternal blessing for your princely gift. It is so long since I have had any money that I could call my own that the possession of this completely dazzles me, and although I am tempted to use it immediately to go home with, my sober second thought deters me and bids me wait to see whether other purposes may not be more benefited by the gift than the delightful measure of going home: especially do I incline not to use the money for this purpose since you tell me that you will surely come West sometime during the winter. Were it not for the promise coming directly from you, I should start tomorrow for Boston and let prudent considerations go. I am on crutches today, stiffened with an attack of rheumatism in my foot wound. It is the first day of the attack and therefore is very severe; tomorrow I shall have come fully under the influence of Blair's pills, and will undoubtedly be on the mend again. It must seem strange to you to be in America again: how much I should give to see you.[80]

Wilkie decided to visit Henry after all, and he arrived in Cambridge in December. Henry Jr. then proceeded to Washington, D.C. In January, Mrs. James became seriously ill, and Bob was with her in Cambridge at the time, having again left Milwaukee as suddenly and as inexplicably as he had arrived.

It was Bob who informed Henry of his mother's condition on January 28, 1882. Believing that his mother was recovering, he wrote: "The medical man assures me that she is entirely out of danger but the recovery of her strength will be slow."[81]

Soon after Bob wrote to Henry, Mrs. James's condition became critical, and Henry and Wilkie were sent for. They did not arrive in time, and Mary James died on the evening of January 30, 1882. Henry reached home the next morning, and Wilkie did not arrive in Cambridge until the morning of his mother's funeral. It was Henry's "princely gift" which had enabled Wilkie to travel home the month before to see his mother alive for the last time.

For the first time since before the Civil War all five James children were together for their mother's funeral. It was also to be the last.

Bob remained in Cambridge, and on January 31, 1882, he wrote to Mary, who had remained in Milwaukee with the children.

Dear Mother died at 6:45 Sunday evening. Five days previously she was taken with asthma complicated with bronchitis which apparently was getting better. . . . I was constantly with her through those five days and in feeling had retreated to the old time relation of a boy to his mother. And she was so grateful and pleased for any attention I showed her.

And now we are all conscious of the loss not to be measured but so grateful and happy to think of Mother having gone from death into everlasting life. Isn't it pleasant to know that she is sheltered for ever and that but for this poor body of ours we could touch her hand. I was the only boy at home, Willy and Harry arrived this a.m.[82]

Mrs. James had possessed indomitable strength, but in the last years of her life it had been sorely tested. Henry, her favorite son, the one who had given her the least amount of trouble, had been in England, and she sorely missed him. At the time of her death, Mrs. James knew that William was settled and prospering, but even he had been a trial with his poor health and vacillations. For almost twenty years, Mrs. James had cared for Alice, with little respite. Knowing that Alice would never be able to care for herself, Mrs. James left her entire estate to her daughter. Wilkie had almost died during the Civil War and Mrs. James had nursed him for months. His life after the Civil War had disheartened her: first the monumental and costly failure in Florida, then his marriage to a woman for whom Mrs. James cared very little, and finally his bankruptcy. The last year of her life was spent, for the most part, caring for Bob, whom she had accurately described as "belligerent." She could not have been pleased to see him return home to Cambridge as she lay ill, knowing that it meant that he had again left his wife and his two young children. She had never had the opportunity to enjoy her four grandchildren—in fact, she had barely seen them. As for Henry James, Sr., whom Mrs. James loved devotedly, one can only wonder how much patience was required to live with a husband whose goodness often interfered with his ability to function in society.

In a second letter to Mary, Bob described his mother's funeral, and although it provides valuable information, it also reflects the pious, sentimental religiosity which so annoyed his sister.

Dear Mother's funeral occurred on Wednesday—We four boys took her coffin to the grave and kissed her quiet face for the last time. Mr. James Freeman Clarke read a simple burial service at the house—some scriptures and at our request omitted any reference to her personally—a thing no one could have done for us and have spoken out thoughts. I sometimes think father's loneliness must be appalling but he gives no sign of it save in physical weakness. His union with her was a perfect one both in heart and mind. No marriage could have been more perfect. It is often that people love each other, perhaps not always that they understand each other. The secret of their union was a religious one. It had its inception during their engagement when mother relinquished all the narrow sectarian habit in which she had been bred to his and her own everlasting peace.

There have been no mutations on that score between them. We have been all educated by father to feel that death was the only reality and that life was simply an experimental thing and for this reason it may be that it is we have taken mother's going as such an orderly transition. None of us would recall her for we feel that we are more near to her now than ever before, simply because she is already at the goal for which we all cheerfully bend our steps. An hour after we laid her out I do not think that either father, Alice or myself have shed a tear. But the boys coming later were very much shocked. Harry especially who had a passionate childlike devotion to her.

I feel as if I had not much else in life to live for now but keep very close to father and dissipate, as much as possible, the loneliness in which he must remain. I sleep beside him in mother's empty bed and we have quite happy talks at night about Mother's nearness and about our pride in her. The last two weeks of my life have been the happiest I have known since you and I were engaged. No one who has any vital belief in God can have any other thought for father than one of thankfulness that his own end is so very near. And what a privilege it is for a son to be beside him constantly as his sun is setting. . . . I am wakeful now by necessity in caring for Father—but no unquietness can invade my mind any more. At these seasons I confirm my mind more and more in the Christian truth I get from Swedenborg's writings. Their sufficiency has been tested now and I feel that no accident of life can avail to harm one who believes in the Lord Jesus Christ. No one can say how long it may be before you and I meet again. But all anxious care to meet you has vanished. If we are spiritually married we need not care for the marriage of the flesh.[83]

Two months after his mother's death, Bob abruptly decided to travel to Fayal, one of the islands forming the Azores, located near Portugal. His conduct seemed bizarre, even to himself, and he tried to explain it to his brother Henry.

Dear Harry,
    You will be surprised to learn that I am on my way to Fayal.

For the sake of pleasing Willy I have tried hard to think it wise to go back West. The more I have tried to convince myself it would be wise to do this, the less I have been able to think so. I look upon the West with nothing but horror. . . .

I am sorry dear Harry that I have not been able to see you more familiarly since we have been together. But I begin to see a rift in the clouds at last and possibilities of future friendliness with those I care for which all the conditions of my past life rendered impossible.

It seems like a dark thing sometimes to be sailing away on this hazardous sea—away from you all, especially from dear father, but I can't get rid of the feeling that there is harmony at the centre of it all.

I have enough money to take me to Fayal—and pay my way there for three months. If you feel that you are able to let me draw on you from time to time, write me to that effect. But if there is the slightest obstacle to this I hope you will trust me enough to tell me of it.

I want to stay away a year if I can and if possible without spending any money in moving about. With this idea in view I hope to have the fortitude to stay in Fayal or at the next island—St. Michael.[84]

This letter, particularly the last paragraph, is ironic, and sad. Henry and William had written in a similar vein when they first traveled to Europe to regain their health or to discover their goals. Their plans were often uncertain, they were to draw on their father's account, and they promised to be as frugal as possible. But poor Bob was thirty-six years old. Such fanciful and spontaneous trips were meant for young bachelors; Bob had a wife and two children to support, and he was an alcoholic.

Bob remained on Fayal for two weeks and then sailed to St. Michael and Lisbon. The sea voyage had been rough, and he was experiencing severe headaches and backaches which led him to resort to chloroform. He traveled from Lisbon to London, where he waited for his brother Henry to arrive from America, and remained with him for the summer. Henry wrote to Mary that Bob was nervous, and a trying companion, primarily because "his very constitution and character are so unhappy."[85]

Bob returned to Boston (where Henry James, Sr., and Alice had settled after selling the house on Quincy Street) in September of 1882, hoping to find a permanent position either as an art instructor or as a commercial artist. His hopes had been raised by Moore, the art teacher who had instructed him in Cambridge in 1881, who had assured him that he had real talent as an artist. But he could find nothing and Henry James, Sr., convinced him to return instead to his wife and children in Milwaukee. Part of the reason for this may have been Alice's strong and growing dislike of Bob. (After the death of Henry James, Sr., William's wife told William that Alice had not sent for Bob until the last possible moment, because "Alice so dreaded to have Bob about.")[86]

Bob remained in Boston for less than a week, and at this time his father made him promise to overcome his hatred for his father-in-law. "The one thing in life is for you to conquer your dislike of Holton," Henry James, Sr., had admonished Bob, "for remember one man is as another, no good, no bad."[87] It is impossible to imagine how Henry James, Sr., could ever have thought that such a thing was possible, especially since he himself had found Holton's behavior repulsive.

Bob returned to Milwaukee on September 22, 1882, and apparently he did coexist with his father-in-law. Mary noted in her datebook that they passed "another Thanksgiving under the hospitable roof of Highland Home."[88] That November, Henry James, Sr., in one of the last letters he wrote, was able to report to William that "Bob, wonderful to say, is living in the utmost cordiality with Mr. Holton, and he never alludes to disagreement with him." The cordiality lasted for only six months, but Henry James, Sr., would never know that.

In the same letter to William, Henry James, Sr., delivered somber news of Wilkie's health, but he certainly never suspected that Wilkie would die in less than a year:

Wilky has made us a visit for 10 days in order to see Dr. Hodges who diagnosed him with remarkable care and reported his heart as valvarily enlarged. He has grown very thin, but I never saw him so sweet and good natured, enjoying a lighthearted *repartee* with Alice, and conducting himself altogether as if he were already a denizen of the Elysian Fields. Dr. H. told me that he only required to be prudent in his diet and in his exercise, to enjoy a good many years of life in spite of his disease, and he sent him off in capital spirits to resume his work. It will be considerably lightened by an assistant.[89]

Wilkie had lost none of his geniality, however, and Henry James, Sr., concluded his letter by noting that Wilkie "saw all his old friends while here. They all called upon him, and treated him with extreme friendship."[90]

Less than a month after Henry James, Sr., wrote this letter, he became ill, and Henry, who had returned to London only six months earlier, was sent for. William, who was also in Europe at this time, intending to study and write, remained in Henry's flat in London and waited to hear from his family about his father.

Aunt Kate kept Wilkie and Bob informed through her letters to Mary. On Thursday evening, December 14, 1882, she wrote a lengthy report of his condition:

> His pulse is becoming weaker very slowly, and keeps perfectly regular. He has no pain of any sort, and no physical discomfort but from extreme weakness. . . . His mind is at times confused, but in the realm of his accustomed thought it works clearly. He is very happy in the thought of the immortal life, upon which he says he has already entered. He insists that he has passed through death and that it has no sting, and wants to tell every one how delightful it is to die. . . . He may live yet a month or more, his strength holds out marvelously . . . Father persists in his refusal to eat, saying that life is sustained by "God Almighty," and needs not bread and meat, and any difference from him irritates him extremely. It is hard to see him sinking from this cause, but it would be harder, Alice says, to see him living with a diseased brain.[91]

Aunt Kate referred frequently, in this letter and in others she wrote, to "Anemia of the Brain," "Brain trouble," and "softening of the brain." This infuriated William, who wrote to his wife asking for an explanation. She responded: "I very likely don't know what softening of the brain is. I can only say that to the very last father's mind seemed to me the strongest part of him. And as I told you, Jim

Putnam said there was no more disease in the brain than in any other organ—life was exhausted."[92]

Aunt Kate did not limit herself to letter-writing. She also spoke of Henry James, Sr.'s, disease, and of many other private matters as well. Alice wrote to her husband: "I wish dear Aunt Kate would not talk to anyone but ourselves—she doesn't know how much she unintentionally tells."[93]

Henry James, Sr., died on December 18, 1882, less than a year after his wife. He had missed her terribly and had talked constantly of joining her. Bob arrived in Boston shortly before his father died and remained for the funeral, which was held three days after Henry James, Sr.'s, death. That evening, he went to the station to meet his brother Henry, no longer junior, who had not arrived in time to bid his father good-bye. Wilkie did not make the trip from Milwaukee— he was too ill—and Bob departed for Milwaukee the next morning.

It fell to Henry to read, over the grave of his father, the letter which William had written from England, hoping that it could be read to Henry James, Sr., before he died. It is a poignant letter, but one too often quoted to reproduce here, except for one promise made by William:

> As for us, we shall live on each in his way, feeling somewhat unprotected, old as we are, for the absence of the parental bosom as a refuge, but holding fast together in that common sacred memory. We will stand by each other and by Alice, try to transmit the torch in our offspring as you did in us, and when the time comes for being gathered in I pray we may, if not all, some at least be as ripe as you.[94]

Little did William suspect that his father's actions would precipitate the first instance in which the James children would have to "stand by each other." Henry James, Sr., had excluded Wilkie from his will.

6
PAINS AND SUFFERINGS
AND MISTAKES:
Wilkie's Death

"My dear Bob," Henry wrote to his brother less than two weeks after their father's death, "Father appointed me Executor of hs will, and I have had to open it and take the necessary steps in consequence. One of these is to send you a copy of it which I have asked Aunt Kate to make. I enclose it herewith." Henry had anticipated that his role as executor would be a perfunctory one, but it proved to be one of the most trying of his life. His letter continued:

> You will notice that Father has placed a limitation upon your share of the estate, but what will strike you more than this is the fact that he has omitted Wilky altogether. I won't make any remarks upon either of these facts now, because I have just written a long letter to Wilky, and because I mean very soon to come out to Milwaukee, to see both of you and to talk with you about the whole matter. Wait till then dear Bob, and we shall all understand each other. The estate is roughly estimated at $95,000, so much for the present.
>
> I hope you had a comfortable journey back from here and that you have taken up your work with a good spirit. If you only stick to it I am sure it will bring you happiness.
>
> Here we are very quiet. Alice was rather ill the day you left, and went into the country (Beverly) with K. Loring as a kind of desperate measure. It agreed perfectly, and she has come back wonderfully better. I also found myself ill and had to take to my

bed for four days. But that is over and I am able to look around me.

You may imagine how we miss father—how we feel his personal absence. But since the night I arrived I have heard everything about his end, and I am glad he has given up a life of which he was so weary.

Give much love from me to Mary and the boy and girl, and believe me ever dear Bob your affectionate brother,

Henry James, Jr.[1]

Henry longed for nothing more than to return to London and his writing, but for over six months after his father's death, although he did some literary work, he was preoccupied with the settling of his father's estate. It was comprised primarily of real estate: commercial buildings in Syracuse, the house in Boston, and railroad bonds.

Alice was disheartened over her father's decision to exclude Wilkie, and she, along with Bob, immediately agreed with Henry that they should redivide the estate, much as Henry James, Sr., and his brothers and sisters had done with their own father's will. William did not agree to the redivision, primarily because he believed that Carrie's wealth far exceeded his own and that therefore Wilkie did not need money. His wife agreed with his argument, as always, but, she believed that Wilkie should receive his share and wrote to William about it.

I think it was just and wise [of Henry James, Sr.], since Wilky's wife and children have such a large fortune assured to them in the future, but it strikes me that for the few years Wilky has to live it would be right to share with him. Alice mustn't for she needs money—all she has. And Bob told me he had lost heavily through Wilky in times past—so he ought not—but we can do it and lest you should be for one instant checked by what might be mistaken consideration of me, I hasten to speak of this. What we have not had we shall not miss. Bob told me Wilky looked very ill and I know Dr. Hodges considered him unfit for work. Father did not think of this for feeling that Carrie and the children were secure and knew he thought Wilky would not live long.

Aunt Kate thought father should leave all he had to Alice,

to which he agreed, but when Alice heard of it she declared she would share with her brothers or break the will. She objected strongly to the exclusion of Wilky from an equal share, but father insisted that he would put on record what he considered justice to his children.[2]

William was still not convinced, and finally, on January 8, 1883, Henry wrote to William that "your own voice alone is now wanting" in order to arrange for the redivision. "The redivision will be a perfectly simple transaction," Henry insisted, "not demanding in the faintest degree your presence."[3] (Henry had insisted, all along, that William remain in England, although William repeatedly expressed a determination to return home.)

When Wilkie learned of his exclusion from his father's will, his reaction was understandably bitter. He wrote to Bob on the day after Christmas 1882.

My dear Bob,
I shall do or say nothing in the matter of the will, until I hear its contents. Then I shall place the matter very deliberately into the hands of a lawyer for contest, and the entire breaking of the will, making voluntarily the discrimination against myself in its benefits of a sufficient sum to pay you the rest of my indebtedness, and the $5,000 lost by father in my bridge business. I shall utterly and entirely disclaim any liability on account of the Florida enterprise. I never in any way gave my note for it to father. The property was purchased in his name, and he gave me power of attorney to run it for him. I labored with it for six of the best years of my life trying to save it, have never received one dollar of benefit from it since I left there in 1871, but on the contrary, burdened myself for life with indebtedness to other people in order to save it to the family, paid its taxes from my salary for 5 years, and in every way made father's estate liable to me for every dollar I have spent upon it. Not an acre of the Gordon property has been sold to anybody since I left it eleven years ago, and its title remains in father's name, subject to the mortgages which he induced me to give to Wetmore for its defense. I have in my possession a complete chain of accounts of the whole property, also letter after letter of father's trying to

induce me to abandon the whole property and fathering the ill-judged investment himself.

The more I think of this discrimination against both of us, the more unjust and damnable it seems to me. I don't see why you should in any way submit to the one made against yourself. The farm I always understood was a gift forced upon you by father and mother, they deeming it very disadvantageous to you to remain in Prairie du Chien.

It was a base cowardly act of father's, a death stab at two of his children to whom he owed every gratitude a father could owe to his flesh and blood; a death stab at the only two of his children who dared fight through the war for the defense of the family and the only two who attempted while very young to earn their own living and have earned it steadily ever since. It seems to me that the circumstances surrounding the whole transaction are very peculiar: why he should suddenly make a will after refusing 72 years to do so, why he should do so in a way privy to Aunt Kate alone who made it her boast last winter to me that she forced mother fairly to make her will for the benefit of Alice alone, why he should discriminate against the only two of his children whose health are too much impaired to make a living, all these facts, together with the fact that he broke his own father's will for his own benefit, make it absolutely apparent to me that he was greviously and strenuously influenced in his last hours. This in connection with the very characteristic remark made by Aunt Kate that "why leave Wilky any money, he may die at any moment," only makes the assumption on my part a very justifiable one.

> Yours affecty,
> G. W. James[4]

Wilkie's observation that he and Bob had fought during the war and had later supported themselves, unlike Henry and William, is the only reference ever made by any of the Jameses to this sensitive issue. However, the accusation seems to have been a belated one, inspired by Wilkie's desperate circumstances and his shock over having been excluded from the will rather than by any long-festering resentment. Wilkie never begrudged his brothers their success; in fact, he had saved in his scrapbook along with his Civil War momentos, Milwaukee newspaper clippings announcing the publication and success of Henry's books. One senses that Wilkie, in his letter, was trying to rile Bob up sufficiently so that Bob would join him in contesting the will. The limitation of Bob's share was a deduction of seven thousand dollars which Henry James, Sr., had given him to purchase the farm in Milwaukee in 1874.

One can appreciate Wilkie's anger upon learning of his exclusion from his father's will. He felt betrayed, but more important, his financial affairs were in disarray and he needed money more than any of the other children. His need for money intensified as his health failed. He was often unable to work, and he was not paid for days not worked. He had tried, to no avail, a water cure in Michigan, again incurring a loss of salary. Within four months of his father's death he would be forced to resign from a job he had taken with the Internal Revenue because of his failing health. As a result, he had no income with which to support his family, much less to pay his debts.

Upon the death of his father, Wilkie must have anticipated the financial relief which an inheritance would have provided; instead, his financial problems remained, and he had to endure in addition the mortification of others learning of his situation. This is evident from a newspaper article which appeared in the *Milwaukee Sentinel* on January 12, 1883, as a "special dispatch":

> Boston, Jan. 12—The will of the late Henry James . . . has been filed in the Probate Court, and will probably be approved on Monday. The deceased left no widow, his heirs being four sons—and one daughter, William James, of Cambridge, Henry James, the novelist, whose residence is in Boston, Alice James, of Boston, and Robertson and Garth Wilkinson James of Milwaukee, Wis. Miss Alice James, who was a great favorite with her father, comes into the possession of the household furniture, silverware, ornaments . . . together with Henry, William, and Robertson. She is also one of the residuary legatees, and it is particularly directed that her portion shall be disposed as to be most convenient for her. The estate has not yet been appraised, but will probably amount to a considerable sum. Garth Wilkinson James, at his own request, is not made one of the residuary legatees. He is understood to be doing a very good business in Milwaukee. The excellent philosophical

library of the deceased, the copyrights of his books and all his manuscripts are bequeathed to William James. Henry James is made the sole executor with bonds.[5]

Obviously, the information that Wilkie was "doing a very good business" and thus had not been made a legatee at his own request was supplied by one of the Jameses in Boston to spare Wilkie embarrassment, but anyone who knew Wilkie in Milwaukee knew that he was, in fact, doing no business whatsoever and in debt to creditors and friends, and was therefore able to surmise that Wilkie had been excluded against his will. Despite the protection of the bankruptcy laws, Wilkie still felt morally responsible for the money he had borrowed from friends and from his brother Bob. In addition, he had other debts not covered by his bankruptcy, some of which even Carrie did not know about. Wilkie was intentionally evasive, even disingenuous, about such matters; only after his death would the severity of his financial problems come fully out into the open.

Clearly, Henry James, Sr.'s, decision to exclude Wilkie was not "a base cowardly act," given the financial backing which he had provided to Wilkie both in Florida and in Milwaukee, but it was unexpected. Wilkie's suspicions about Aunt Kate's involvement in Henry James, Sr.'s, decision were probably justified. Henry James, Sr., had always functioned in a magnanimous and impractical way when dealing with his children: he gave as much as he could to those who needed it. He once wrote to Bob, that if necessary, he would sell his house and property in Albany to finance Alice's trip to Europe. He made spontaneous offers of help the moment he detected a need: he helped Henry and William in financing their studies and travels; he offered Bob and Mary help in purchasing the farm and in paying for a horse and a nurse for the children. His will was certainly not consistent with his lifelong habits, and his disdain for wills in general, after his own father had written such an odious one (Henry James, Sr., had been excluded from his father's will), does lead one to suspect that the will which Henry James, Sr., wrote was not altogether his idea. The efficient arrangements made in his will sound very much like something Aunt Kate would devise. In her own will, she bequeathed Alice a lifetime interest in a shawl.

Some of the correspondence dealing with Wilkie's exclusion is missing. However, it seems that Carrie's diamonds, which had so offended the Jameses in the past, had again been mentioned. Wilkie wrote to Henry in February of 1883, and this letter helps one to realize how difficult it must have been for Wilkie to accept his exclusion from his father's will:

Dear Harry,

I have been waiting patiently till I got through my present sufferings to answer your letter of the 12th. . . .

I have been in bed ten days with rheumatism and other *isms* and have had a vast amount of pain. The children's condition [scarlet fever] added also to my anxiety, although we are now all of us on the way to recovery. Poor Carrie is down again with exhaustion and fatigue, but there is no use of worrying about her, as her condition is a natural one. I cannot write a long letter, as I am weak and unfit to write much. But I must answer certain questions in your last letter of importance. First I want it thoroughly understood, that I want no benefits, nor no relief from father's estate, which is to be at all contingent upon anybody's solicitude as to my wife's action about her own property and belongings.

Carrie has done nothing but make sacrifices for me ever since my business misfortunes. She has been a singularly unself-ish and devoted wife. She offered Bob her jewels six years ago, to pay my debt. The offer was refused. She sold all her *valuable* jewelry to pay some of my debts; her earrings were recovered by her father, under the promise that she should never part with them again, and all she now has is them and two rings, and a pearl ring, her engagement ring. She has paid during the last year over 2,000 dollars, to pay for the long period of idleness during my illness from last April till the present time, in which time I have lost $1,000 of income, and was subjected to the expenses of two visits home for myself, and one for Bob at the time of father's funeral, and my long absence and illness at the water-cure in Michigan. For herself since her marriage she has never expended a dollar. She had literally never taken a day of rest since her marriage, and in nine years she has never been away from her home, simply because she could not afford to go. Her trip to the farm house in the country, last summer and the summer before last, have been her only alleviations from the grind and dreariness of our misfortunes since our marriage, and of sore trials she has had plenty.[6]

Even before Wilkie wrote this letter, Henry had decided to visit Wilkie and Bob in Milwaukee to discuss the redivision in person. William had correctly anticipated Henry's reaction to the uncivilied lifestyle he would find there. Henry not only found Wilkie's living conditions deplorable, he wrote to William on January 23, 1883, that "the thermometer at Milwaukee was 20° below zero." William had still not agreed to the redivision, and Henry again tried to convince him to do so, based on his findings on his trip to Milwaukee:

> It had been an immense load off my mind in seeing Wilky and Bob that before I did so I should have written you my proposal for your assent to an equal re-division of the estate. If I made you that proposal *then* with eagerness, I should have made it now with an even greater desire that it be realized. I wrote you last of Alice's entire assent to it—and Bob of course is only too glad. That Father's will should have been made just as it was, has been a source of the greatest unhappiness to all of us here. . . . Time—each succeeding day—has only made the thing more regrettable. . . . It will however be a great pleasure to me to write to Wilky and Bob on the earliest day that you *do* assent to the redivision. You probably will yourself have written to them to this effect. I stayed with Wilky at Milwaukee, and found him, I am sorry to say, a sadly broken and changed person. I am afraid he is pretty well finished, for his spirits have gone a good deal, as well as his health, though all his old gentleness and softness remain. When I got there he was in the grip of a rheumatic attack, but it left him thirty-six hours after my arrival, and then he was very much better. I think he might, in spite of his double malady, get on decently well in the future if he has some small idea of taking care of himself, or if his wife had some idea of taking care of him. But they have absolutely none—as is shown in their whole manner of life, and Carry's imbecility is especially deplorable. I lectured and preached them much; I hope with some effect. Bob strikes me as a good deal better than he used to be; he has become a landed proprietor. That is, he

and Mary have, by her father's advice, invested $7,000 of hers in the purchase of a country residence or rural retreat about five miles from Milwaukee and about two from Holton's residence. It is a small but solid brick house, with a Grecian portico, and a really very charming domain of thirty-five acres. It needs to have a little money spent on it—but it is, says Holton, a very wise investment.[7]

Bob had decided to return to the East permanently and was beginning to tempt Mary to join him, and this was Mr. Holton's way of keeping his daughter and grandchildren near him. Bob tried the arrangement, but within six months he fled to Boston. Mary and the children, however, remained in Milwaukee, near Mr. Holton.

William now insisted that Wilkie be given five thousand dollars less than the others. Once again, Henry tried to persuade him to agree to an equal division. As a safeguard, Henry adopted the tack of simply assuming that William would agree with him and proceeded on that basis. He wrote:

I agree in all you say as to the *principle* of Father's holding Wilky responsible for the $5,000 advanced to him before his failure, and I can only repeat that if the circumstances were now more favorable to our cutting down his allowance it should certainly be done. But they are as little as possible.

I have now decided to assent to his *own* request to accept $5,000 from the amount I am to put into trust for him (i.e. the rest of his equal share), to enable him to pay his debt to Bob and two or three other "debts of honour." . . . To cut off more than this would be rather grievous—and his state of mind and of health together are such that I shrink from carrying out such a plan. Just now both his children are ill with scarlet fever (it appears to be light) and in the midst of this addition to his other troubles I feel like letting him off easily. You may think that I am rather weak about this; and I am, I admit. But I put it all on the ground of Wilky's generally collapsed condition. If it were a palpable injury to any of us, I should not urge my own project in preference to yours. But as the difference between the two is so small . . . I think we had better abide by the fact that having Wilky equal with us and not insisting on the forfeit in order to justify Father, will be the thing which satisfies most of the proprieties of the case. The will was unfortunate, in its wholesale character, and the best way to justify Father is simply to assume that he expected us (as he *did* expect us) to rearrange equally. . . . I shall let (Wilkie) suppose that you have simply assented to it, and shall leave it to your confidence that I am acting for the best as the circumstances appear to me here, to justify me.[8]

One must remember that Henry James had a fastidious nature, and he had been appalled by what he observed in Milwaukee. However, he obviously hid his disgust well from Wilkie, upon whom Henry's visit had a salubrious effect. Wilkie wrote with love and gratitude:

Your invitation, with Alice's, to go East and spend a few months of rest and repose with you in Boston touches me very much, and fills my heart to the bottom with gratitude and love for you and Alice. Your visit here, the fact of your coming here this long distance to see us, has prepared me for almost any exhibition of kinship from you. Your extreme kindness and kinship to me while you were here, your loving, tender, moderate and wise counsels to me had peremptorily disarmed me of all the fancied abuses and isolations under which my existence labored, and of which I had written to you so fully and so unjustly as it seems to me now. In a word, your visit had the effect of shaking off in a day, almost all the evil omens and surroundings which my mind had . . . invited to me. . . . And so your visit left me, in mind and body, when your and Alice's letter reached me, which both go still further in confirming this attitude of mine.[9]

At about the same time Henry received Wilkie's letter, Bob wrote to him about his plans for his share of Henry James, Sr.'s, estate:

I think it more than likely after the appraisal is known that if there is any way in which I can draw my share out it would be the best thing I can do. I view my interest in the estate as wholly my wife's—as I have no prospect ahead of me of ever being able to accumulate money. I am bound to provide for her and the children in the event of my death by securing to her whatever I can. She will decide when the time comes as to what to do. Her father strongly recommends me to profit by any opportunity which may offer of withdrawing my share from Syracuse, not that Syracuse property is other than desirable but because the same amount of money invested here will yield 50% more income. I am convinced of this also, but there is time enough to decide it.[10]

As usual, Mr. Holton was involved. However, Bob's provisions for Mary were not being made simply in the event of his death; Bob knew that his marriage could not endure much longer. He intended to use his legacy to buy his freedom—freedom from financial responsibility for his family, freedom from his father-in-law, and freedom to paint and write in the East.

An equal distribution was finally agreed upon, but Wilkie's health was deteriorating rapidly, and his financial condition was so grim that he was unable to remain with his family in Milwaukee. He wrote to Henry on February 21, 1883, of the dissolution of his home and family:

I have today resigned my place as Deputy Collector and Cashier here.

I shall go East next month, say about the 10th of March . . . if it still seems agreeable to you and Alice. William's arrival home may possibly make it now seem better to give him up my room. Otherwise I shall go. I prefer, however, to go there with the purpose of immediately finding some occupation, and paying my board to you and Alice while I am there.

As soon as the children get well, I think Carrie and they will go East to spend a few months with some of her relatives in New York State, near Syracuse and Utica. I think this will do them all a vast amount of good, especially to Carrie, and it will break up our house here for good and ever I trust. You offered to send me some money some time since. I am obliged to you very much, but I can get along without any for the present and for the near future.[11]

Wilkie did not travel east immediately; rather, he headed south to Florida. His friends were concerned about him; he had formed relationships in Milwaukee as strong as those he had formed in the Sanborn School and later in the army. A letter has survived which shows the extent of the affection Wilkie's warm and trusting nature engendered. The letter is written on Chicago and North Railway Co. stationery, and on it is printed the title "Office of Second Vice President." It is signed "Edward," and no last name appears.

My dear Wilkie
  Knowing that you have chosen the royal road to good health—I would accuse myself of indifference to your welfare should I omit to give you (with many good wishes) a passport over that portion of the journey within my control. I expect to hear what the plans are for arriving and leaving Chicago with a view of having a parting benediction.[12]

Wilkie probably visited his old plantation in Florida. From there, he traveled through the Carolinas, perhaps visiting the sites of his old battles, and met Henry in Washington, D.C. Henry reported on Wilkie's condition in a letter to Bob, written soon after Henry and Wilkie arrived in Boston:

I brought Wilky back with me . . . and he is now settled here for the time. His condition, poor fellow, is not brilliant—on the contrary: the bad conditions, fatigues and discomfort of his . . . journey were very unfavorable to him, and did him more harm than good. He is very weak and suffers much, with his heart. On the other hand, he already looks much better than when I met him in Washington, and is at present in circumstances which (when they have time to act upon him) must . . . relieve and refresh him. Dr. James Putnam is looking after him, and promises him improvement. He has fortunately almost no rheumatism.[13]

Less than a month later, however, Henry reported to Bob that Wilkie's "rheumatism has come back to him, and he suffers a good deal."[14]
  In that same letter, Henry expressed, as subtly as he could, a fear

which he and William had been harboring. Bob had asked for his entire share of the estate in cash so that it could be invested in Mary's name in Milwaukee, with the advice of Mr. Holton. Henry and William trusted Mr. Holton, but they did not believe Bob's decision to turn the entire share over to Mary was wise. Henry inquired if Bob had any "definite use to put" the money to, "or manner to invest it." William wrote to Bob: "I hope you won't realize on your share until you are sure that the contemplated Milwaukee investment will bring in a much more rapidly augmenting return than the Syracuse one."[15] And in June, William again wrote to Bob, explaining that it would be a "pity to sell" the "thriving" property in Syracuse; if they waited until January or February "the store in question might bring $30,000" as opposed to a lesser price immediately. Wilkie needed five thousand dollars immediately, but William hoped that Bob would "agree in waiting." Bob did finally agree to hold on to the Syracuse property, but he insisted on turning his entire share and its control over to Mary. "I should have written to you from Syracuse directly recommending patience," wrote William to Bob, "but I did not know the outlandish name of your permanent address."[16]

Bob's address was Wauwatosa, Wisconsin, the location of the farm which Mary had purchased, at her father's recommendation, in January of 1883. Bob and Mary moved to Wauwatosa in April, and Mary's datebook entry was all too predictable: "Bob worked very hard for three months but got into nervous excitement again and left for Boston."[17]

This time, Bob intended to stay away from Milwaukee. In July of 1883, he informed Mary that he had settled in "a respectable boarding house . . . for six dollars a week" in Arlington, a suburb of Boston. He worked out a budget on which he and Mary could survive. He intended to occupy himself "with painting," and he told Mary: "Your letters will mean more to me than anything else."[18]

Bob wrote to Mary frequently, often daily, advising her on financial matters and assuring her that he was having the papers drawn up to transfer the Syracuse property into her name. Henry and Wilkie, who were living with Alice, assured Bob that one of his pictures was "the best thing" he had done. Bob made arrangements to take lessons from an art instructor in Boston, and he urged Mary to either rent or sell their farm in Wauwatosa, since he intended to study with this instructor, Mr. Crowninshield, a successful commercial artist, for two years. He asked Mary to send his stock of drawing paper and, of course, his Swedenborg books.

Bob wrote to Mary of the "cheerfulness" and the "feeling of thankfulness" he felt at being able to provide her with some financial security. "You will be in all respects," he wrote, "as free a woman as you were before I married you, holden to me for nothing, and free to seek your pleasure wherever it may lead you. The gratitude I feel in being able thus to release you from any mistake you may have made in marrying me is beyond any words of mine to express." Of course, Bob was suggesting divorce, but Mary steadfastly ignored such references; one did not get divorced in Milwaukee in 1883. Bob's goal, he wrote to Mary, was to become "a self-supporting, independent, and industrious man," a goal not very different from the one he had wished for when he was only fourteen and wanted his father to set him up in a drygoods store. Nor was his goal very different from the one he had at nineteen, when he returned from the Civil War and refused to be satisfied until he found a job. Now, however, he wanted to earn his living as an artist, and at the age of thirty-seven, he was desperately trying, he told Mary, "to retrieve the past."[19]

Wilkie had returned to Milwaukee in August of 1883, in great pain and distress from the combined symptoms of his heart ailment and his rheumatism. He was, of course, unable to work. It is not clear whether or not Carrie and the two children had ever taken the proposed trip to Utica, New York. In any event, Carrie began to nurse Wilkie, who was permanently confined to bed.

Mary kept Bob informed of Wilkie's illness; her letters have not survived, but Bob mentions a letter in which she "gave so bad an account of Wilkie."[20] In mid-September, Bob again mentioned Wilkie's condition, and told much of his own, in another letter to Mary:

> I rec'd a letter from you yesterday which must have been at the studio a good while. You very properly censure my apparent want of interest in Wilkie's condition—but it is only an apparent want—for I feel how bitter his suffering must be. I wrote him a couple of weeks since a letter of affection and sympathy—but when I thought of how little any of you have to remember me by which is pleasant it seemed to me as if he would not care to

hear from me. I ought not to have had the feeling I am sure and should have mailed it—but did not. Do not think that I cannot love others Mary—I may not seem to, it is too true. God grant I may go back to the old days of innocent confiding feeling in others.[21]

Bob's various symptoms had begun to return, and he was often unable to go to the studio for instruction. This greatly upset Mary, since Bob had paid for his lessons in advance. He returned to Milwaukee that fall, probably in part as a result of Wilkie's grevious condition, and his sudden return upset Mary. She had managed the farm alone for months, but at Bob's urging she had finally rented it. Now they had no place to reside and went to live again with the Holtons at Highland Home, the same living arrangement which had precipitated Bob's drinking bouts in the past.

In what may have been the last letter Wilkie ever wrote—or to be more precise, dictated—he explained his circumstances to William on September 25, 1883, two months before he died:

My dear William,

I have recently heard nothing from you except your letter from Mrs. Tappan. I have written but little because I have been waiting to find out more accurately what my true condition was. I do not know it definitely even now; a consultation of Doctors has been had recently, which confirms the suspicion of Doctor Putnam that I have elements of Bright's disease. . . . So let it be it now makes little difference what happens. Severe kidney trouble is present within me and the heart disease has become simply one of the elements of that. I cannot write any more except to say that I am trying to gain strength if I can to bridge over the increasing demands upon any vitality. This I do very slowly having lost nearly all my appetite—so that it looks as if it would not be long before I shall peg out. Excuse this very unsatisfactory letter for I am too weak and tired to dictate details to you, getting no rest or sleep without the aid of drugs; I have no rheumatic suffering whatever and no acceleration of other pains resulting from kidney troubles. All this is a relief over my condition when you last saw me and the only pains which beset me or discouragements come from my fast declining strength. I will try to write to you again when I feel stronger and in better spirits.

With much love to Alice and yourself I am,
Your affectionate brother, Wilkie

Please send this letter to Harry, as it is so tiresome for one either to dictate or to write, but I will write him fully tomorrow or next day.[22]

Alarmed by this letter and by a telegram from Mary, William immediately traveled to Milwaukee, and he related the sad details of his visit to his sister:

I am stopping between two trains on my way home from a flying visit to Wilky, made in consequence of a telegram received from Mary Saturday PM to the effect that he was sinking and could not live many days. When I arrived however, yesterday at 2, I found him over his attack and temporarily sitting up. He still has a good deal of strength and flesh, and *may*, poor fellow, last weeks or even months. On the other hand it is possible he may suddenly go any day. He is excitable and nervous as he never was before—not as apprehensive of dying, but about every passing thing—and his mind is weak and flighty. Carrie is evidently an excellent nurse and caretaker, he has Gerry and another male nurse, and half the ladies of the neighborhood seem struggling to help. My presence evidently was too exciting for him, every thing that interests him brings on attacks of hard breathing—so I spent the night at Wauwatosa with Mary and her children, and am now returning, having seen eno' to warrant me in concluding that I had best not come again as long as poor Wilky lives, since all he wants is complete quiet and repose. His children are a charming looking pair, and seem very healthy.[23]

Henry had returned to London ready to resume his writing. He had, through enormous patience and labor, finally settled his father's estate and had turned the management of it over to William. Henry was satisfied with the redivision: Wilkie would receive an equal share; Bob assigned his share of the estate over to Mary but agreed to keep the Syracuse property intact; and Henry signed his share of the estate over to his sister, Alice. Upon his arrival in London, however, Henry found William's letter informing him of his intended trip to Milwaukee. Henry wrote to his good friend Elizabeth Boott of Wilkie's imminent death.

I have indeed at present a good many sad and anxious thoughts; but they come from America and not from London. My last letter gave an account of poor Wilky's rapid decline, and the very last of all was a note from William telling me that he was about to start for Milwaukee immediately. I am therefore in painful suspense—though my foremost feeling is an earnest wish to hear that Wilky has laid down forever the burden of all his troubles. All the last news of him is a record of unmitigated suffering, and he was long ready to go. I have before me now a little pencil drawing that William made of him, years ago, after he was brought home wounded from Fort Wagner and when he thought he was dying. It was taken at a moment when he looked as if everything was over, and is a most touching, vivid little picture. I say to myself as I look at it that it probably represents the dear boy now. Peace be to his spirit—one of the gentlest and kindest I have ever known.[24]

It was a terrible change of circumstances: Wilkie had always been the healthiest and happiest of all the James children. They had teased Wilkie endlessly about his weight; Henry had once inquired in a letter about Wilkie "the fat and faithless one,"[25] and William had once described Wilkie's "plump curpusculus" and called him "Wilky the rosygilled."[26] Now, Wilkie was emaciated and broken in health and spirit.

Wilkie died on November 15, 1883, at 5:10 P.M. He was thirty-eight years old, and the official cause of death was given as "Bright's disease of Kidney." He had been married to Carrie for ten years and three days. Wilkie's son, Joseph Cary, was nine years old; his daughter, Alice, was almost eight. Every Milwaukee newspaper carried notice of his death, and the *Milwaukee Sentinel* printed a column-long tribute to him. His valiant Civil War service was mentioned; even the poem which Louisa May Alcott had written for Wilkie when he was wounded was printed. The obituary concluded:

"He possessed rare conversational powers, and was eminently social in his nature. He was a delightful companion, genial, unpretending, genuine. Everybody that knew him loved him, and his death will cause unaffected sorrow through the wide circle of his friends. He was genuine and kindly, and without guile."[27]

Wilkie had not changed at all from the nine-year-old whom Henry would describe many years later in his *Autobiography*: ". . . his successful sociability, his instinct for intercourse, his genius for making friends. It was the only genius he had, declaring itself from his tenderest years, never knowing the shadow of defeat."[28]

Henry was notified immediately of Wilkie's death. "A telegram from Carrie about poor Wilkie's blessed liberation came to me two hours before yours," Henry wrote to William.

> I instantly wrote to Carrie, and afterwards to Alice, who will have forwarded you my letter. It is a great weight off my spirit—not to see him lying there in that interminable suffering. . . . You will, I hope, have had news to send me about his last hours. May they have been easy—I suppose they were unconscious. I like to think that somewhere in the mysterious infinite of the universe, Father and Mother may exist together as pure, individual spirits—and that poor Wilky, lightened of all his woes, may come to them and tell them of us, their poor *empetres* children on earth. . . .
>
> P.S. As I must always worry about something, I worry now, as regards Wilky, about his burial-place. It would be a great regret to me if he doesn't lie beside Father and Mother, where we must all lie. I hope, at any rate, you have had no trouble—that is no discussion and no excessive correspondence or fatigue about it—and above all no expense. I have sent Carrie 42 pounds, to contribute to Wilky's funeral (and other expenses).[29]

Carrie wanted Wilkie's body to remain in Milwaukee, and he was buried in the Forest Home Cemetery, one of the most prestigious cemeteries in Milwaukee, far different from the modest cemetery in Cambridge where the Jameses were buried. Henry was disturbed by this, and he wrote to Bob: "Your letter implies that Wilky was to be buried at Milwaukee, and this is a great disappointment to me. I had hoped he would lie in Cambridge beside Father and Mother and not in the place and in the company, in which I am afraid he has been laid."[30] Bob alone of all of the Jameses was present at Wilkie's burial, but one of the obituaries noted that "the attendance was very large."[31]

After Wilkie's death, it became evident that his financial affairs were far worse than anyone had realized. William wrote to Bob shortly after Wilkie's death, and his letter reflects the financial disarray which was slowly being discovered:

> Your note relative to Carrie's affairs came a couple of days ago and this very second as we are writing comes your other one of Nov. 26th, saying that the $2,000 is certainly squandered. It is a grievous thing to leave behind. The whole money side of Wilky's life is a mystery to me, as well as to every one else I suppose, covering one thing by another and acquiring such a bad conscience towards every one that at last he was afraid to tell even his wife that he hadn't been able to cover this sum.[32]

Bob realized the desperate condition in which Wilkie's finanial affairs had been left, and he took it upon himself to write to a man named Wetmore, from whom Wilkie had borrowed by using his ten-thousand-dollar insurance policy as collateral. The letter, in which Bob implored Wetmore to consider forgiving Wilkie's debt because Wilkie "left his two children totally unprovided for,"[33] is an eloquent one, but it did not have the desired effect. Wetmore kept the ten thousand dollars.

Shortly after Wilkie's death, William became concerned that should Wilkie's children not reach their majority, Wilkie's share of Henry James, Sr.'s, estate—namely, the property in Syracuse—would revert to the Carys. William was determined to get assurances from Carrie that this would not be the case. When Bob learned of his actions, he immediately wrote in shock and anger over William's attitude. Bob believed that William's strong distaste for Carrie was instigating his behavior, and Bob strenuously defended Wilkie's widow:

> Dear William:
>   I cannot tell you how sorry I am to learn from you of your attitude toward Carrie. Indeed I am more than sorry. I cannot

believe that you will persevere in it when you reflect upon what we owe her as the only ones who can make any reparation to her for Wilkie's pitiful and almost criminal want of providence for her and the children. I don't treat that matter at all as a reparation to the Cary Estate. God knows that is bad enough, and beyond all reparation.

You have misunderstood my motive entirely in supposing I had any such idea. My simple motive was to make some amends to Carrie for what I consider has been her social treatment from the Jameses in Cambridge up to the time of mother's and father's death. Coupled with the fact that her husband legally at least made no provision for her or her children; but died on the other hand leaving a heavy debt of honor unpaid to her father. I don't know whether you living at a distance have been able as I have been able to—to realize with what conspicuous indifference she was always treated during the lifetime of father and mother. I can readily understand that you can not entertain the idea fully by reason of the distance which separates us. But it is nevertheless a sad certainty and notwithstanding her uncompromising patience and good temper, I have reason to know that she has felt this indifference keenly.

Every woman has the right to expect upon marrying into the family of a reputable husband at least some social interest if not a display of affection. But during the nine years of Carrie's married life she not only never received an invitation to visit Cambridge, but was acutally repelled from coming when her husband tried to provoke some expression of willingness that she should be allowed to go. Men of more keen sensibilities would have felt and resented this unpardonable attitude toward a wife, but Wilkie apparently did not feel it enough to temper the mortification which she has felt. But I have been made aware more than once that all of Carrie's own friends commented upon it and did resent it as well as herself.

You say speaking of changing the arrangement, "I don't wish to give the money to Carrie out and out." If I proposed this—of which I have no recollection—I certainly did not mean it, altho' if it were left to me alone I would not hesitate to make that disposition of it—having no fear that she would "leave it to some Cary relative." All that I plead for is that we should take the most generous way of righting the undoubted wrong which a brother of ours has done to a woman who trusted him. It seems to me it is a niggardly way to show our affection and respect for a woman who made a most loyal and patient wife to one who can no longer repair the error he has himself committed—I say it seems to me a niggardly way to do a tardy justice to her to decline placing her children's money as a trust in her own hands. *It seems to me that our sense of honor ought to be touched and that we ought to be touched* and that we ought to be too glad to wipe out as far as we may and in as generous a manner as we can what seems to me at least a dishonorable and the only dishonorable chapter in the history of our family. . . .

Love to Alice.

P.S. You sadly misjudge Carrie or rather you sadly underestimate her if you could suppose that she would ever allude to any of these matters herself.[34]

William remained adamant, however, and responded to Bob: "Yours rec'd. I hold to my opinion about the reversion. It won't in the least degree prevent Carrie's freedom in dealing with the property, because if lost, there is nothing to hold her responsible, and I wish her to feel this. But I do wish to hold on to the infinitesimal chance of my children getting it instead of the Carries, whom Wilkie hated, and to whom I don't feel as if anything from Father's estate was due."[35] In fact, Carrie *did* agree with William's request. Eventually she inherited large amounts of money and property from her father's and brothers' estates, and, ironically, she outlived both of her children.

Later letters indicate that the relationship between Carrie and the other Jameses deteriorated even further, and eventually Bob withdrew his support. Writing to his daughter in 1906, he described Carrie as "an ignorant person never having had any noble ideas of life or loyalty or affection," and accused her of "refusing to pay her husband's debts, money for which ($20,000) we had sent her."[36] Henry expressed his disgust over Carrie when he learned that she had instructed Bob's wife not to have anything to do with William's family. Henry wrote to William that it made him ill to hear "of Carrie's instructions . . . to Mary not to come and see you. Carrie is really atrocious, and I can't pretend, now, to maintain my relations of correspondence with her. If she asks me why, I will plainly tell her. She is not worth doing anything at all to keep. I am sorry for her children—what an ass she is for them!"[37]

Despite Henry's protests, he did valiantly persist in maintaining contact with Wilkie's wife and children "for the poor Wilky-ghost's sake."[38] It was not always easy, and Henry complained to his sister of the difficulty of doing so "for want of topics."[39] The one topic they had in common, however, was Wilkie himself, and in 1913, when Henry borrowed Wilkie's letters from Carrie in order to write *Notes of A Son and Brother,* he recalled with sorrow and affection Wilkie's too-short life, and tried to put it in some sort of acceptable perspective. It was Wilkie's memory, more than anything else, to which Henry remained faithful. He wrote to Carrie:

. . . so trying, so upsetting indeed to nerves and spirits do I sometimes find it to plunge into this faraway and yet so intimate ghostly past, where everything and everyone lives again but to become lost over again, and what seems most to come forth are the old pains and sufferings and mistakes. And yet Wilky's war letters are an extraordinary picture of young courage and cheer and happy reaction of every kind—making me recall so vividly the times we received them, and all that convulsed public and private history, that they seem the story of another life and world altogether. He was touchingly young to have such big things, and difficult and trying things, happen to him, and I see how he bore the mark of them for good and for harm (to his poor overstrained and injured physical man) ever afterwards. It's not the war letters that are saddest, but those (though not numerous,) of the dreary attempt at cotton raising in Florida afterwards (it was so unsuccessful and delusive and dismal as to life, even had better things come of it) where his extreme youth for such wretched responsibilities—his and Bob's—again bring tears to my eyes.[40]

7
LITTLE SAVE MEMORY
TO LIVE WITH:
Bob's Death

After Wilkie's death, there began to be a balance of burdens: Henry, who felt true sympathy for Alice's condition, absorbed more and more responsibility for her until her death in 1892, and William patiently and compassionately arranged for Bob's financial and physical needs when Bob was unable to do so himself. There was nothing premeditated about this arrangement; in fact neither Alice nor Bob desired such treatment. Despite this, they often needed help, and Henry and William gave it unstintingly. Alice was lonely in America after her parents' death. She was too witty, independent, and intelligent to be able to bear residing with Aunt Kate, and William and Alice were suspicious of her relationship with Katherine Loring, Alice's friend and constant companion. William's wife and William's sister had never developed a fondness for each other. In October of 1884, Alice traveled to England to be near Henry, and she remained there until her death. Henry often described her condition in his letters to William, and in return, William often detailed Bob's activities and condition to Henry. For several years, however, Bob's circumstances altered so rapidly that William's news was often outdated before his letters had reached Henry in England.

In retrospect, Bob's behavior does not seem to be as erratic and capricious as it did to his family at the time. It is difficult to justify his actions, but it is less difficult to recognize the regularity with which he tried to live with Mary and her family in Milwaukee, failed, and tried again. Each failure manifested itself in behavior which grew progressively worse. Bob finally managed, many years later, to learn to control both his emotions and his alcoholism, but only after he had left Milwaukee permanently and spent several years in a sanitarium.

Mary's datebook provides a skeletal outline of what must have been an excruciating period for Bob, Mary, and their two children. Bob's son, Ned, was in 1884 eleven years old, and his daughter, Mary, was nine, difficult ages at which to witness such distressing incidents:

> 1884—Still at Highland Home. May—While Mother and Father are South Bob gets into deep waters and I conclude that life as such cannot last and he must try life away from me. He accordingly went to Delafield and North Lake [Wisconsin] for the summer. July—Children and I went to Morristown and then with . . . Carrie to Ocean Beach. Sept.—returned to Milwaukee and H. H. again. Rob in trouble leaves for Boston.[1]

Aunt Kate's letters to Mary provide the missing and painful details. In March of 1884, Bob was appointed curator of the Milwaukee Art Museum, a seemingly suitable position for him, given his artistic taste and talent. However, this was Milwaukee in 1884, and it is easier to understand the type of position Bob was accepting when one realizes that the museum was located, according to local newspapers, in "the rear of Poposkey's," an art and photographic store in downtown Milwaukee. Bob's predecessor had been dismissed because of unreconcilable differences over whether the curator or the director of the museum should open the mail. After three months, Bob could no longer endure either the position or Milwaukee, and he abruptly left for Boston. Aunt Kate wrote to Mary, referring to Bob's drinking and hostile behavior. Her letter provides evidence of Alice's and Aunt Kate's growing aversion to Bob, along with proof of William's unfailing patience and loyalty.

> A fortnight before I left Boston, I heard that a telegram had been received by William from Rob, telling him that he would be with him that evening. I was lunching with them, and replied I am very sorry to hear it, and wish much that he had delayed his coming until after my departure, for I have no wish to see him. William said neither does Alice, she told me some time ago

that she did not even wish his name mentioned to her, that she could do nothing in his case, and that a knowledge of him and his ways only excited and distressed her and that peace in reference to him came to her only in her hearing nothing about him. Katherine Loring told me that Alice had a nervous dread of seeing him, and that if he was to be in Boston, it was a sufficient reason for Alice leaving there. So we were all on our guard that she should not become aware of his being in Cambridge. I was fortunate in not meeting him. His conduct to me at the time of his mother's death, and his misrepresentation of me after his father's, to Wilkie, made me feel him to be a wholly unreliable person, and one to be kept out of the way of, as much as possible. . . .

William thought he ought to be occupied, and his only salvation to be in getting something to do, and that he might in accordance with his tastes find occupation in "household art" in some studio, or rooms in Boston. William is so hopeful and merciful, and deals with Rob in the most truly fraternal way, but my hopes are few, and his long habits of idleness are much against him. He told Mrs. Alice that he never felt better in his life, and felt just like hard work; but alas—how utterly unreliable are his words, and what a gift of fine talk he has.[2]

Encouraged by Aunt Kate's sympathy, Mary confided to her that Bob had, while still in Milwaukee in 1884, been involved with another woman. (Bob had asked Mary for a divorce on at least one occasion, but Mary had refused.) Aunt Kate continued to fuel Mary's indignation:

My dear Mary:

I am more pained, shocked, disgusted with what you tell me of Rob's recent course than I can express. Truly he is degrading himself very rapidly; and I should think you would feel yourself well rid of him, and that he should keep himself out of sight of the children is doubtless to be wished.

You say this woman who has shown herself so devoid of morality, decency and common sense, as to accept the overtures of a married man, and of such a reprobate as Rob must be known to be, is thought well of in your community. Whatever esteem she may have formerly been held in, I should think her social position must now be utterly sacrificed. I do not understand dear Mary, why you should dread a divorce, you can never be a sufferer but only a gainer by it, and the less the children have to do with, or know about their father the better for them, I should think.

I grieve that William has got this burden upon him. . . .

There was some confusion on Mary's part over Aunt Kate's position, and Aunt Kate hastened to make herself understood:

> I have just received your letter and hasten to disalude [sic] your mind of a false impression received by you from the letter I wrote you in reply to the one in which you told me of Rob's last brutal treatment of you, when he proposed a divorce. You seemed so shocked by this proposition . . . and viewed his getting it, as somehow (I couldn't imagine how) as bringing disgrace, you said, upon you and your children, that I hastened to tell you I should think, and all the world who knew you, would look upon it, as a great blessing to you.[3]

Aunt Kate was residing in New York at this time, and she wrote to Mary whatever news she heard of Bob. In the letter quoted above, she wrote: "In my letters from Cambridge nothing is said of Rob, which does not seem to me a good sign." Actually, William and his wife were fully aware of Aunt Kate's habit of repeating and sometimes distorting news, and they were intentionally reticent when writing to Aunt Kate. For a few months, William was successful in maintaining some semblance of privacy about Bob's affairs, but "Whilst on a visit to Newport in January," Aunt Kate wrote to Mary, "William came there and I had an opportunity of asking about Rob." Aunt Kate proceeded to describe, at length, Bob's behavior and her predictions for his future:

> He had had a breakdown about three weeks before, and William said had since been in a state of abject humiliation. *I* say in a state of mental and physical reaction after his cups. So William felt called upon to deal with him pretty decidedly, and show up his evils to him; I wondered what the effect would be, as he has

not hitherto been prone to forgive any honest dealing with him in this line; and I find the old course has been followed and he has packed up *all* his belongings, big chest and all, I suppose, and decamped to Concord, where Carry tells me he writes as supremely happy. This will last I suppose, until he disgraces himself there, and then another move will take place. He left on apparently good terms with William, and writes to him frequently I believe, but my impression is, that he never forgives *plain* dealing with, showing how little he really sees his evils, and how little he *really* desires to overcome them.[4]

William continued, somewhat successfully, his attempts to keep Aunt Kate at bay, for Aunt Kate wrote to Mary in another letter: "William has had a frequent correspondence with Bob but I have not seen his letters as they have all been Wm. says about business affairs. I have no interest."[5]

William followed the same course with his sister in England. Aware of her disdain for Bob, he mentioned Bob briefly and only when the news was good. In December of 1884, he wrote: "Bob continues angelic as few human creatures can be. He says it's all the result of getting his domestic troubles settled. He lives across the street and 'boards' with us for five dollars a week, and is very useful, doing all the Syracuse correspondence, running of errands, etc."[6]

In March of 1885, William informed Alice that "Bob keeps in first rate condition. Lives on 500 a year. Is now at Concord."[7]

Bob grew fond of Concord and was to live there until his death, although he spent several years away from Concord in a sanitarium in New York State for treatment of his alcoholism. In Concord, Bob found the time and peace to paint and write, and one of his paintings still hangs in the Concord Free Public Library. Many years later, after Bob's daughter had married and moved to Pennsylvania, Bob wrote to her joking of the provinciality of the town: "Well, Mary—I can't say I've read the two books you speak of. I can't get them in the Concord Library. I suppose they are immoral. There's a great tidal wave of immorality in literature about to consume us, but thank heaven I'm safe in the Concord Library. They won't even have Tolstoy's books there. I hope when I die I won't wake up in Concord. I'm not afraid of Hell."[8]

Mary Holton James would also come to love Concord. In

October of 1885, almost a year after Bob left Milwaukee, Mary brought the children east. William described her decision to his sister: "Bob's Mary turned up yesterday afternoon from Concord, whither she had come a few days previous, to try the experiment of living with Bob again, away from her father's neighborhood. I cannot hope it will be a long experiment, but it is worth trying for a while perhaps. She was blooming as ever in appearance and reported the children well."[9]

The experiment was not always successful, but it was long. Mary liked the people and the schools, and Ned's asthma seemed to improve in the New England climate; Mary too remained in Concord until her death.

In March of 1885, in the midst of such turmoil, Bob achieved a great personal and literary success. One of his poems, entitled *The Seraph Speech,* was published by William Dean Howells in the *Atlantic Monthly.* It contains all of Bob's personal and religious struggles and reflects his disgust with the Gilded Age.

There is an outcast multitude
Of forms, forgotten and unheard,
By Love untouched and Hope unstirred,—
A pallid army of Despair,
Which mutely faces Want and Care.

God does not give to all a voice
To utter that which goes untold
Of heart-break which their bosoms hold;
However bitter be the strife,
Unheard they live their tragic life.

Their eyes know not the meadows green,
Nor dream they in the city's gloom
Of singing birds and flowers which bloom;
And vapors of the poisoned street
Fall on them as a winding-sheet.

But when their pain within our own
Has stirred the tongue so long unused
With words to them so long refused,
'Tis then the speech we think our own
Is uttered by a voice unknown.

'Tis then the silent spaces ring
With seraph echoes far and near;
And seraph music fills the ear,
When mortal lips cannot express
The measure of their dumb distress.[10]

As early as 1877, when Bob was still working for the railroad, he wrote poetry in his spare time, and he had sent some of his poems to Henry. Henry wrote to his mother of them: "They have great and real beauty, in spite of their queerness and irregularity of form, and I shall be curious to see whether this form will grow more perfect. They are soft as moonbeams in a room at night—strangely pure in feeling."[11]

Bob's poems did not grown "more perfect"; rather, they grew more conventional, and many of his later poems are sentimental, even for the period. One can only wonder what would have happened had Bob been able to dedicate his life to art, as Henry had done. Although Bob did not begin to paint regularly until middle age, those paintings which have survived reflect real talent. For all the years Bob spent in Milwaukee, his audience was dull and unresponsive. Mary's taste in poetry leaned toward uplifting rhymes such as the one she had copied into the first page of her datebook:

Our happiness is formed when we some joy impart;
Peace, when we soothe and calm a broken heart;
Success, while helping others up life's rocky step"[12]

and so forth through Wealth, Health, and Faith.

However, Bob never abandoned his literary pursuits, although his writing habits were irregular at best. He wrote many of his poems while he was in the Dansville Asylum, and he attempted to write his autobiography. He wrote his Civil War essay and an essay dealing with the Boston draft riots while he was in Concord. In 1902, after he had achieved some financial and personal comfort, he traveled to Canada in search of literary work, but he was no more successful than when as a young man he had traveled to Colorado with his infant son in search of a career in journalism. Bob read extensively, and he corresponded occasionally with William Dean Howells. He once traveled to New York to attempt a career as an actor, but he discovered that he was, by then, far too old to endure the rigors of such a profession.

In March of 1889, Aunt Kate died in her house in New York City. Except for a brief, unhappy marriage, Aunt Kate had been entirely absorbed with her sister's family. Alice wrote of her, shortly after her death: " . . . the truth was, as her long life showed, that she had but one *motif,* the intense longing to absorb herself in a few individuals.[13] Aunt Kate's will surprised the James children, leaving the bulk of her estate to cousins in Connecticut, cousins whom she had occasionally mentioned in letters to Mary Holton James but with whom she had never been intimate. She left William ten thousand dollars; Henry and Alice were left very little. Alice, who had strenously and successfully sought independence from Aunt Kate, was incredulous at Catherine Walsh's bequest to her: a life interest in Aunt Kate's silver and a shawl, which, after Alice's death was to revert to a male heir. Mary Holton James had confided for years in Aunt Kate; Aunt Kate rewarded her confidences with a thousand dollars. The pragmatic Mary used the money to make repairs on her house in Concord.

Aunt Kate had been as kind to her niece and nephews as she would have been to her own children. She lived with the Jameses and helped to care for the children from the time of Henry James, Sr.'s, marriage to her sister until his death,, with the exception of a short period of time when she was married to Charles H. Marshall, a marriage which Henry James, Sr., termed "a frightful mistake."[14] She traveled with Alice to Europe and to New York City when Alice underwent treatments for her nervous ailments. She contributed to William's finances when he traveled to Brazil. She had lost money in the Florida enterprise, and letters show that she sent Bob and Wilkie monetary gifts regularly when they were in Milwaukee. In addition, Bob once thanked her for a sewing machine which she had purchased for Mary. In all of the letters which the James children sent to their parents, they included love for Aunt Kate, and Bob called her *Tante* when he was studying French.

Catherine Walsh was, however, like her sister in personality: loving but firm, subservient but demanding. As the James children reached adulthood, they seemed to find her desire to incorporate herself into their lives far less appealing, and Alice found Aunt Kate's company tedious. Catherine Walsh's letters to Mary Holton James reflect a highly inquisitive woman very set in her ways, and Wilkie never forgave her for her purported influence over Henry James, Sr., concerning his will. There is no record of Bob's reaction to her death, but he certainly must have resented his aunt's interference, and support of Mary, in their marital problems. When Bob recorded some of his childhood memories, he accused his mother of recklessly confiding her offspring to others, citing as evidence the fact that he was made to share a room with Aunt Kate. Henry, William, and William's wife, Alice, continued to show respect for their aunt, but Alice's comment at the time of Henry James, Sr.'s, death that Kate "doesn't know how much she unintentionally tells" indicates the potential difficulty of Catherine Walsh's personality and behavior in delicate situations.[15]

It was assumed that Alice would reside with her aunt after the death of Henry James, Sr., but she moved to England instead. Near the time of Catherine Walsh's death, Alice imagined her aunt "as usual lying with folded hands fostering her own aches and pains."[16] Catherine Walsh's letters to Mary Holton James, containing minute descriptions of the illnesses and deaths of various relatives and acquaintances, confirm this impression. Perhaps Aunt Kate sensed such an attitude in her niece and nephews, a perception that would account for the manner in which she disposed of her property.

By 1890, Bob and Mary had finally achieved some financial security. Bob had liquidated his share of his father's estate, and that income, coupled with Mary's money from the sale of the house in Milwaukee provided them with enough to meet their needs. Despite this, their relationship was still often stormy. Their two children had developed into intelligent young adults who often sided with their mother in her marital problems. Bob was often harsh with his son, who at one point during his college career took refuge in the home of Ellen Emerson for six weeks.

There was only occasional news of Carrie, which William passed on to Alice in England:

> Mary . . . has seen Carrie this summer who is nursing her brother Ed on his deathbed. It seems that the eldest brother Charles died a year ago. C. left his money to Carrie, and according to Mary, Ed has made her his sole heir, so Mary says she is a rich woman. The boy, Mary says, has been kept at home

the past winter apparently doing nothing. Mary has induced Carrie to get a tutor for him, and to send Alice to school at Utica. She says that Carrie would be willing to have him go to college, only he seems insusceptible of being "fitted" therefor. It's a rather sad business. We have asked Carrie (when East with the children) to come and see us at Chocora. Neither time could or would she come. If the end of our summer had not been so broken up, we should have invited the children alone this year, so as to learn to know them. But with such a mother what can they be? "Take a hole and pour iron around it" was the classic Irish receipt for cannon making. Take nothingness and pour blind maternal instinct and dead obstinacy around it, and you have Carrie. The trouble with the children is that they are now so old, that the mischief of their bad education or no education is probably irretrievable. But I don't want to rile you up about them—this is the first news I have had from them in so long a time that it ran out of my head.

Bob's son had begun to study at Harvard College, and in referring to Ned, William was able to give Alice better news: "Ned has a pleasant room here [in Cambridge], and is a really prepossessing young fellow. Two of my colleagues have spoken to me of him as having attracted their attention."[13]

Henry continued to wonder and worry about Wilkie's family, and William's wife, Alice, tried to keep him informed. Her news of Carrie was frequently unpleasant, but her final paragraph in the letter below about Mary Holton James's niece must have amused Henry, whose career had been devoted to depicting variations on the very theme Alice described.

I . . . wish to tell you how nice I found Mary Holton. I had resigned myself to her uncomfortable trust of me, and when we met—it was gone. Perhaps Bob's absence from the scene helped. She is such a sound, energetic, major key sort of a woman and so really good that I like to be friends with her. I assure you she seemed like a tower of strength beside Carrie. If you could have seen William's touching attempts to "get acquainted" with Wilky's children you would have groaned in spirit. They were so cold, so absolutely indifferent. Alice evidently disapproved of him, and he seldom makes a greater effort to be agreeable than he did with them. The call William made on Cary [Wilkie's son]—he being out—he did not return till he came to say goodbye. He could not dine with us because he was "engaged to Detroit friends." In short, they were so evidently eager to escape us that I never again shall feel the slightest responsibility toward them. Carrie's only effort was directed to evading every question as to her plans on travel. And tho she had written to ask William's advice about Cary, every reference to his future was met with the same evasion. And he ought to be well drilled by a tutor before he is a month older. Their coming saddened W. as I am sure it did me. . . .

Perhaps I ought not to write you of this, I started to tell you how attractive I found Mary and Mamie. Poor old Mrs. Holton cried all one evening because her granddaughter is engaged to an Englishman, the disaster being aggravated by his title—Sir Philip Gray Egerton. I suppose few English mothers would take her view.[18]

In March of 1892, Alice James died of breast cancer. She was forty-four years old, and she and Bob had not corresponded for over six years. Bob was, of course, aware of Alice's attitude toward him. In writing to Fanny Morse, Bob referred only to their innocent and trouble-free childhood, in which they had pretended together in the nursery to be Mary and Henry, and he concluded: "I hope some part of my heart has gone with hers, away from the poor shams in which most of us have to live."[19] Henry tried to soften the impression of Alice's attitude toward Bob at the time of her death. He wrote to Bob and Mary: "She sent on the 6th a cable message to William—a message of tenderest love and farewell, addressed to him, but intended, as you will have seen, for all of you."[20]

Toward the end of her life, Alice had admonished William not to mention Bob in his letters to her. Her opinion of Bob had hardened into a particularly cruel and unsympathetic one, and she once wrote to William:

I am indeed distressed to hear about Bob. Poor, poor Mary. She has need of all her courage, how bad it must be for the children now they are getting so old. As Bob has been drinking ever since he was in the army, off and on, my unpsychic intelligence leads me to decide that his "progressive nervous degeneracy" is effect and not cause, the result however is equally distressing and disastrous. The poor creature seems to have no inner existence of any kind, he has always made upon my mind the impression of a human bladder.[21]

Alice steadfastly refused to make any connection between her own nervous ailments and Bob's. She had once written: "How profoundly grateful I am for the temperament which saves [me] from the wretched fate of those poor creatures who never find their bearings, but are tossed like dried leaves hither, thither and yon at the mercy of every event which overtakes them. Who feel no shame at being vanquished, or at crying out at the common lot of pain and sorrow."

Jean Strouse noted that Alice was comparing herself to people like her brother Bob. She wrote in her biography of Alice: "By 'those poor creatures' Alice may have meant the invalid men and hypo-chondriacal brother(s) she had determined to prove herself superior to. She looked at her own limited life without complaint and without the distortions of religious optimism or justification."[22]

This is true enough, and one cannot deny that Alice was intelligent, perceptive, and witty about her own illness. However, her life was far simpler than Bob's. She was financially secure both before and after her parents' death; it was acceptable for a woman in the nineteenth century to be crippled by such nervous ailments; and from the time of her parents' death until her own, Alice had Katherine Loring as a constant aide and companion. (Alice had her worst breakdowns when Katherine Loring was unable to be with her.) In the late 1890s, when Bob was finally able to attain some degree of financial and emotional stability, he too behaved far more stoically. He was able to abstain from alcohol, and his self-pity evolved into a sharp and witty sense of self-satire and irony.

The contents of Alice's will were predictable: to her adored brothers, William and Henry, she left approximately twenty thousand dollars each; she left the same amount to Katherine Loring. Bob and Mary received only ten thousand dollars, because, Alice rationalized, Bob had a rich father-in-law. To Wilkie's daughter,

Alice James, Alice left twenty-five hundred dollars and her gold watch. She had already given Bob's son, Ned, a thousand dollars toward his tuition at Harvard. Bob's daughter, Mary, and William's daughter, Peggy, each received twenty-five hundred dollars. There were other, smaller distributions, but Carrie James was not mentioned in the will, nor was Carrie's son, Cary.

In 1892, Mary's father, Edward Holton, died, and the bulk of his huge estate was divided equally among his wife and three daughters. Edward Holton, in the final clause of his will, divided the sum of twenty-one thousand dollars fifteen ways: the final allocation reads: "To my son-in-law, Robertson James, as a token of regard and remembrance, if he will accept it, a thousand dollars."[23]

Mary's datebook indicates her pleasure in her financial independence: she would remain married to Bob, but she would do as she pleased. Mary had always been an attractive, friendly, extroverted woman. She began to travel extensively with her mother, her sisters, and her children, especially her daughter, Mary. Henry James and "the two Marys," as he referred to them in his letters, met in St. Augustine, Florida, in 1905. As they became better acquainted, they grew sincerely fond of each other. Over thirty letters from Henry James to his sister in law and his niece have survived, and they reflect an affection as strong as the one Henry had for William's wife. Mamie (the younger Mary's nickname) was the primary source of those now famous anecdotes telling of Henry James's horror at the decline of the English language in America.

Mary recorded her almost frenetic activity in her datebook: "1893—after a most successful year abroad . . . we returned home . . . Rob meeting us in Boston. . . . In Dec. Rob again falls and goes to Arlington Heights where he remains about three months." "1894—Mother comes and makes me a visit of two months or so. . . . Rob returns . . . invests his money in Concord real estate. I buy the lot on Wheeler Hill and we . . . make arrangements to build." "1895—January, I spend this month in Milwaukee with Mother. Mary keeps house for her father while Edward does well in Cambridge." The datebook continues in this way, entry after entry: trips to Milwaukee, Florida, California. But in effect Mary was simply making the best of a bad situation. Bob's behavior had not yet stabilized appreciably, and in November of 1897, Mary wrote: "The twenty-fifth anniversary of my marriage and a sad day to me. I am in Milwaukee where I have come to see my mother and Edward. . . . Rob in Boston."[24]

Henry James instinctively enjoyed and admired Mary's undaunted exuberance for life. He said little of Bob; under the circumstances there was little he could say; he could only hope, as he did on one occasion, that Bob was "in quiet waters." Of Carrie, he wrote: "I have had not long since, a few lines telling me she meant to go to Florida. . . . She seems to me at this distance rather a lone, worn, wandering thing—but I hope she has some friends and some success." Of his nephew, Wilkie's son, Henry said in a letter to Mary: "I'm afraid Cary is not much an element of success and I find it difficult to construct any theory of his future." He wrote in the same letter: "I should rejoice indeed if Bob would do me a water-colour. Please tell him how grateful I should be."[25]

To his nephew Edward, who was considering a career in writing and who had had some success in having his short stories published in the *Harvard Magazine,* Henry offered nothing less than the philosophy which he had so successfully employed in his own long career:

For the stories in the Harvard Magazine I am . . . gratefully indebted to you. I have read them with the searching of spirit (to begin with) inevitable to one who has in a manner set an example and who sees it (in his afternoon of life) inexorably and fatally followed. (By fatally I don't mean that you are dashing to your doom—but only that the happy poison is to all appearance, distinctly in your blood.) I find your prose full of good intentions, and with the tales bright and lively.

I think *Cloistered* much the better of the two, and I think you will really write if you care to enough to go through, for the purpose, the long grind of one's apprenticeship. I hope with all my heart you do, for the pleasure is worth the pain. You will however find out for yourself all sorts of things which will be the steps of your growth, and the joy probably, of your soul. . . . Nothing that is worth doing is easy to do . . . the more one gets in, the more one sees, and . . . when one is young, one's successive stages and pleasures are at best provisional and momentary. One must take the business as seriously as possible—but one's success in it, *not* (for a long time, at least) too much so. These "efforts" (excuse the patronizing term), seem to me to show a disposition which makes me want to give you all sorts of good advice. But that will come little by little as occasion offers—it *can't* come all at once, like a recipe for a pudding. There is only one recipe—to care a great deal for the cookery. If you do all you can for this story-telling mystery, it will do a good deal for you. Live your life as your life comes to you; but, for your work, remember that an art is an art and that you must learn it with every sort of *help*, with the aid of all the implements. Read—read—read much, read everything. You will always observe and live and feel; but for God's sake do be as accomplished as you can. If you go in for literature be a man of letters. You have probably an heredity of expression in your blood (from your father through his father), and I see symptoms in your stories of the sense and gift for that. So gird your loins and store up your patience. Take the most important subjects you can, and write about the most human and manly things. We live in a frightfully vulgar age; and twaddle and chatter are much imposed upon us. Suspect them—detest them—despise them. Send me all you do I shall always be delighted to see it. And I will send you my stuff. . . . I hope you have a quiet scribbling-hole in that charming Concord house. Receive, my dear nephew, the love and the blessing of your faithful old uncle.[26]

Early in 1897, Bob began to manifest symptoms far worse than any he had displayed before. But though his behavior became more disruptive and erratic, Mary still refused to grant him a divorce, and in March of that year he suddenly decided to travel to England. He remained for only one week, during which time he visited Henry. As was often the case during this period, Bob misrepresented Henry's opinions to Mary, and Henry sought to set the record straight in a letter written soon after Bob's visit:

My dear Mary
    I am much stricken by the melancholy news I have just had from you. . . . I should be amazed at Bob's report of my opinion on the matter you write me about, could I, after all that has

come and gone, be amazed at anything he says or does. You will
have heard from him of my having . . . gone down to Liverpool
to see him. I passed thus a day with him—which proved a much
less disagreeable one than I had expected; but on that day not a
word was exchanged between us on the question you put to me.
. . . I was with him but for those few hours—during which he
both looked, talked and behaved much better than I had feared;
and not having seen him for years and feeling that I should
perhaps never see him again, I made no move upon any
contention or discussion, anything that could bring on a scene.
I only wanted to get off without one and not have a horrid
memory of my practically sole interview with him in so long a
stretch of time. He, on his side, didn't let loose the dogs of war;
and we parted after much pleasant, but studiously superficial
talk. Therefore it is only one of his customary madnesses to
quote me to you as approving his proposal—his pressure on
you—for the act you speak of.[27]

Bob had told Mary that Henry believed she should grant the divorce
which Bob so eagerly sought, but Mary remained adamant. She
explained to Henry that given Bob's behavior, a divorce would not
free her from worry, and she believed that it was wiser from a
financial standpoint to remain married to Bob. But the real reason
was that Mary continued to love Bob, as hard as that was for
everyone, including Mary, to comprehend. In describing her house
in Concord, Mary wrote in her datebook: ". . . our home grows
more attractive each year. This year I should have rented it for the
sake of economy, but thought Rob might come home again and I
wished to have the door open for him if he should wish to come."[28]

Mary was often unaware of Bob's whereabouts, and she was
often traveling herself. Given these circumstances, coupled with
Henry's great distance, the responsibility for Bob's care fell to
William and his wife, and it was a trying one. Over the course of
Bob's separations from Mary, his drinking, and his earlier frequent
flights from Milwaukee to Boston, William and Alice had made him
welcome in their home. Were it not for them, Bob's life would
literally have been in danger at times.

The first week of January 1898, Bob again paid Henry an
unexpected visit in England, and although Henry was as compas-

sionate as possible, he feared for Bob's sanity, and wired William and
Alice to expect the worst upon Bob's return. Alice, already preoccupied with William's poor health, wrote to Henry to describe the
events which followed:

> It is nearly a week since Bob arrived and neither William nor I
> have sent you tidings of him. This has been due partly to our
> profound immersion in his problems, partly because we waited
> till we could report some solution of it. I may as well anticipate
> the story of the week and tell you that William started with Bob
> today for Dansville, a great sanitarium near Buffalo, which by
> way of climate and general good repute promises better than
> any other place we could hear of. The miracle is that Bob goes
> gladly.
>
> Your dispatch and letter . . . prepared us for his return. He
> came Friday evening very drunk. The cabby who brought him
> and lifted him onto the porch told me that he found him in
> Boylston Square "knocking about." After some difficulty the
> man got the name of our street and number and so brought him
> out. Billy luckily appeared just then and got him to bed. William
> had been very nervous all day and I had urged him to go to his
> club dinner in town, so he did not see Bob till the morning. To
> judge by experience this meant days or weeks of anxiety and
> care. Imagine our amazement therefore at finding Bob in the
> library next morning perfectly sober and strangely sane.
>
> After breakfast he had some talk with William then came
> upstairs to bed. He referred to his previous evening and asked
> me if I had ever thought that his mind was failing. I was so
> wretched about him that I told him the whole truth; that it was
> failing, that he was much broken, and that another six months
> of such racking of himself could have but one end. He agreed,
> not only to this but to the place for his cure, the placing himself
> under restraint for months. He called William in and asked to
> have the doctor sent for. That very afternoon he came and the
> papers were filled out by which he can be taken to Foxboro at
> any time. Inebriates are no longer allowed in the state insane
> asylums and the inebriate asylums are filled with the very
> offscouring of the police courts. In short, Foxboro is a semi-
> penal institution where the men are all locked in together in a

common ward. Oh horrible! William told Bob how bad it was (and he never flinched) and how inevitable if his drinking returned, but that it never should be tried until milder measures had failed. William was very wise to confront him with so dreadful a remedy for when he proposed the sanitarium as a mild alternative poor Bob fairly clutched at it. He instantly set about arranging his money affairs. . . . I believe at all events he has placed his money out of reach so that by no possibility can he run away from Dansville. But I can give you no idea of the change in him. His mind has begun to live again, his arm is better, his eyes are blue as the sea and all the old defiance gone. He has been careful about himself in every respect—and lovable in his patience and docility. He has talked constantly of you, of your kindness to him and your goodness. He was thankful that he had not "broken down" while with you. Don't let him know that I have told you of his arrival. Luckily the servants did not see him so none but William, Harry, Billy and I know of his condition that Friday night. He could not have got over it so quickly if the drinking had lasted long. We heard that he had been most agreeable on the steamer. Very few people know that Bob was here, and he wanted to see no one.

I must believe—and I exult in it, that Bob is on his feet at last. It is the inward change that I feel, tho' I cant' in the least describe it—that moves me. William . . . feels quite as I do Bob's change of heart.[29]

Bob was displaying all of the charm and guile of an alcoholic at the Dansville Asylum. Alice's next letter to Henry concludes: ". . . I am less hopeful than I was. If ever a human creature was in the odour of sanctity, he was when he left here, but he forced W. to leave some money with him 'to buy a pair of shoes,' and as soon as William had gone he went to the village and got drunk. The doctor there gave him all attendant and hence forward Bob is to have no money, but go to the doctor for everything. Now I must write to Bob—we try to send him a letter every week."[30]

Alice did write to Bob at least once a week, and she was correct: after the one incident she mentioned to Henry, Bob did improve. He wrote often to Alice—long, often amusing letters. He observed that "there are 37 saloons in Dansville—one for every forty of the population."[31] Mostly, Bob remembered the past and Wilkie. He remembered their excursions on Lake Geneva: "the distant and sombre blue range of the Jura—the village priest who thrust a heated knife into Wilkie's adder-bitten finger, and saved him from death in the mountains—the stables of the Swiss chalets and the fragrance of the clean fodder on which we slept—the mystery of night as it locks in the life of the valley—all these things are more real and vivid to me now than they were in boyhood."[32] Bob was strongly attracted to the Catholic church while at Dansville and wrote lengthy letters about its teachings, but it is not clear whether or not he actually converted. He later followed the teachings of the Christian Scientists, and finally he returned to Swedenborg.

The Dansville Asylum (the name was later changed to the Jackson Health Resort) was a quasi-resort, with accommodations for two hundred "guests," which had been established in 1858 by Dr. James Caleb Jackson, who was described in a brochure published by the institution as one "known throughout America and internationally as . . . the pioneer in the employment of Hydrotherapy." In effect, Bob received little more than bath treatments, just as William and Henry had had many years earlier in Europe, when they were suffering from various symptoms and were unable to work.

But Bob's treatments reflected American "progress." He drank "All-Healing Spring Water" and received therapy in the "Moliere-Thermo Electric Bath," the "Autoconduction Cage and Autocondensation Couch," "High Frequency and Morton Wave Currents," and "Electrical Diathermy." Presumably, none of these treatments was harmful, and Bob must at least have enjoyed the 5,000-volume library and the beautiful surroundings: over forty acres overlooking the Genesee Valley, in Livingston County, New York, near Buffalo. A fire destroyed the main building and all medical records shortly after World War I, so one can only wonder whether Bob benefited from such innovations as "The American Costume," devised by Dr. Jackson to "allow a natural position for the internal organs," and the Granula Cereal, a specialty of "Our Home on the Hillside," the name which Dr. Jackson preferred to use in describing the facility.[33]

Bob never grew independent of alcohol, but he improved. It took a long time, however, and he remained at the Dansville Asylum for over five years. When he finally returned to Concord in 1901, his children were grown and his wife was financially independent, and he wrote to William that he needed a "visible use" in life.[34] He painted daily, but he also became somewhat eccentrically involved in other things as well. He helped some local farmers uncover a fraud in the state Bureau of Agriculture, and he and William experimented in group séances in which they tried to communicate with spirits. He formed and became president of the "League of the School Republic," "to extend instruction in moral and civil training in the schools."[36]

Bob still had occasional lapses, and on one occasion in 1904 he did so in the presence of his son's in-laws, the very wealthy and prominent Mr. and Mrs. Cushing. Mary recorded the incident in her datebook: Bob arrived "badly off with liquor. . . . Particularly unfortunate as the Cushings come to Concord and so realize the situation."[37] Bob, however, described the incident in a different and more humorous light to his sister-in-law Alice. Speaking of Mr. and Mrs. Cushing, he wrote:

> The old man is a corker. Kindly heart, I guess, but his head wobbles . . . as he talks and he asked questions all the time and never affirmed anything. I won't state the questions—they were like an air blowing on your cheek, leaving no impression. The mother I rather liked. I mean she seemed the most sincere of the company and it was a relief when she allowed me to dissent with her as to Henry James, Jr.'s lack of patriotism. Why had he not remained in his native country? Why couldn't he write here? I observed that he was executing a work of art—a product, a fruit, a something for which America did not provide. The right soil! Why did not America produce the right soil? Because there is a difference in soils, Europe having one and America another, so far as impulses to create pictures and books were concerned! Could she not see (this very politely) that strawberries do not mature in Alaska or polar beans in Florida. But she could not see it. Still I liked her a good deal. . . .
>
> I looked at the two butlers creeping around the table and got called down by the most servile of the two for having placed my butter on the wrong plate. . . .
>
> I hope they [the Cushings] won't criticize me as I have criticized them.[37]

Bob's son, Ned, had married Louisa Cushing in 1899. They had three children, all daughters, one of whom married Alexander Calder, the prominent American artist.

Mary, Bob's daughter, became engaged to George Vaux, of a well-known and highly respected Quaker family from Bryn Mawr, Pennsylvania. Bob refused to attend her wedding, but he later apologized to her for his petulant reason: "the Friends," he thought at the time, "were against the spirit of Christ in insisting on denominational forms"[38]—this from a man who had been christened in an Episcopalian church, considered converting to Catholicism, felt the healing powers of the Christian Scientists, and read Swedenborg's writings daily. Bob did send his daughter a telegram on the day of her wedding: "You have my whole heart's love."[39]

In 1906, Mary noted in her datebook that Bob's heart was "in bad condition," but nothing more was said of the matter.[40] He had probably had his first undiagnosed heart attack.

After Mary's wedding, Bob and his wife began to live together again in Concord, at least when Mary was not traveling. Bob had become philosophical about most things, and he wrote to his daughter of her mother's frequent trips: "I get nice letters from your mother, but her never-ending sight seeing I should think would break the strongest constitution."[42] Bob was not exaggerating: Mary traveled to Milwaukee frequently, and she and her mother, who was over eighty years old, toured California together. Soon after, Mary spent a week with her daughter in Bryn Mawr, a week in New Haven, and another week in New York, only to return to Bryn Mawr for the birth of her first grandson, George Vaux, in 1908.

Bob's ideas grew more and more like his father's, but they lacked Henry James, Sr.'s, munificence and wit. Of organized religion Bob observed: ". . . it takes a stronger stomach than mine to resist the temptation I see in all of them to foster spiritual pride and a sense of superiority." Of the value of higher education, he observed: "I know of no more degrading place for most boys than one of our fashionable universities."[42] He confessed that he had considered suicide but wrote to his daughter: "I don't believe God likes a coward."[43] Bob never really forgave his parents for not preparing him for a particular profession, and writing to his sister-in-law Alice of her son Francis's desire to be a painter, he said: "I wish our own father had steered his sons into the Soap or Baking Powder line."[44] Finally unencumbered by the need to earn a living, Bob wrote, in true Henry James, Sr., fashion, of the general state of corruption he sensed about him: "My great interest in life is centered in the present national struggle to become a decent people. . . . The labor element just as much as the wealthy class seem to have surrendered the old-fashioned ideas about honor and integrity."[45]

Bob quickly suspended his criticism of society, however, when his grandson, George, whom he referred to in his letters as Flub Dub, visited Concord. His letters to his daughter about the baby are refreshingly devoid of cant; they are simple messages of grandfatherly pride and happiness: "His visit was certainly an event in our lives. I constantly keep picturing him to myself as I remember him before breakfast every A.M. His adorable bow legs prodding my stomach as I held him under his arms—his philosophic rotundity of brow inclined toward mine—lifting his . . . eyes absorbed with wonder at New England facts of nature. . . . Write as often as possible about the baby."[47]

And, finally, Bob began to understand himself better. William's daughter Peggy sent Bob a tie, and he wrote to thank her in 1907, describing himself with ironic detachment:

> Your necktie arrived to fulfill its appointed function in life. . . . Your Aunt Mary says I look very pretty in it—but I don't care so much what other people think, so long as I feel pretty—and I do that. Dear Peggy, it's all in the feeling. I've galloped through all kinds of feelings during my career, but the problem of getting a feeling to stay by you more than 24 hours, I am still hammering at. I think the necktie will help me to keep on feeling pretty, for quite a while, because it is made of durable silk, and among so many fleeting possessions (like the paper collars I wear) I am glad to have something which is durable.[48]

Bob's relationship with his brother Henry, which had been strained during their meetings in England, also improved, to the satisfaction of both brothers. Through letters, they resolved their differences and determined to maintain better contact with each other. "Remaining for so long in such imperfect communication with you," Henry wrote after finally receiving a letter from Bob, "has been to me ever as a sort of dull ache or vague pain, that craved a balm." Henry knew, however, that it had been Mary who prodded Bob to write to him, for Henry concluded his letter:

> Good night then, dearest Bob—and good night, dear Mary, to whom I shall soon separately and specifically write, with a great deal of sense meanwhile of her gentle and beneficent nudging of your still elbow—as I surmise—in respect of your blessed breach of silence to your ever-affectionate old brother.[48]

In November of 1909, Bob again had another drinking bout, for Mary wrote in her datebook that she found Bob "so badly drugged that it ended in a sharp climax and I make up my mind that I must leave him alone for another period."[49] Consequently, Mary sailed for Paris that December. She met her mother and sister in Italy, and they traveled to Austria, Switzerland, and Germany. Bob would die alone while she was abroad.

In June of 1910, Bob heard that William, who was also in Europe, was seriously ill. Bob wrote to his daughter: "The James brothers are beginning to crumble fast and are a good deal more than half way on a return to the paradise in which they grew up."[50] That was the last letter Bob wrote.

On July 3, 1910, while Bob was alone in his house in Concord, he suffered what was probably another heart attack and died. He was sixty-three years old. His neighbors did not notice anything amiss, and his body was not discovered for two days. When it was, his daughter arrived quickly from Bryn Mawr, but his wife and son were in Europe, as were Henry, William, and William's wife. Mary's granddaughter, also named Mary, was only six years old at the time, but she was in Europe with Mary Holton James and still remembers her grandmother's reaction to the news of Bob's death. Mary did not cry; she simply muttered in disbelief, over and over, several times, "Bob is dead. I can't believe that Bob is dead."[52]

Peggy James, William's daughter, wrote to her mother on July 9, 1910, six days after Bob's death, to tell her of the events which had taken place:

> This has been a dreadful shock to us all—this death of Uncle Bob, and I am constantly thinking of you and Dad and Uncle

Henry. He just passed out, smiling, in his sleep, and the poor storm-tossed spirit is at rest. It was the most beautiful way to go. I went up from here Wednesday as soon as I got Mary Vaux's telegram. The funeral was at five and my train being four hours late, I did not get in till half past four. No body had let the boys know, and they had not seen it in the paper so there were none of us there. Harry and I felt terribly, but it could not have been helped.

Harry and I went out to Concord the next morning and found Mary and George Vaux. They were packing up everything in the cottage to move out and shut it up, so that Aunt Mary could come back to the big house and less harrowing associations.

I felt full of pity of Mary because she has some remorse coupled with her grief. She kept saying to me "I would have done more for Father, if he had let me, but he never would and now it is too late." Those fatal words "too late"—they grip one by the throat and make one fairly suffocate under the load of chances lost. We must draw the circle closer while we are here together, and do all we can for one another while it is still time.[52]

Actually, Peggy could not fully appreciate the extent to which Bob's daughter was feeling remorse. Mary had been a great source of comfort to her father and wrote to him regularly, letters which pleased Bob, particularly when they mentioned his grandson. In one response, Bob wrote to his daughter: "It is a great comfort for me to know that you are so near dear Mary—for I feel as if I had been abandoned by all my own."[53] But in another letter, Bob had asked his daughter about the train schedule to Bryn Mawr and the cost of the fare, explaining that he had lately been visited "with a half formed idea of going to Philadelphia for a day or two to see you and the Vauxs."[54] Mary must have written in strong opposition to the idea, for in his next letter, Bob wrote apologetically: "I don't think that it ever occurred to me for a moment that my friendly suggestion of going on to Philadelphia was going to be looked upon by you as adding to the 'strains both physical and nervous' which you say you have been under. How would you have expected me to be in any way 'entertained' or looked upon as a guest I can't imagine. If going to a hotel for a couple of days and running in to see you now and again is alarming to you, I shall know enough not to go."[55] Mary harbored a legitimate concern for her father appearing drunk before her Quaker in-laws, but she must certainly have been thinking of her sharp rebuke to her father as she packed his letters and papers shortly after his death.

Bob was buried in the Sleepy Hollow Cemetery in Concord, Massachusetts. The *Boston Transcript* printed Bob's obituary on July 9, 1910, and it is a kind but astute summation of Bob's entire life:

> Robertson James, youngest brother of Henry and William James, and with talents as brilliant as theirs, had they been as steadily exercised, has . . . suddenly died at Concord, where he had lived for 30 years past. He was educated in Switzerland and at Concord in the years just before the Civil War, entered the union army instead of college, and was an officer in a colored regiment at the battle of Fort Wagner. . . . He was by turns journalist, artist, man of leisure, and occasional contributor to the magazines,—a charming talker, and in religion a constant seeker, without finding rest in any form of faith. His family was absent, his wife and son and grandchildren in Paris; his married daughter, Mrs. Vaux, at Philadelphia,—when death came. He is buried in the Sleepy Hollow cemetery not far from his father's friends and his own,—the Emersons, Alcotts, Channing, Thoreau, Wasson and others.[57]

William James was dangerously ill, and when he was told of Bob's death, he said: "It fills me with a new respect for Bob, and how I should like to go as quickly."[57] What else could William say? William had cared for Bob for many years, with affection and patience, but he had also observed him (as he had observed himself, on occasion) with clinical detachment. William's biographer, Gay Wilson Allen, noted that William had Bob in mind when he described, in *The Varieties of Religious Experience,* the difference between "the healthy minded," and the "sick souls." The difference was psychological, a sick soul being one "whose existence is little more than a series of zigzags, as now one tendency and now another gets the upper hand. Their spirit wars with their flesh, they wish for incompatibles, wayward impulses interrupt their most deliberate plans, and their lives are one long drama of repentance and of effort to repair misdemeanors and mistakes."[58]

Bob had never received psychotherapeutic intervention of any sort. William had recognized Bob's problems and sufferings, but there was little which he, or anyone else at that time, could do for Bob. Bob, like his sister, Alice, had been born too early to benefit from the work which their brother William had just begun. William had insisted that Bob enter the Dansville Asylum, but no diagnostic or therapeutic treatment was available there or anywhere else at the time.

The discoveries which have since been made by psychoanalysts, particularly Erikson's theory of personality development, contribute to a far greater understanding of Bob's struggles with himself and others. Ericson concluded that if a happy personality does not evolve through certain stages, a manifestation of symptoms will develop instead which seems to reflect a disgust with others, with life in general, and with institutions, but which actually signifies "the individual's contempt for himself."[59] As Henry had written to Mary shortly after Bob's visit to England: "His very constitution and character are so unhappy."[60]

Many years after Bob's death, his nephew, Henry James III, criticized the way in which Anna Robeson Burr had described his uncle in her book. Yet he too had difficulty in defining his uncle: "Burr covers up so completely his faults, and misadventures of his life that were associated with them, that she . . . does nothing for him but to veil him over with vague intimations that he was a nervously disordered and hysterical sort of person. In that, of course, there is an element of truth, but it is such an inadequate explanation of such a complicated, and in some ways, interesting personality."[61]

Nowhere does his complexity show more than in a letter which Bob wrote to his sister-in-law Alice from the Dansville Asylum. The letter is as fragmented as Bob's troubled life had been, but it is also rich in experiences and images, capturing the essence of the unique Jamesian childhood which all of the Jameses had shared, with very different results.

Dansville Feb'y 24, 98

Dear Alice

It occurs to me tonight that I had better write to you. In your letter rec'd today you speak of an autobiography. Would that I could write one—for—curiously enough memory of days gone by lightens up again with me—now that I have little save memory to live with. But the facts of it are so meaningless. Down the palm of my left hand runs the so called line of Fortune and of Luck. Sufficiently defined is the line of the left hand, but badly broken. On the right palm the line not half so distinct and badly broken—which signifies that Destiny of itself gave me bad fortune and that with my own right hand I made that Destiny worse. It would have to be the biography of broken fortunes. Still the lines show this in both hands. At the beginning and the ends the lines are both well marked and straight—the breaks are all in middle life. More and more I take comfort in omens and portents and go to swell the ranks of those who lean on oracles. It is the return to childhood—which would bring me back to 54 West 14th St. in N.Y. What a troop of figures come out of the shadows. Alice James and the nursery there and scarlet fever, measles, the Irish nurse whom I have never yet forgotten, and the precious brooch she wore with a green crystal in which came to me the first wonder and mystery of color. When the light struck it first, something wondrous and from heaven awoke in my stomach—so lasting that today the effect of a green crystal is to make me weep inwardly. There are no end of figures which come and go in that New York house. Uncle William from Albany who throws his nightgown, night cap, brushes etc. from the omnibus window *en passant* from the Albany train to the lower roadway from which he is to return late in the day—signaling to the awe-struck servant on the steps that these things are his and that he will return for the night. "Tell Henry and Mary" is lost in the rumble of the wheels on the high cobbles of the roadway. Charles Dana at Saturday dinners. George Ripley. Mr. Bayard Taylor who tells of his frozen nose in the north. Mr. Bryant's son-in-law—name forgotten—but not forgotten the homeliest countenance in America which was his. Uncle Edward. John and Uncle Gus. The McBrides the Van Zandts Grandma James—her silk dress—peppermints, lace mittens and gentle smile. The Senters the Costers the Ironsides. Then also my mother who walked down Sixth Avenue to Washington Market *with a basket on her arm (of this I am sure)* every morning—for I tagged after her aged 6 years, and held to her shawl. The Vanderpoels and the Vanderbergs come next.

And then the dancing school. William will remember the name—Gen. Ferano—the master distinguished himself later on in our war as a soldier. You see this goes far back and takes in the marriage of Capt. Marshall and his subsequent discomfiture. I was a witness to his wooing, being near to Aunt Kate at that time and not supposed to be an observer—sharing her bed in fact and carrying with me to this solemn hour the hurt I felt at her mandatory ways. A mother does wrong to confide her offspring recklessly to others than herself. I might go on indefinitely writing you of these memories. Some of them are very plain like the sight of Gen. Kossuth seen in a procession of welcome on Broadway. There are plenty of others left in New York. But on the other side they come thick and fast. A riot in Regent's Park where the mounted men charged the populace in the Bread Riots. The night in London when it was aflame with fireworks over the Crimean Peace. The Queen who sits in the gilded coach on her way to Parliament. The Christmas Pantomine—the Rat Catcher's Daughter—Berkeley Square—Fanny McDaniel—Dr. Wilkinson—the Horse Guards. Mr. Thackeray who carried me on his shoulder, and then Boulogne-sur-Mer and the College Municipale and its stone vaulted ceiling where Wilkie and I went and failed to take prizes. But the day when the Mayor of the City distributed these I do remember, and somehow I think that tho' it was not a prize we both had souvenirs or a reward of some kind—for I recall a beautiful book with gold figures. But around the mayor who stood on a platform with great civic splendor and officials in uniform, I see yet the fortunate scholars ascend the steps of his throne, kneel at his feet, and receive crown or rosettes, or some symbol of merit which *we* did not get. The luck had begun to break early!

The only thing to say of it is that it was a beautiful and splendid childhood for any child to have had, and I remember it all now as full of indulgence and light and color and hardly a craving unsatisfied. Especially those daily growing revelations of heavenly landscape in Switzerland and the long cold winter at the Boarding School three miles out from Geneva. The break-fasts in the stone vaulted and sided and floored refectory—no butter—nothing but the bowl of coffee and dark bread. The house or part of it had been a monastery and was encircled with a great stone wall which had issues from it closed at nightfall with huge iron gates very old very ornamented and handsome. In the distance the purple Jura Mountains rose and nearer was the junction of the Soane and the Rhone whose waters do not mingle—two streams running side by side—one yellow with mud and the other clear and clean refusing to be defiled.

I don't know why I should have written you all this save to kill time. I am glad the old man who was tired of seeing himself in the glass has gone. I have seen Sidney Colvins, Keats letters, but I find it hard to get interested in books.

I hope you will not allow William's famousness to inflate him too much. I think when I get thoroughly restored here and everything is permanently disposed of as to my future . . . I may end my life in Europe somewhere.

Yours affectionately

R. James[62]

AFTERWORD

Mary Holton James continued to live in Concord after Bob's death and became increasingly active in volunteer work, particularly the suffrage movement. Above all, however, she enjoyed her grandchildren. In addition to Ned's three daughters, Mary James Vaux gave birth to a second son, Henry James Vaux. (He is now in possession of Bob's papers and letters, and his daughter Alice owns Alice James' diary.) Mary Holton James continued to visit her children, her sisters, and her mother. Among the many entries in her notebook, Mary noted the death of her brother-in-law William a little more than a month after Bob's death. Mary and Henry kep 'n close contact, and Mary and William's wife began to have a better friendship after Bob's death. Alice described Mary to Henry as "most friendly and responsive."[1] Carrie James was not mentioned at all in Mary's notebook after Robertson's death. In 1916, Mary noted the death of Henry James; he was, she wrote: "the last of his generation. Makes me sad."[2] In September of 1922, Mary made the last entry into her notebook, writing that William's wife had died. Two months later, while Mary was riding a streetcar in Concord, she collapsed and died instantly at the age of seventy-three. It was a more appropriate setting than it seems for she had always loved to move and to travel. She was buried beside Bob in Sleepy Hollow Cemetery in Concord. Her son, Ned, in describing her after her death, appreciated the difficulties she had endured throughout her life with Bob: ". . . she bore all, and overcame all, and forgave all, amid trials that would have crushed and disheartened others, she had the patience and the iron will to fight for and save her family and hold it together as a unity, never trying to have an easy time for herself, always holding the laboring oar."[3]

Long after Wilkie's and Robertson's deaths, Henry's devotion to them remained strong. In 1897, Henry had been delighted that a sculpture by Augustus Saint-Gaudens was dedicated in Boston to the memory of Robert Gould Shaw and his black regiment. (William delivered the dedication address.) Henry wrote to William, asking for details of the ceremony and for "the finest and biggest photograph of the sculpture that can be found."[4] Henry, more than any other James, always suspected that Wilkie's subsequent failures were a result of the harrowing experiences which he had endured during the war. In 1913, when Henry wrote *Notes of A Son and Brother,* he recalled, as gently as he could, the lives of his younger brothers. After his sister-in-law Alice had read it, she wrote to tell Henry that he had "interpreted Bob and Wilky and done honor to each as faithfully as to William."[5] This must have pleased Henry for his task in presenting Bob and Wilkie had been difficult. They were, as he said in his book, "so constitutionally different," not only from each other but from the other Jameses.[6]

In 1908, Wilkie's daughter, Alice, married David A. Edgar, an engineer who worked on the building of the Erie Canal and who later formed his own highly successful investment firm. It was a happy but relatively short marriage; Alice James Edgar died of a heart ailment in 1923, childless, at the age of forty-eight. She is buried beside Wilkie in Milwaukee. One of the last glimpses any of the Jameses had of her was in 1913, when Henry met her for the first time in many years. She was thirty-eight at the time, the age at which Wilkie had died. Henry wrote to William's wife about the meeting, and Alice's response was a poignant one: ". . . she made on me exactly the impression you describe. She suggested something to me which I found myself momentarily waiting for—and it did not come. And it left me with an odd sense of disinheritance—as if she had been kept out of her birthright."[7] (In the same letter, Alice told Henry that an old family friend had observed a resemblance between her son Henry and Wilkie as he had looked as a soldier.)

Wilkie's son, Joseph Cary James, achieved great prominence and financial success in Milwaukee. His biographical sketch in the *Memoirs of Milwaukee County* attests to this. In 1907, he married Antoinette Pierpont (from one of the most prominent families in the country) and eventually became one of the wealthiest men in Milwaukee as a real estate broker and by operating one of the largest sand-and-gravel businesses in the state. Cary and Antoinette were described in the society columns as "members of the young and popular social set of the city."[8] They had one son, born in 1909, whom they named Garth Pierpont James, after Wilkie. Joseph Cary James died in 1925 at the age of fifty-one.

Carrie James's life must have been a lonely one after the death of her two children. She outlived all of the Jameses and died on November 24, 1931, at the age of eigthy-one, in a sanatarium in Milwaukee. She was described in her obituary as the widow of a Civil War hero, and as "a pioneer resident and social leader of Milwaukee."[9] Her sizable fortune, which included valuable Milwaukee commercial property (Carrie's three brothers had never married, and she inherited their estates), was divided among the three survivors of hers and Wilkie's small family: her daughter-in-law, Antoinette Pierpont James; her son-in-law, David Edgar; and her grandson, Garth P. James. In addition, Carrie remembered several charities, particularly St. Paul's Episcopal Church in Milwaukee.

The James nieces and nephews—William's four children and Bob's two children—corresponded occasionally, but they were more preoccupied with their own marriages and families than with being Jameses. Furthermore, William's children and Bob's children had never had much contact with each other, even when their parents were alive.

However, in 1933, while Ralph Barton Perry was completing his biography of William, William's son Henry James III, suggested that Perry contact Mary James Vaux, knowing that she had her father's papers, which included many letters from Henry and William. But Mary refused Perry's request to reprint some of the letters, declaring that she herself intended to use the papers "at some future date."[10] Perhaps the knowledge that Perry was completing a biography spurred Mary into action, for it was at about this time that she hired Anna Robeson Burr to write a book about Bob, Wilkie, and Alice.

Mary may also have been inspired to do something in her father's memory as a result of the guilt she felt over having repulsed her father's suggestion that he travel to Bryn Mawr to visit her shortly before his death. One suspects that Mary, in packing up her father's letters and papers and taking them with her when she returned home directly after his funeral, may have been harboring from that time the idea of using the papers in some commemorative way.

In addition to Bob's letters and papers, Mary also acquired Alice James's diary from Katherine Loring. Katherine was happy to turn the diary over to Mary, since she believed that Alice had always wanted the diary to be published.[11] Mary also contacted Wilkie's grandson, Garth Pierpont James, who lent to her Wilkie's Civil War and Florida letters. Mary's sons, George and Henry Vaux, who were teenagers at the time, spent their summer vacation typing transcripts of Wilkie's letters so that the originals could be returned to Garth.

Mrs. Burr worked quickly, and the result was published in 1934. The title of her book reflects the awkward coupling of Alice's diary with an essay about the James family: *Alice James: Her Brothers—Her Journal.* The book begins with an eighty-two-page essay which attempts to delineate the family, the trips to Europe, the war, and William's and Henry's careers, while glossing over most of the troubled circumstances of the adulthood of Wilkie, Bob, and Alice. The book concludes with Alice's diary, but Mrs. Burr deleted newspaper clippings which Alice had pasted into her diary and thus deprived the reader of crucial references. In addition, as Jean Strouse notes in her biography of Alice, Mrs. Burr took the liberty of editing the diary without acknowledging having done so.

Despite this, the book was well received. John Chamberlain, of the *New York Times,* described Alice's writing as "vigorous, frank, and brilliant in expression."[12] The reviews also reflected the public's interest in all of the Jameses. The *New York Times Book Review* of Sunday, May 20, 1934, reviewed the book on the front page, calling the Jameses "America's Most Distinguished Family of Intellectuals,"[13] and pictures of Henry, William, and Alice appeared prominently on the first page. Ironically, Bob and Wilkie were somewhat neglected, even in the review of a book intended to rescue them from obscurity.

The other Jameses were not pleased with the book: Mary's brother, Ned, believed that Alice's diary should have been published separately, and he later gave R. B. Perry permission to use several of his father's letters, permission which Mary had withheld. William's children liked the book even less. When it was published, Henry James III, who was the executor for both his father's and his Uncle Henry's estates, wrote to Perry of the book's many flaws. And when

Henry wrote to his sister Peggy of a particularly scathing comment by one of the reviewers about Mrs. Burr, he told her that he "chuckled over it with malicious glee."[14]

Although Mrs. Burr's book was generally well received, its success reflects the interest Americans had in the James family more than the quality of the book itself. *Alice James: Her Brothers—Her Journal* soon went out of print and was later eclipsed by such major scholarly works as Perry's and Allen's biographies of William, Edel's five-volume biography of Henry, and Strouse's biography of Alice.

Of course, the lives of Garth Wilkinson and Robertson James are of interest primarily because they are Jameses, and knowing more about them leads to a better understanding of William and Henry. It is unfortunate, though, that Wilkie and Bob have been relegated to the background of the James family biographies, where they appear only as failed, shadowy figures whose troubled lives sometimes disturbed the lives of their siblings. It wasn't like that at all. It is true that relationships sometimes became strained, particularly between Alice and Bob, but among the four men there was never a sense that William and Henry, because they achieved prominence, were superior to Wilkie and Bob. Throughout their lives, they loved and cared for each other as equals, as brothers.

NOTES

Unless otherwise indicated, the material cited is in the Houghton Library, Harvard University. A date in brackets indicates that no date was given in the letter but that the author was able to determine the date based on the letter's contents. Henry James's *Autobiography* refers to the Criterion Books edition, edited by Frederick W. Dupee, which combines James's three autobiographical works: *A Small Boy and Others, Notes of a Son and Brother,* and *The Middle Years*. The following initials are used to identify the material quoted and its location.

AHJ	Alice Howe Gibbens James (William's wife)
AJ	Alice James
CJ	Caroline Eames Cary James (Carrie, Wilkie's wife)
CW	Catherine Walsh (Aunt Kate)
EHJ	Edward Holton James (Ned, Bob's son)
EP	Elizabeth Peabody
FRM	Frances Rollins Morse
GWJ	Garth Wilkinson James (Wilkie, GWJ's spelling; his family often used the "y" ending)
HJ	Henry James (brother)
HJ Sr.	Henry James, Sr. (father)
JMF	John Murray Forbes
MHJ	Mary Holton James (Bob's wife)
MJ	Mary Walsh James (mother)
MJV	Mary James Vaux (Bob's daughter)
MJP	Margaret James Porter (Peggy, William's daughter)
RJ	Robertson James (Bob, or occasionally Rob)

RWE   Ralph Waldo Emerson
WJ   William James (brother)
CFPL   Concord Free Public Library, Concord, Massachusetts
DJ   Collection of David E. M. James
GV   Collection of George Vaux
HJV   Collection of Henry James Vaux
MB   Collection of Mrs. Slater Brown (Mary Brown)
MHS   Massachusetts Historical Society

INTRODUCTION

1. Henry James, *Autobiography* (New York: Criterion Books, 1956), 4.

1

1. William James of Albany's estate was valued, at his death in 1832, at $3 million, ranking him, along with such families as the Astors and the Van Rensselaers, as one of the wealthiest men in the nation. His estate was divided equally among his children, but only after Henry James, Sr., and his brothers and sisters fought a successful court battle to break their father's will. As a result of his inheritance, Henry James, Sr., was financially independent for his entire life. Had the court case not been successful, however, he would have inherited far less than his siblings, and trustees would have had enormous control over the estate.
2. *The Diary of Alice James,* ed. Leon Edel (New York: Dodd, Mead, 1934), 72.
3. AJ to HJ Sr., March 11 [1860].
4. MJ to Mrs. J. J. Garth Wilkinson, November 29, 1846.
5. James, *Autobiography,* 162.
6. Ibid., 165.
7. Ibid.
8. F. O. Matthiessen, *The James Family* (New York: Vintage Books, 1980), 88.
9. James, *Autobiography,* 310.
10. Fragment of autobiography typed by Robertson James, HJV.
11. James, *Autobiography,* 279.
12. Anna Robeson Burr, *Alice James: Her Brothers—Her Journal* (New York: Dodd, Mead, 1934), 24.
13. Allen, *William James,* 63.
14. WJ to parents, August 19, 1860.
15. HJ Sr. to RWE, August 31, 1849.

16. F. W. Dupee, *Henry James* (New York: William Sloane Associates, 1951), 20.
17. James, *Autobiography*, 278.
18. Ibid., 126.
19. Matthiessen, *James Family*, 70.
20. Ibid., James, *Autobiography*, 127.
21. Ibid., 99.
22. *Diary of Alice James*, 128.
23. James, *Autobiography*, 239.
24. Ibid., 260.
25. RJ to AHJ, February 24, 1898.
26. GWJ to HJ Sr., December 1859.
27. RJ to AHJ, April 19, 1899.
28. GWJ to parents, July 1, 1858.
29. WJ to T. S. Perry, [1858].
30. HJ Sr. to Edmund Tweedy, July 18, [1860].
31. Ralph Barton Perry, *The Thought and Character of William James*, 2 vols. (Boston: Little, Brown, 1935), 1:200.
32. HJ Sr. to Mrs. Francis G. Shaw, July 22, [1859].
33. Matthiessen, *James Family*, 70.
34. *The Notebooks of Henry James*, ed. F. O. Matthiessen and Kenneth B. Murdock (Chicago: University of Chicago Press, 1974), 40.
35. WJ to parents, August 19, 1860.
36. HJ to MJ, January 24, [1876].
37. Dupee, *Henry James*, 25.
38. Matthiessen, *James Family*, 12.
39. GWJ to parents, [November 1861], DJ.
40. WJ to parents, November 15, 1861.
41. WJ to MJ, December 1861.
42. Edward Emerson, *The Early Years of the Saturday Club* (Boston: Houghton Mifflin, 1918), 328.
43. James, *Autobiography*, 133.
44. Ibid., 14.
45. Ibid., 369.
46. HJ Sr. to Edmund Tweedy, July 18, [1860).
47. James, *Autobiography*, 313.
48. Ibid., 369.
49. Matthiessen, *James Family*, 22.
50. HJ Sr. to RWE, March 26, 1861.
51. Gay Wilson Allen, *Waldo Emerson* (New York: Viking Press, 1981), 341.
52. James, *Autobiography*, 18.
53. Burr, *Alice James*, 28.
54. HJ Sr. to Caroline Sturgis Tappan, quoted in James, *Autobiography*, 369.
55. Ibid.
56. James, *Autobiography*, 370.

57. Ibid., 369.
58. HJ Sr. to RWE, quoted in Perry, *Thought and Character,* 1:3.
59. *The Memoirs of Julian Hawthorne,* ed. Edith Garrigues Hawthorne (New York: Macmillan, 1938), 85.
60. Franklin B. Sanborn to Theodore Parker, February 12, 1860, CFPL.
61. Franklin B. Sanborn, *Recollections of Seventy Years* (Boston: The Gorham Press, 1909), 453.
62. Sophia Hawthorne to Franklin B. Sanborn, quoted in James R. Mellow, *Nathaniel Hawthorne in His Times* (Boston: Houghton Mifflin, 1980), 536.
63. Ibid.
64. *Memoirs of Julian Hawthorne,* 81.
65. Ibid.
66. Ibid., 86.
67. Ibid., 86–87.
68. WJ to family, September 16, 1861.
69. GWJ to parents, November 1861, DJ.
70. James, *Autobiography,* 258.
71. HJ Sr. to HJ, [1869].
72. The sketch is located in the Houghton Library Collection, Harvard University.
73. WJ to family, quoted in James, *Autobiography,* 327.
74. GWJ to Tom Ward, May 24, 1861.
75. WJ to family, [June 1862].
76. WJ to family, Christmas, [1862].
77. HJ Sr. to unidentified correspondent, fragment of a letter, HJV.
78. HJ Sr. to EP, July 22, 1863, MHS.
79. Abraham Lincoln to Horace Greeley, August 22, 1862, quoted in Carl Sandburg, *Abraham Lincoln, The War Years,* 4 vols. (New York: Harcourt, Brace, 1939), 1:567.
80. *War Papers,* a collection of war recollections of the Commandery of Wisconsin, Loyal Legion, Milwaukee, 1891, 4 vols. Wilkie's address is titled "The Assault on Fort Wagner," 1:9. The address was originally published in the *Milwaukee Sentinel* in 1883. Wilkie's handwritten copy is in the possession of David James.
81. HJ Sr. to EP, July 22, 1863, MHS.
82. *The Letters of William James,* ed. Henry James III (Boston: Little, Brown, 1926), 47.

2

1. Otto Friedrich, *Clover* (New York: Simon & Schuster, 1979), 57.
2. Ibid.
3. Charles B. Fox to his wife, July 1863, Papers of Charles B. Fox, MHS.
4. Luis Emilio, *A Brave Black Regiment, History of the Fifty Fourth Regiment 1863–1865* (Boston: The Boston Book Company, 1894); reprint ed., (New York: Johnson Reprint Corp., 1968), 2.

5. James M. McPherson, *The Negro's Civil War* (New York: Pantheon Books, 1965), 163.
6. Ibid.
7. Ibid., 162.
8. Emilio, *Brave Black Regiment,* 3.
9. Governor Andrew formed a committee to direct the raising of recruits; its members were some of New England's most prominent citizens: George L. Stearns, Amos A. Lawrence, John M. Forbes, William I. Bowditch, LeBaron Russell, Richard Hallowell, Williard Phillips, and Francis G. Shaw.
10. Emilio, *Brave Black Regiment,* 6.
11. Ibid., 3.
12. Ibid., 6.
13. James, *Autobiography,* 456.
14. Emilio, *Brave Black Regiment,* 9.
15. *War Papers,* 11.
16. *Three Years' Service with the Fifty-Fifth Massachusetts Volunteer Infantry,* an address delivered by Robertson James in Concord, Massachusetts, March 10, 1886. The address is forty-five pages long and is bound together with the recollections of other soldiers; 293.
17. Emilio, *Brave Black Regiment,* 7.
18. Ibid., 23.
19. Ibid., 7.
20. Wilkie took these letters, along with his scrapbook and Bible, with him when he moved permanently to Milwaukee. Had he not done so, they probably would have been destroyed when Catherine Walsh burned bundles of family letters after the death of Henry James, Sr. After the death of Wilkie's widow, her grandson, who served during World War II, preserved the letters. They are now in the possession of Wilkie's great-grandson, David James, who served in Vietnam.
21. GWJ to parents, January 27, 1863, DJ.
22. GWJ to parents, November 7, 1862, DJ.
23. General von Moltke, quoted in J.F.C. Fuller, *The Generalship of Ulysses S. Grant* (Bloomington: Indiana University Press, 1958), 15.
24. GWJ to parents, December 29, 1862, DJ.
25. Ibid.
26. GWJ to parents, January 18, 1863, DJ.
27. Ibid.
28. GWJ to parents, January 27, 1863, DJ.
29. *War Papers,* 11.
30. Ibid., 12.
31. Emilio, *Brave Black Regiment,* 19.
32. Ibid., 20.
33. Although the Fifty-fourth and the Fifty-fifth regiments fought in many of the same battles, Bob and Wilkie did not serve in the same place at the same time because of their injuries. As a result, it is more practical to discuss Bob's service separately in the next chapter.
34. James, *Autobiography,* 456.

35. Ibid., 457.
36. Ibid., 446.
37. Ibid., 457.
38. *War Papers*, 13.
39. Peter Burchard, *One Gallant Rush* (New York: St. Martin's Press, 1965), 92.
40. Burchard, 93–94.
41. RJ to Edward Henry Clement, November 22, 1900.
42. Emilio, *Brave Black Regiment*, 3.
43. Ibid., 48.
44. Ibid.
45. *War Papers*, 14.
46. Though Wilkie's letter has been lost, HJ Sr. quoted it in his letter to Elizabeth Peabody, July 30, 1863, MHS.
47. *War Papers*, 15.
48. Emilio, *Brave Black Regiment*, 60.
49. Ibid., 61.
50. Ibid., 62.
51. Ibid.
52. HJ Sr. to EP, July 30, 1863, MHS.
53. Emilio, *Brave Black Regiment*, 64–65.
54. Ibid., 77.
55. HJ Sr. to EP, July 30, 1863, MHS.
56. Emilio, *Brave Black Regiment*, 78.
57. Ibid., 74.
58. Ibid., 75.
59. Burchard, *One Gallant Rush*, 136.
60. Emilio, *Brave Black Regiment*, 82.
61. Ibid., 91.
62. Ibid., 84.
63. Ibid., 95.
64. *War Papers*, 22–26.
65. Burchard, *One Gallant Rush*, 143.
66. James, *Autobiography*, 383–84.
67. HJ Sr. to Caroline Sturgis Tappan, quoted in James *Autobiography*, 381–82.
68. HJ Sr. to EP, August 11, 1863, MHS.
69. HJ Sr. to Francis G. Shaw, July 28, 1863, MHS.
70. WJ to Katherine Prince, September 12, 1863.
71. HJ Sr. to Mrs. C. P. Cranch, 1863.
72. WJ to parents, November 1863.
73. James, *Autobiography*, 467.
74. GWJ to parents, January 4, 1864, DJ.
75. HJ to Henry James III, quoted in Edel, *Henry James, The Untried Years*, 1:138.
76. James, *Autobiography*, 469.
77. GWJ to HJ Sr., December 20, 1864, DJ.

78. GWJ to parents, December 22, 1864, DJ.
79. GWJ to parents, December 25, 1864, DJ.
80. GWJ to parents, February 17, 1865, DJ.
81. GWJ to parents, February 19, 1865, DJ.
82. Newspaper clippings pasted to sketch, DJ.
83. WJ to AJ, March 15, 1865.
84. GWJ to HJ Sr., February 22, 1865, DJ.
85. GWJ to WJ, February 1, 1865, DJ.
86. GWJ to family, February 5, 1865, DJ.
87. GWJ to HJ Sr., April 27, 1865.
88. GWJ to parents, December 31, 1864, DJ.

3

1. HJ Sr. to RJ, August 29, 1864, HJV.
2. Ibid.
3. *Three Year's Service*, 290.
4. Ibid., 291.
5. Ibid.
6. James, *Autobiography*, 457–58.
7. *Three Years' Service*, 292.
8. Ibid.
9. Ibid.
10. Ibid., 300.
11. RJ to MJV, [1905], HJV.
12. Emilio, *Brave Black Regiment*, 109.
13. *Three Years' Service*, 302.
14. Ibid., 303.
15. Charles B. Fox to his wife, October 11, 1863, MHS.
16. *Freedom: A Documentary History of Emancipation, 1861–1867*, series II, "The Black Military Experience," ed. Ira Berlin (New York: Cambridge University Press, 1982), 1.
17. RJ to parents, February 14, 1864.
18. *Three Years' Service*, 317–18.
19. Ibid., 307–09.
20. Emilio, *Brave Black Regiment*, 148.
21. *Three Years' Service*, 310–11.
22. Ibid., 314.
23. James, *Autobiography*, 458.
24. Ibid.
25. *Three Years' Service*, 323.
26. GWJ to parents, March 20, 1865, DJ.
27. GWJ to parents, March 22, 1865, DJ.
28. HJ Sr. to RJ, August 29, 1864, HJV.
29. HJ Sr. to RJ, September 13, [1864], HJV.
30. Ibid.

31. HJ Sr. to RJ, August 31, 1864, HJV.
32. HJ Sr. to RJ, September 13, [1864], HJV.
33. HJ Sr. to RJ, [March 1865], HJV.
34. HJ Sr. to RJ, April 28, 1865, HJV.
35. HJ Sr. to RWE, March 9, [1865].
36. Bob's discharge papers, MB.
37. *Three Years' Service,* 333.

4

1. HJ Sr. to JMF, November 4, 1865.
2. Lawrence N. Powell, *New Masters: Northern Planters during the Civil War and Reconstruction* (New Haven: Yale University Press, 1980), 6.
3. Ibid., xii.
4. MJ to GWJ, March 14, [1866], DJ.
5. AJ to FRM, February 14, 1866.
6. AJ to FRM, May 7, 1866.
7. GWJ to HJ Sr., March 27, 1866, DJ.
8. Ibid.
9. Ibid.
10. HJ Sr. to GWJ, March 13, [1866], DJ.
11. GWJ to HJ Sr., March 27, [1866], DJ.
12. GWJ to HJ Sr., April 27, 1866, DJ.
13. GWJ to HJ Sr., April 7, 1866, DJ.
14. GWJ to HJ Sr., April 14, 1866, DJ.
15. GWJ to HJ Sr., June 26, 1866, DJ.
16. AJ to FRM, June 17, 1866.
17. GWJ to HJ Sr., June 26, 1866, DJ.
18. MJ to GWJ, June 21, 1866, DJ.
19. MJ to RJ, June 28, 1866, DJ.
20. MJ to GWJ, July 2, 1866, DJ.
21. MJ to GWJ, July 15, 1866, DJ.
22. Ibid.
23. GWJ to HJ Sr., July 21, 1866, DJ.
24. GWJ to HJ Sr., July 9, 1866, DJ.
25. HJ Sr. to GWJ, August 2, [1866], DJ.
26. GWJ to HJ Sr., August 6, 1866, DJ.
27. GWJ to HJ Sr., August 9, 1866, DJ.
28. GWJ to HJ Sr., August 15, 1866, DJ.
29. GWJ to WJ, September 29, 1866, DJ.
30. HJ Sr. to GWJ, October 9, [1866], DJ.
31. AJ to FRM, October 21, 1866.
32. HJ Sr. to GWJ, February 8, [1867], DJ.
33. RJ to Mrs. John Murray Forbes, December 30, 1866.
34. GWJ to parents, February 1, 1867, DJ.
35. MJ to GWJ, March 18, [1867], DJ.

36. MJ to GWJ, March 1, [1867].
37. MJ to GWJ, March 18, [1867], DJ.
38. GWJ to HJ Sr., March 24, 1867, DJ.
39. GWJ to HJ Sr., July 21, 1867, DJ.
40. MJ to RJ, [1867], HJV.
41. MJ to WJ, May 27, [1867].
42. GWJ's scrapbook, DJ.
43. HJ Sr. to GWJ, August 18, [1867], DJ.
44. MJ to GWJ, [1867], DJ.
45. RJ to Edward W. Kinsley, October 27, 1867, MHS.
46. MJ to GWJ, October 20, [1867], DJ.
47. MJ to WJ, November 21, 1867.
48. Powell, *New Masters,* 146.
49. GWJ to MJ, January 27, 1868, DJ.
50. MJ to GWJ, January 26, 1868, DJ.
51. GWJ to parents, April 8, 1868.
52. GWJ to parents, November 8, 1868, DJ.
53. Ibid.
54. GWJ to parents, November 15, 1868, DJ.
55. GWJ to parents, December 31, 1868, DJ.
56. GWJ to AJ, April 28, 1869.
57. Savage & Haile to GWJ, August 25, 1869.
58. HJ to WJ, March 8, 1870.
59. James, *Autobiography,* 461.

5

1. WJ to RJ, January 27, 1868.
2. MJ to WJ, November, 1867.
3. MJ to HJ, September 6, [1868].
4. RJ to AJ, February 28, 1868.
5. MJ to RJ, [1869], HJV.
6. WJ to RJ, November 14, 1869, HJV.
7. WJ to RJ, August 1871, HJV.
8. WJ to RJ, June 22, 1872, HJV.
9. WJ to RJ, September 1872, HJV.
10. WJ to RJ, June 22, 1872, HJV.
11. James B.A. Thayer, *A Western Journey with Mr. Emerson* (Boston: Little, Brown, 1884), 6.
12. HJ Sr. to GWJ, June 4, [1871], HJV.
13. HJ Sr. to RJ, [1872], HJV.
14. HJ Sr. to RJ, [1872], HJV.
15. MJ to AJ, July 18, 1872.
16. HJ Sr. to WJ, August 7, 1881.
17. MJ to HJ, December 15, 1872.
18. GWJ to MJ, August 7, 1872.

19. GWJ to HJ and AJ, August 28, 1872.
20. HJ to parents, October 10, [1872].
21. Holton family diary, 1872, GV.
22. HJ Sr. to HJ, [1872].
23. HJ to WJ, September 22, [1872].
24. RJ to HJ Sr., October 23, 1872.
25. HJ Sr. to RJ, December 10, [?], HJV.
26. RJ to HJ Sr., January 28, 1873.
27. AJ to FRM, [December 1873].
28. HJ to HJ Sr., December 22, 1873.
29. MJ to HJ, December 8, 1873.
30. MJ to RJ, December 16, [1873], HJV.
31. MJ to RJ, February 18, 1874, HJV.
32. RJ to HJ Sr., January 28, 1873.
33. HJ to MHJ, July 8, 1873, HJV.
34. CW to HJ, January 13, 1873.
35. MH to HJ, [1873], HJV.
36. MJ to HJ, February 28, 1873.
37. HJ to AJ, April 25, [1873].
38. MJ to HJ, May 25, 1873.
39. MJ to HJ, September 12, 1873.
40. RJ to MJ, [1873], HJV.
41. HJ Sr. to RJ, [1873], HJV.
42. MHJ's notebook, 1873, GV.
43. HJ Sr. to WJ and HJ, November 21, 1873.
44. MJ to HJ, December 8, 1873.
45. MJ to RJ, December 16, [1873], HJV.
46. HJ to HJ Sr., December 22, 1873.
47. MJ to WJ, January 23, 1874.
48. WJ to GWJ, November 16, 1873.
49. MJ to HJ, April 3, 1874.
50. MJ to HJ, May 18, 1874.
51. WJ to RJ, April 26, 1874, HJV.
52. HJ Sr. to RJ, [1874], HJV.
53. MJ to RJ, September 27, [1874], HJV.
54. MHJ tp parents, November 19, 1874, HJV.
55. WJ to RJ, July 12, 1875.
56. MHJ's notebook, 1875, GV.
57. MHJ's notebook, 1876, GV.
58. Ibid.
59. WJ to RJ, September 15, 1877.
60. HJ to RJ, December 6, 1876, HJV.
61. HJ Sr. to RJ, December, [1875], HJV.
62. MHJ's notebook, 1877, GV.
63. MJ to RJ, [1877].
64. WJ to MHJ, May 12, 1878.
65. MHJ's notebook, 1880, GV.

66. Ibid.
67. AHJ to HJ, April 11, 1892.
68. MJ to GWJ, April 1, [1881].
69. HJ to WJ, January 28, [1878].
70. MJ to RJ, Sunday, [1878], HJV.
71. CW to MHJ, [1878], HJV.
72. HJ to Mrs. Frances Mathers, February 13, [1882].
73. HJ to WJ, March 14, [1876].
74. HJ Sr. to MHJ, March 16, [1881], HJV.
75. CW to MHJ, March, [1881], HJV.
76. James, *Autobiography,* 459.
77. HJ Sr. to WJ, August 7, 1881.
78. CW to MHJ, [1881], HJV.
79. HJ to RJ, January 27, [1882].
80. GWJ to HJ, [1882], DJ.
81. RJ to HJ, January 28, 1882.
82. RJ to MHJ, January 31, 1882, MB.
83. RJ to MHJ, [February 1882], MB. Bob's references to his mother's devotion to his father's beliefs were probably intended as a contrast to Mary's behavior, who did not pay any attention whatsoever to Bob's passionate interest in Swedenborg.
84. RJ to HJ, March 26, 1882.
85. HJ to MHJ, May 25, [1882], HJV.
86. AHJ to WJ, January 6, 1883.
87. AHJ to WJ, January 15, 1883.
88. MHJ's notebook, 1882, GV.
89. HJ Sr. to WJ, November 7, 1882.
90. Ibid.
91. CW to MHJ, December 14, 1882, HJV.
92. AHJ to WJ, Christmas 1882.
93. AHJ to WJ, December 31, 1882.
94. WJ to HJ Sr., December 14, [1882].

6

1. HJ to RJ, December 30, [1882], HJV.
2. AHJ to WJ, December 22, 1882.
3. HJ to WJ, January 8, 1883.
4. GWJ to RJ, December 26, 1882, HJV.
5. *Milwaukee Sentinel,* January 12, 1883.
6. GWJ to HJ, February 21, 1883.
7. HJ to WJ, January 23, [1883].
8. HJ to WJ, February 11, [1883].
9. GWJ to HJ, February 6, 1883.
10 RJ to HJ, February 4, 1883.
11. GWJ to HJ, February 21, 1883.

12. "Edward" to GWJ, [1883], DJ.
13. HJ to RJ, May 1883, HJV.
14. HJ to RJ, June 4, 1883, HJV.
15. WJ to RJ, April 1883, HJV.
16. WJ to RJ, June 1883, HJV.
17. MHJ's notebook, 1883, GV.
18. RJ to MHJ, July 1883, HJV.
19. RJ to MHJ, August 12, 1883, HJV.
20. RJ to MHJ, September 16, 1883, HJV.
21. RJ to MHJ, [1883], HJV.
22. GWJ to WJ, September 25, [1883].
23. WJ to AJ, October 2, 1883.
24. HJ to Elizabeth Boott, October 14, 1883.
25. HJ to WJ, August 12, 1869.
26. James, *Autobiography,* 312.
27. *Milwaukee Sentinel,* November 17, 1883.
28. James, *Autobiography,* 162.
29. HJ to WJ, November 24, [1883].
30. HJ to RJ, December 2, 1883, HJV.
31. Unidentified newspaper clipping in GWJ's scrapbook, 1883.
32. WJ to RJ, December 2, 1883, HJV.
33. RJ to Wetmore, [1884], HJV.
34. RJ to WJ, November 26, [1883], HJV.
35. WJ to RJ, January 7, 1884, HJV.
36. RJ to MJV, March 31, [1906], HJV.
37. HJ to WJ, June 1, 1895.
38. HJ to AHJ, April 11, 1913.
39. HJ to AJ, February 29, [1884].
40. HJ to CJ, July 31, 1913, DJ.

7

1. MHJ's notebook, 1884, GV.
2. CW to MHJ, October 25, 1884, HJV.
3. CW to MHJ, November 2, 1884, HJV.
4. CW to MHJ, November 20, 1884, HJV.
5. CW to MHJ, March 30, 1885, HJV.
6. WJ to AJ, December 7, 1884.
7. WJ to AJ, March 9, 1885.
8. RJ to MJV, [no date]. Robertson was probably alluding to the fact that the Concord Free Public Library had banned Mark Twain's *Huckleberry Finn,* calling it "trash of the veriest sort."
9. WJ to AJ, October 19, 1885.
10. *Atlantic Monthly,* March 1885.
11. HJ to MJ, January 31, 1877.
12. MHJ's notebook, inside cover, GV.

13. AJ to WJ, March 22, 1889.
14. HJ Sr. to RWE, June 18, 1855.
15. AHJ to WJ, December 31, 1882.
16. AJ to WJ, January 29, 1889.
17. WJ to AJ, November 1, 1891.
18. AHJ to HJ, March 4, 1892.
19. RJ to FRM, March 14, 1892.
20. HJ to RJ and MHJ, March 8, 1892, HJV.
21. AJ to WJ, April 23, [1887].
22. Jean Strouse, *Alice James* (Boston: Houghton Mifflin, 1980), 125.
23. Edward Holton's will, on file in Probate Records Office, Milwaukee.
24. MHJ's notebook, 1893-1897, GV.
25. HJ to MHJ, April 27, 1895, HJV.
26. HJ to EHJ, February 15, 1896, HJV.
27. HJ to MHJ, May 28, 1897.
28. MHJ's notebook, 1897, HJV.
29. AHJ to HJ, January 13, 1898.
30. AHJ to HJ, February 14, 1898.
31. RJ to AHJ, April 19, 1899.
32. Ibid.
33. Brochure from the Jackson Health Resort, 1858–1917, courtesy of the Dansville Historical Society and W. J. Rauber, historian.
34. RJ to WJ, October 10, [?], Concord.
35. Motto printed on RJ's stationery.
36. MHJ's notebook, 1904, GV.
37. RJ to AHJ, January 14, 1904.
38. RJ to MJV, [no date], HJV.
39. Telegram, RJ to MJV, April 3, 1907, GV.
40. MHJ's notebook, 1906, GF.
41. RJ to MJV, [no date], HJV.
42. RJ to MJV, [no date], HJV.
43. RJ to AHJ, October 28, 1898.
44. RJ to AHJ, February 9, 1898.
45. RJ to MJV, [no date], HJV.
46. RJ to MJV, [no date], HJV.
47. RJ to MJP, September 2, 1907.
48. HJ to RJ, October 14, [1909?].
49. MHJ's notebook, 1909, GV.
50. RJ to MJV, June 7, 1910, HJV.
51. Interview with Robertson's granddaughter, Mary Brown.
52. MJP to AHJ, July 9, 1910,Bancroft Library, University of California, Berkeley.
53. RJ to MJV, [no date], HJV.
54. RJ to MJV [no date], HJV.
55. RJ to MJV [no date], HJV.
56. *Boston Transcript,* July 9, 1910.
57. AHJ to MHJ, September 6, 1910, MB.

58. Allen, *William James,* 433.
59. Erik H. Erikson, "Identity and the Life Cycle," *Psychological Issues,* vol. 1, no. 1, monograph 1 (New York: International Universities Press, 1959), 98.
60. HJ to MHJ, May 25, [1882], HJV.
61. HJ III to R. B. Perry, May 10, 1934, Harvard University Archives.
62. RJ to AHJ, February 24, 1898.

AFTERWORD

1. AHJ to HJ, April 27, 1913.
2. MHJ's notebook, 1913, GV.
3. EHJ to his cousins, December 8, 1922, HJV.
4. HJ to FRM, June 7, 1897.
5. AHJ to HJ, March 14, 1914.
6. James, *Autobiography,* 4.
7. AHJ to HJ, May 17, 1913.
8. *The Milwaukee Blue Book of Selected Names,* 1911–1912.
9. *Milwaukee Sentinel,* November 24, 1931.
10. MJV to R. B. Perry, January 27, 1931, Harvard University Archives.
11. Strouse, *Alice James,* 320–26.
12. *New York Times,* May 17, 1934.
13. *New York Times Book Review,* May 20, 1934.
14. Henry James III to MJP, January 9, 1935, Bancroft Library, University of California, Berkeley.

INDEX